The Raymond Chandler Papers

The Raymond Chandler Papers

Selected Letters and Nonfiction, 1909–1959

RAYMOND CHANDLER

Edited by Tom Hiney and Frank MacShane

Atlantic Monthly Press
New York

Contents copyright © 2000 by the Estate of Raymond Chandler
Introduction copyright © 2000 by Tom Hiney
Editorial arrangement copyright © 2000 by Tom Hiney and Frank MacShane

First published in the United Kingdom in 2000 by Hamish Hamilton Ltd., an imprint of
the Penguin Group

Published simultaneously in Canada
Printed in the United States of America

FIRST AMERICAN EDITION

Library of Congress Cataloging-in-Publication Data

Chandler, Raymond, 1888–1959.
    The Raymond Chandler papers : selected letters and nonfiction, 1909–1959 /
Raymond Chandler ; edited by Tom Hiney and Frank MacShane.
        p. cm.
    Includes index.
    ISBN 0-87113-786-0
    1. Chandler, Raymond, 1888–1959—Correspondence. 2. Authors, American—
20th century—Correspondence. 3. Detective and mystery stories—Authorship. I.
Hiney, Tom, 1970–   II. MacShane, Frank. III. Title.

    PS3505.H3224 Z48 2001
    813'.52—dc21
    [B]   00-054314

Atlantic Monthly Press
841 Broadway
New York, NY 10003

01 02 03 04   10 9 8 7 6 5 4 3 2 1

Contents

Introduction

'In a general way I am completely disgusted with the anthology racket. People who have given nothing to the world in the way of writing (and never will) presume to use other men's work at nominal, and by God I mean nominal, prices, for their own benefit and profit and to justify themselves as editors or critics or connoisseurs, in furtherance of which they write pukey little introductions and sit back with an indulgent smile and all nine pockets open.'

Letter to Sheridan House publishers, 24 November 1946

Six years ago, I began work on a biography of Raymond Chandler. In so doing, it quickly became clear to me that the best source of material concerning the subject was that written by Chandler himself. This was in part by virtue of necessity. He had been a reclusive man, who had left no wife or children after his death in 1959. Nor were there any brothers or sisters; or even second cousins. He had been an only child and a childless man, and, clocking up over 100 addresses in the course of his life, rootless. The man *Time* magazine once described as 'the poet laureate of the loner' appeared to be the genuine article. 'To know me in the flesh,' he warned one correspondent, 'is to pass on to better things.'

But while he may have been a recluse, Chandler was a compulsive letter-writer; and here lay many clues to the man behind Philip Marlowe. The surviving carbons of his letters are divided between a large collection at the Bodleian Library in Oxford and one at the University of California at Los Angeles. In those letters, of which thousands have survived, Chandler talks openly about life, writing and modern Californian society. Many of the letters included here were written late at night, spoken into a Dictaphone for his Mexican secretary Juanita Messick to type up in the morning. He was often drinking when he dictated them, and they serve as an unusually honest and freewheeling journey into the mind of a man who had seen a lot, read a lot, drunk a lot, thought a lot and steered perilously close to insanity in the process. He was as capable of fierce self-scrutiny as he was of antisocial virtuosity – no one, I came to believe, could be more perceptive or informative about Chandler than Raymond Chandler himself.

The letters lie firmly at the heart of his written legacy, and there have already been two selections since his death in 1959: *Raymond Chandler Speaking* in 1962 and *The Selected Letters of Raymond Chandler* in 1981. I am indebted to both here, and particularly to the work of the late Professor Frank MacShane. Frank MacShane died in 1998. His work on Chandler in the 1970s and 1980s helped to convince the intellectual powers-that-were that Raymond Chandler was more than just a whodunit writer, but in fact a modern Californian shaman and an American literary treasure – something his fans took for granted. MacShane's valiant work lives on in this selection, which expands on, and bases itself on, his 1981 selection. I would also like to express my gratitude to the Chandler estate for having approached me to prepare this edition.

After spending a lot of time myself with the Chandler papers, I believe I have found some interesting new material. There is one main reason for this. The majority of Chandler's letters were to men and women he dealt with professionally: publishers, agents, lawyers. Most of these letters began with a matter of business at hand, and would then veer off into soliloquies concerning whatever fired Chandler's thoughts at that moment. Thus, for example, a letter to his accountant about tax matters might end up discussing cinema and chess (the latter described by Chandler as 'the greatest waste of human intelligence outside an advertising agency'). In the midst of an argument with his European agent about Italian translation rights, Chandler might offer an insight into General MacArthur's performance in World War II. And so on. Realizing how much still remained embedded within the avalanche of his business correspondence (which could easily fill two large wardrobes), I decided to resurvey his correspondence, from start to finish. I was rewarded, as I had hoped, with some classic lost Chandler moments. Readers familiar with the two earlier selections of Chandler's letters will therefore find plenty of new material to enjoy here. In addition to that retrieved from existing papers (including never previously seen journalism) several new letters have come to light in the last ten years – notably Chandler's two-year correspondence with a fan-turned-lover named Louise Loughner.

Raymond Chandler's letters and journalism are worth reading even by those not acquainted with his fiction. As the *Washington Post*'s critic wrote in reviewing MacShane's selection in 1981, Chandler's letters are 'compulsively readable'. At moments, in fact, they match the lucid heights of his fiction.

A potted sketch of Chandler's life will be useful for those not familiar with his story. For, in a century dominated by dislocation, Raymond Chandler had had a particularly unsettled background. Born in Chicago in 1888, he was the only child of an Irish-born mother and a Pennsylvania-born father. Both were lapsed Quakers, and his father was an alcoholic, whose job as a itinerant rail engineer meant Chandler saw little of him while growing up. Chandler and his mother spent his first years in a rented house in Chicago, then in a series of inexpensive hotel rooms, and increasingly with relatives in the prairies of Nebraska.

In 1895, Chandler and his mother, whose marriage was now over, sailed with their belongings for Ireland. There, they lived as outcasts amid the genteel Protestant community of Waterford in which Florence Chandler had grown up. The boy was later sent to London, to live with his grandmother and – at the expense of an uncle – eventually to attend Dulwich College, a smart Victorian private school where he had to wear tails. The uncle was not prepared to pay for him to attend university, so removed Chandler from Dulwich a year early and sent him to tutorial colleges in France and Germany, in preparation for sitting the British Civil Service examination, a familiar recourse of well-spoken young men with no capital.

Following his year on the Continent, Chandler passed third out of 500 in the exams and began working in the British Admiralty, in the office of munitions. He disliked the job, and resigned after a few months. Over the next five years, he lived at an assortment of shabby addresses in London, earning a meagre living from writing for literary magazines. His uncle refusing to continue to subsidize his ward any longer, Chandler emigrated alone to America in 1912, the same year the *Titanic* sank. He had no money other than that borrowed (to be repaid, with interest) from his uncle. After jobs as a tennis racquet-stringer, fruit-picker and shop assistant, he eventually found work in Los Angeles as a junior accountant.

In 1917, Chandler journeyed north of the United States border in order to enlist with the Gordon Highlanders. Only the twentieth century could produce the scenario of an American-born Anglo-Irishman travelling to Canada in order to join a Scottish regiment to fight Germans in France. Chandler served in the ranks as a soldier, and rose to the rank of Sergeant. On his return to California (via Seattle) he married a twice-divorced ex-model and found work within the state's now booming oil industry. The Chandlers moved house constantly in and around Los Angeles over the next thirteen years and had no children. Possibly unbeknown to Chandler, his wife was seventeen years his senior, and had altered her birth date on their wedding certificate by ten years. After his sacking from the oil business for drunkenness in 1932, the couple continued their nomadism, though in shoddier suburban Angelino addresses. Chandler began to write for pulp crime magazines. In 1939, he completed and published his first full-length novel, *The Big Sleep*, introducing a hero-narrator called Philip Marlowe. Seven years later, having made his fortune via Hollywood, he settled and bought a luxurious house near San Diego. Both he and Philip Marlowe were by then famous, on screen and on the page.

Following his wife's death in 1954, Chandler lived out a lonely and manic end in European and southern Californian hotels. He had managed to sustain no real long-standing friends in his life, and he had no family. Only seventeen people attended his funeral in 1959, including a local representative of the American Mystery Writers' Association.

Add the recurring demon of alcoholism to this story, and it is little surprise that Chandler once described it emotionally at least as 'a rather forlorn sort of life'. It was sometimes more than forlorn: he made a drunken suicide attempt in 1955 that landed him a state psychiatric cell. But qualities other than desperation are often found on the boundaries of sanity, and Chandler held those in spades. The payback for a life of odd ends was the sort of raw wit that appears in print only once or twice a century. The sort of eye that can see straight through what people say to what they mean. Few writers of his own generation have dated so little. This is as true of his letters as it is of his novels and screen work, and this collection, I hope, will offer fresh testimony to that.

The material here includes not just letters, but other writing outside his novels and screenplays. It is presented chronologically. No correspondence from Chandler's early London adulthood survives, and I have instead included a few of his essays and poems which he wrote for literary magazines at that time. The letters themselves start in 1939, though it is from 1943 until his death in 1959 that most were written. He very rarely wrote fiction after dusk (he said he found efforts to do so too 'ghoulish' in result when read by daylight), and dark instead was when he wrote or dictated his letters. These are very much the chronicles of a midnight man, often spoken aloud as he sat up alone, electrified with an insomnia he had known since he was a young man.

As well as the letters never seen before here, other non-fiction pieces are resurrected for the first time, including an unpublished account of a fascinating meeting with the exiled gangster Lucky Luciano, held at a Naples hotel two years before Chandler's death. Also published for the first time since it appeared in print in 1948 is his memorable eye-witness description of that year's Oscar ceremony, a masterpiece of satire by a man on the cusp of retiring from Hollywood.

But like most great writers, Chandler's papers begin with some very bad poetry . . .

Tom Hiney

Republic of South Africa, March 2000

Act I (1909–1912)

Chandler's papers start with his first creative output – poems and essays – written in London shortly before the outbreak of World War I. Chandler was in his late teens and early twenties at the time, having finished his education at Dulwich College in south London, and a year learning German and French on the Continent. Several of his pieces found publication in three literary magazines of the day: the Westminster Gazette, *the* Academy *and* Chamber's Journal. *Chandler lived, however, at the indulgence of a growingly impatient uncle. His career as a published writer ended in 1912, at the age of twenty-four, with his emigration to the United States of America. He would not write for publication for another twenty years, and then as a pulp crime writer. He later described his early poetry as 'Grade B Georgian'.*

'A Woman's Way',
Westminster Gazette, 22 April 1909.

Come with me, love,
Across the world,
Ere glory fades
And wings are furled,
And we will wander hand in hand,
Like a boy and girl in a playroom land.

Stay with me love in the city's murk,
Where the sun but dares
Shyly to lurk,
And we will watch life hand in hand,
Like a boy and girl in a grown-up land.

Go from me, love,
If thou'lt not stay;
Follow thy bent,
'Tis the better way.
And I will seem to hold thy hand,
Like a child in dreams of fairyland.

I must leave thee, love?
'Tis I must go?
Then as thou wilt,
For thou must know.
Let me but think I hold thy hand,
I'll roam content in any land.

'Destiny',
sent to the Westminster Gazette, *never published.*

When no more shadows veil the silent city,
And down the hunted way no phantoms go,
When no more kings are proud or ladies waiting,
And no more pale narcissus decks the row,
When all the sighs are hush'd and musics broken
Along the moon-dazed garden chill'd and grey,
When fades each bud that was a lover's token,
Shall our love wither too and pass away?

When all the lost are worn and lonely,
And all the tunes are dim and sad and old,
When all the burning dreams we dream are only
Dead leaves too dead to tremble in the cold,
When no more roses droop or lillies falter,
When all the useless hours are wept and [unreadable]
God and silence by the broken altar
Shall our love be a hollow in the night?

Chandler's reviews and sketches from this time, written for the same London journals, show more of the voice that was later to emerge.

'The Remarkable Hero',
the Academy, 9 September 1911.

The time is not distant beyond the memory of living men when the hero of a typical novel had to be, if not a person of title, at any rate a man of tolerable family. If, in the days of his affluence, he did not possess a valet, or if when leaving home under a cloud he could not bestow his last sovereign on a head gardener, he was not likely to have many admirers. The snobbishness of those days was not greater than the snobbishness of these, but it was far simpler and more straightforward. It demanded quite honestly, on behalf of the middle-class reader, to mix with its social betters. No doubt it was perfectly right; if a man cannot choose his company even in novels things are in a bad way. But, however that may be, the distinction of the hero of that time was on the side of birth and breeding. He might be compelled by circumstances to associate with coalheavers, but even when his coat was shiny at the elbows the cabmen called him 'My lord'. When he told the landlady of his humble lodging that he had come into a marquisate and forty thousand a year, she always reminded him that she had known him at the first for a 'real gent'. His brains might be of feeble quality – indeed they usually were – but his manners were of the best. He might not know how to counter the most childish plot, but he invariably knew what to do with his hands in a drawing-room, a problem which has puzzled more people than ever troubled about the riddles of life and death.

In these days, however, good breeding is usually left as a minor perquisite to the villain. The hero may, as far as his social position is concerned, be anybody. He may drop his aspirates, he may be a boor, he may be ignorant of the most elementary rules of polite behaviour. Common honesty is not in the least a necessity to him. If he is fiendishly ugly, his adventures are all the more piquant. He may even be deformed, and his Life will sell in tens of thousands. He may squint, he may be club-footed, he may wear ready-made clothes, he may smoke in church, he may shoot foxes, he may browbeat women and patronize old men, he may do any of those forbidden things, for doing the least of which we would cut our dearest friends, and yet he may charm voracious multitudes. We care nothing for his clothes, nor his manners nor his antecedents nor his actions; in these respects we are all tolerant. But there is one quality which we demand in him: he must be a remarkable person. It matters very little in what his fate lies, whether in art, finance, sport, politics, exploration, swindling, or throat-cutting, but his intellect must be of the cast of great men.

The superficial reason is not very far to seek. Satirized out of his old, honest, matter-of-fact reverence for rank and wealth, the commonplace reader has to satisfy his inborn humility by looking up to an intellectual superior. Forbidden to act the flunkey to the aristocrat, he allows himself to adore the prima donna, the brilliant statesman, the swaggering freebooter, or the subtle master of intrigue. As he can no longer delight in the conversation of a duke, he accepts instead the conversation of an eminent house-breaker. And seeing that, however slight his knowledge of aristocratic circles might have been, his acquaintance with men of genius is even slighter – he is seldom able to detect the fraud which is so often played upon him. He may have a shrewd conception of how a duke would behave in a given situation, but a man of genius is above laws, and his actions are therefore incalculable. So the reader takes, with shut eyes and open mouth, whatever the journeyman novelist cares to offer him in the way of inspired heroes. He is unaware that the great detective whom he so much admires is as unlike any possible great detective as he is unlike a Patagonian anteater; these mysterious and incomprehensible actions pass not, as they should, for the well-meaning, but rather futile, efforts of an uninspired writer to simulate inspiration, but for the unfathomable deeds of a demigod. The more extraordinary they are, the more convinced the reader of his hero's genuineness. In the result, one reads of a great realistic author who studies his situations by kidnapping people, and forcing them to act for him; one finds a great thief who lives, surrounded by *objets d'art*, in a castle in the middle of a sea-girt rock; one finds a great poet who, by way of seeking inspiration, wanders like a madman over the face of the earth for several months, then, returning home, scribbles for four days without stopping, and finally falls dead over his completed masterpiece. The convenience for a second-rate author of a public which accepts such creations may easily be estimated. If extravagance be a sign of genius, then it is infinitely easier to portray genius than mediocrity. The man in the street is quite capable of judging his kind, but to judge the weird antics of an inspired soul he has only the unreliable experience of nightmares. He can but devour and hold out his innocent hands for more. So the curious fashion grows, until the remarkable becomes more common than the commonplace; an amusing development enough, if one does not pause to reflect how swiftly this highly-seasoned fare can destroy any lingering taste for the products of a restrained and disciplined art.

'Realism and Fairyland',
the Academy, *6 January 1912.*

Fairyland is Everyman's dream of perfection, and changes, dreamlike, with the mood of the dreamer. For one it is a scene of virgin, summery Nature undefiled by even the necessary works of man. For another it is a place where there exist no codes, conventions, or moral laws, and where people love or hate at sight, having their virtues and vices writ large upon them. For another it is a champaign dotted with fine castles, in which live sweet ladies clad in silk, spinning, and singing as they spin, and noble knights who do courteous battle with each other in forest glades; or a region of uncanny magic, haunting music, elves and charmed airs and waters. For still another it may be an anarchy of the beautiful touched with terror, tenanted by spirits who must be propitiated with cakes left on the window-sill and soft words spoken up the chimney at night. No two minds see fairyland alike or demand like gifts from it, and to the same fancy it alters from day to day, as the winds change which blow about a house, and with as little apparent reason.

Nevertheless it gives by contraries so accurate a reflection of life that the spirit of an age is more essentially mirrored in its fairy tales than in the most painstaking chronicle of a contemporary diarist.

The visions of what is called idealism are only reflections of fairyland and its experiences; they share with the scenes of that wonderful domain the merit of telling the truth about those who see them, and of telling it the more clearly because unconsciously. Yet there have arisen in the last half-century, more or less, certain long-faced, earnest, intent, and seemingly very daring people, who inform us sadly that we must look dull facts in the face if we would see truth, that we must not delude ourselves with rosy dreams of golden castles in Spain. By way of showing us how to proceed they rake over the rubbish-heaps of humanity in its close alleys and noisome slums to find fragments of broken moral crockery, to nose out the vices of unfortunate people, to set upon them the worst possible interpretation for the social system, and, by the simple process of multiplication, to construct from them what they consider typical human beings. Determining to hide nothing, and to show every side of life impartially, they forget that the things which necessarily strike them most in their impartial survey and appear most emphatic in their work are mere offal of the senses; as a man with a delicate sense of smell would find unpleasant odours the chief feature of life in a hovel of disease. Boldly declaring that they will cast aside all factitious optimism, they automatically choose the dark aspect of all things in order to be on the safe side; as a result unpleasantness becomes associated in their minds with truth, and if they wish to produce a faultlessly exact portrait of a man, all they need do is to paint his weaknesses and then, for the sake of propitiating the instinct of kindness left by some oversight in their hearts, to explain that his shortcomings are the inevitable consequences of a mistaken scheme of life. There remains only to set down the man thus portrayed in a *milieu*, the dullness, sordidness, and stuffiness of which is 'reproduced' with a monotonous and facile elaboration hitherto unknown in art, and a masterpiece of realism is obtained. It is hardly surprising that when such stuff is

6

given to tired and overworked men and women with unsteady nerves as a study for their leisure hours, it is apt to cause a certain flavour of despondency and pessimism to become characteristic of the time, with the social result that if any difficult problem of life clamours to be solved those best equipped for solving it have utterly lost all youthful hope and cheer and have no energy for the labour. They pass on with sighs, leaving the task to bureaucrats and party politicians.

It is an old sneer, no doubt, that realism is a picker-up of life's refuse, and it may be just that any point of view which belongs to a large class of people should find representation in art. But it has never been proved to the satisfaction of the most reasonable and easily convinced visionary that the realistic is a definite point of view. For in truth it is only the mood of Everyman's dull and depressed hours. We are all realists at times, just as we are all sensualists at times, all liars at times, and all cowards at times. And if it be urged that for this reason, because it is human, realism is essential to art, the obvious answer comes, that this claim entitles it at most to a niche in the temple, not as at present to a domination of the whole ritual, and that truth in art, as in other things, should not be sought by that process of exhaustion encouraged so fatally in our age by the pedants of science, and by their fallacy that it may be discovered by considering all the possibilities: a method which surrenders intuition and all the soul's fine instincts to receive in exchange a handful of theories, which, compared with the infinite forms of immortal truth known to the gods, are as a handful of pebbles to a thousand miles of shingly beach.

Faulty as its philosophy is, however, the realistic creed which dominates our literature is not due so much to bad theories as to bad art. To be an idealist one must have a vision and an ideal; to be a realist, only a plodding, mechanical eye. Of all forms of art realism is the easiest to practice, because of all forms of mind the dull mind is commonest. The most unimaginative or uneducated person in the world can describe a dull scene dully, as the worst builder can produce an ugly house. To those who say that there are artists, called realists, who produce work which is neither ugly nor dull nor painful, any man who has walked down a commonplace city street at twilight, just as the lamps are lit, can reply that such artists are not realists, but the most courageous of idealists, for they exalt the sordid to a vision of magic, and create pure beauty out of plaster and vile dust.

Before leaving for America and abandoning his early bid for immortality, Chandler wrote a poem, never sent for publication, called 'Free Verse'.

Yes, friend, the old ways are very becoming
To a certain type of mind,
Just as a poke bonnet
Is becoming
To a certain type of face.
But I find somehow that I require
A little more liberty,
To express my immortal soul
(That is, if it is immortal, which one rather doubts
After reading Freud).
You see, it's such a lot of trouble
To learn metre
And rhyming,
And there aren't many metres,
And still fewer rhymes,
And after all, when one has learned them,
What is it all worth?
You have something to say
To make it tell in that sort of cut and dried form.
And I haven't.
Really in this disintegrating civilization
What could one have to say
Except
That it's all an infernal bore,
And everyone knows that already.
But that other sort of poetry
Is like marble.

Anyone, I think, could make a sort of face
Out of putty
Even if only grotesque (and grotesques have their appeal),
But out of marble?
One rather, you know, needs to be a sculptor for that,
That is to say,
A fellow who has taken a little trouble
To learn his beastly business.
Your cameo carver, just think how long he has
To live with that little picture of his
Before it's done.
Mustn't he get sick of it? Of course, you say,
He would
If it wasn't a good one.
And mine aren't, you know.
I'd flatter my ideas by even
Calling them
Moods.
A little twist of phrase or thought
This way or that
To give it an air of meaning such a lot
More than it says.
A mere trifle of nervous reaction
From the sound of the elevated,
Or too much coffee,
Or a bad night after smoking till 2AM
One wouldn't surely use *form* for that sort of thing?
And yet it's worth putting on paper,
Partly because it's amusing
And easy,
And partly because
Occasionally (very occasionally)
One gets paid for it.
This stuff of mine is pure inspiration,
It's as easy as falling off a log,
The only difficulty is knowing where

To stop,
But I get that by just meandering
On
As long as I feel like
And then
Taking every third line
The gaps in the meaning (if any)
Make it all the more
Interesting.
And words themselves mean such a lot,
The cute little things.
Take 'mauve' for example,
What a lot that simple word seems to mean,
So much more than one can say.
I like
To put a word like that down
And just look at it
With my head on one side,
And run around it,
Around and around it
Until I get a bit dizzy,
And then sit down and
babble a bit
About any old thing that comes
into
My head. Finally I gather it up
With my poetic gift, a sort of shovel, you know,
And spatter it whimsically on a
few
Sheets of paper,
And there you are.
A poem more or less. At least
We call it that
For convenience.
However, old friend, I hope you'll regard
All this as confidential,

Strictly *entre nous*, as it were,
Because
Lots of people are talking quite seriously
About our American intellectual
Revolutionists
And one wouldn't want it to get about everywhere
That we're only intellectual
Bankrupts,
With a nice sense of the discords
Of a cracked fiddle
When fiddled by a rather indifferent performer
At the conflagration
Of a rather more than indifferent
Universe.

Act II (1918–1943)

Chandler had no capital of his own, and after jobbing as a shop clerk in Illinois and a tennis racquet-stringer in San Francisco, he qualified by night school as a bookkeeper. He obtained his first salaried job as an accountant at the Los Angeles Creamery. In 1917, aged twenty-nine, many of his English school friends having been killed during three and a half years of trench warfare, Chandler decided to sign up with a Canadian regiment and was shipped as a soldier recruit to Liverpool, and from there to the trenches. He rose to the rank of Sergeant, on several occasions leading men against enemy machine-gun fire. His position was bombarded one night, and most of Chandler's outfit were killed outright, and the survivors shipped to England for pilot instruction. Chandler learned to fly, but the war ended before he returned to action. He wrote a brief sketch of trench warfare while awaiting his shipment back to Canada.

'Trench Raid'.

The strafe sounded a lot heavier than usual. The candle stuck on the top of his tin hat guttered from something more than draught. The rats behind the dugout lining were still. But a tired man could sleep through it. He began to loosen the puttee on his left leg. Someone yelled down the dugout entrance and the beam of an electric torch groped about on the slimy chalk steps. He swore, retied his puttee and slithered up the steps. As he pushed aside the dirty blanket that served for a gas curtain the force of the bombardment hit him like the blow of a club at the base of the brain. He grovelled against the wall of the trench, nauseated by the din. He seemed to be alone in a universe of incredibly brutal noise. The sky, in which the calendar called for a full moon, was white and blind with innumerable Very lights, white and blind and diseased like a world gone leprous. The edge of the parados, lumpy with dirt from a recent housekeeping, cut this whiteness like a line of crazy camels in a nightmare against an idiotic moonrise. Against the emptiness of the night, a nose cap whined down nearby with a slow, intimate sound, like a mosquito. He began to concentrate on the shells. If you heard them they never hit you. With meticulous care he set himself to picking out the ones that would come close enough to be reckoned on as a possible introduction to immortality. To these he listened with a sort of cold exhausted passion until a flattening of the screech told him they had gone over to the support lines. Time to move on. Mustn't stay too long in one place. He groped round the corner of the bay to the Lewis gun post. On the firing step the Number One of the gun crew was standing to with half of his body silhouetted above the parapet, motionless against the glare of the lights except that his hand was playing scales on the butt of the gun.

Back home in Los Angeles, Chandler married a divorcee there named Cissy Pascal, and found work in the oil industry. As the Californian oil business boomed into the 1920s, Chandler's fortunes rose with it, in his capacity as accountant and right-hand man to the tycoon Joseph Dabney. His wife, however, proved to be seventeen years older than him, a disparity it is possible Chandler did not realize at the time of their marriage – there is a ten-year difference between the date of birth given on her birth certificate and that on her wedding certificate. Either way, Chandler certainly began showing heavy alcoholism at this time, an expensive and illegal activity in Prohibition America. He also began disappearing for booze-laden four-day weekends in out-of-town hotels with a secretary at Dabney's. He wrote nothing during this period. Eventually, in 1932, when Chandler was aged forty-four, Dabney sacked him. The Chandlers moved into a cheap rented apartment in Santa Monica, where Chandler began submitting stories to popular crime magazines. He stopped drinking altogether. Managing to sell his first effort to the Black Mask *magazine, and then subsequently work to other pulp magazines, Chandler began to build a reputation among pulp publishers and readers over the following five years. His stories began appearing on the covers, and earned him around $400 a time. But even without children,*

Chandler was struggling financially. Nonetheless, Chandler was noticeably getting better with each story; his dialogue grew tighter, and his characters more believable.

He also wrote private poems during this period, not intended – as far as one can see – for publication, and usually addressed to Cissy.

'Improvisation for Cissy',
29 October 1935.

You who have given me the night and the morning,
The stillness of your eyes. The softness of your lips,
The murmur of your heart like a steady sea,
And a voice like chanting in an Attic glade
(What have I given you?)

Lean years slinking by at the edge of dusk,
Gaunt with memories, hollow with old pain,
Silences into which come the voices of forsworn desires,
And the colors of unattainable delights,
These I have given to you,
And of them you have made jewels to wear in your hair.
This is what love is, this is what love is.
When love is this, how can there be despair?

Chandler's break came in 1938, when a New York agent called Sydney Sanders read some of Chandler's stories. Chandler was signed up by the publisher Alfred Knopf to write his first full-length book. This was to be The Big Sleep. *For the sake of clarity in the letters that follow, book, publication and movie titles mentioned by Chandler have been italicized.*

Letter to Alfred Knopf,
19 February 1939.

Please accept my thanks for your friendly letter and please believe that, whether you wrote to me or not, I should have written to thank you for the splendid send-off you are trying to give me. Having been more or less in business a great part of my life, I have some appreciation of what this involves, even though I know nothing of the publishing business.

Mr Conroy wrote to me twice that you had said something about my getting to work on another book and I answered him that I wanted to put it off until I had an idea what kind of reception this one would get. I have only seen four notices, but two of them seemed more occupied with the depravity and unpleasantness of the book than with anything else. In fact the notice from *The New York Times*, which a clipping agency sent me as a come-on, deflated me pretty thoroughly. I do not want to write depraved books. I was aware that this yarn had some fairly unpleasant citizens in it, but my fiction was learned in a rough school, and I probably didn't notice them much. I was more intrigued by a situation where the mystery is solved by the exposition and understanding of a single character, always well in evidence, rather than by the slow and sometimes long-winded concatenation of circumstances. That's a point which may not interest reviewers of first novels, but it interested me very much. However, there's a very good notice in today's *Los Angeles Times* and I don't feel quite such a connoisseur of moral decay as I did yesterday. They have Humphrey Bogart playing the lead, which I am in favor of also. It only remains to convince Warner Brothers.

As to the next job of work for your consideration, I should like, if you approve, to try to jack it up a few more notches. It must be kept sharp, swift and racy, of course, but I think it could be a little less harsh – or do you not agree? I should like to do something which would not be automatically out for pictures and which yet would not let down whatever public I may acquire. *The Big Sleep* is very unequally written. There are scenes that are all right, but there are other scenes still much too pulpy. Insofar as I am able, I want to develop an objective method – but slowly – to the point where I can carry an audience over into a genuine dramatic, even melodramatic, novel, written in a very vivid and pungent style, but not slangy or overly vernacular. I realize that this must be done cautiously and little by little, but I think it can be done. To acquire delicacy without losing power, that's the problem. But I should probably do a minimum of three mystery novels before I try anything else.

Thank you again and I do hope that when the returns are in, you will be not too disappointed.

Very sincerely,
Raymond Chandler

Letter to a fellow Black Mask *writer called George Harmon Coxe, who had written to congratulate Chandler on* The Big Sleep, *9 April 1939. When Chandler refers to 'Shaw' in the letter, he is referring to 'Cap' Joseph Shaw, pioneer editor of the* Black Mask. *A conscientious former army officer, Shaw had first been appointed editor of the magazine in 1926 when it was publishing all manner of formula pulp material, including romance, adventure and occult stories. Seeing an original new strain of Detective writers (including the young Dashiell Hammett) Shaw had dropped all other genres and concentrated on nurturing the best out of a new modern genre he felt capable of real greatness. A victim of his own vision, Shaw made such a success of his job that, by the end of the 1930s, the market was swamped with poor imitators and cut-throat publishing antics; a world Shaw had no grasp for, and from which he was to be rather tragically flung.*

Thanks for your letter, and I much appreciate your remarks about it and about the detective story business in general. I had a talk with Sanders while he was out here, and after that I'm surprised that anyone writes or publishes the darn things at all. He told me about Simon and Schuster's Inner Sanctum mysteries, for instance. Yet about 150 mystery books are dished out every year. I suppose if you are good enough there is a bare living in it – very bare. However, I'm used to that. I don't think I'd ever make the grade with slick magazines, unless in some kind of story quite different from anything I have attempted so far. I can't read their stuff for my own amusement, and that seems to be fatal. I should never have tried to work for *Black Mask*, if I hadn't, at one time, got a kick out of reading it.

Knopf seems to think that if somebody comes along who can write as well as Hammett, he should have Hammett's success. Knopf being a publisher should know his business, but my feeling is that somebody might come along who wrote a great deal better than Hammett and still not have anything like Hammett's success. But of course these things are quite unpredictable. In my opinion *Thieves Like Us* by Edward Anderson was an infinitely better and honester book than *Of Mice and Men*. Did it get anywhere? I doubt it.

Your letter doesn't sound very happy somehow. I had the idea that you would do well in Hollywood for a long time, that you had enough facility, and that you had enough character not to be impressed by the phony side. Of course I don't know you very well. Personally I think Hollywood is poison to any writer, the graveyard to talent. I have always thought so. But perhaps I have lived too close to it.

I'm terribly sorry about Shaw. He never told me anything about his affairs, always had the attitude (that rather pathetic attitude of small men trying to maintain their pride) that his failures were his own choice. He had left the *Black Mask* on a matter of policy and he had left the agency he was with because too much was going on for a man to do his own thinking. That sort of attitude, not those words. I suppose it's natural enough. It's bad enough to be kicked in the seat of the pants without having to go around and show the bruise. But as to his success or lack of it as an agent I knew absolutely nothing, except what I might deduce from the fact that he had no secretary. I think it was natural for him to think an opportunity existed for a type of agent who might be more than a marketer of merchandise. In the long run, if he could stick it out, and if he was adaptable enough, there might have been. Unfortunately he is not very adaptable and he wants to run his writers. The only kind of writers you can run are the ones who are negative, and they're hardly worth running. It's too tough a racket for people who have to be propped up from behind. Yet Shaw has, strangely enough, a great insight into writing and he can give a man a buck up when he needs it as nobody else I know can, or does. That should be worth a lot somewhere. I agree with you that he ought to have a magazine. I'd like to see him have the magazine which for years I've wondered somebody did not think worth publishing, a high class pulp detective story magazine aimed at the rather large class of people who find the pulps mostly too juvenile and who don't like the big magazines because of their fundamental dishonesty in the matter of character and motivation. He himself thought the market existed, I know, but he was doubtful about the supply of material. In that I think he was wrong, because the magazine would in a short time create its own material. Sanders told me the big magazines are getting steadily more and more starved for material, largely because of the lowering of prices and standards in the pulps. New writers do not appear to replace the ones who go to Hollywood and either stay there or learn how not to write there and never get over it. And the new writers don't appear because there's nothing in the business any more, no encouragement to do good work, and no recognition if, in spite of all practical considerations, you insist on trying to do it. I think the effect of this will be that some of the slick magazines will become more catholic in their tastes, more receptive to stories with unsatisfactory endings. Probably there will be some lowering of rates to balance some loss of cheap chic advertising. But in the long run there will be better and more readable magazines. I'm hoping.

If you come out to the Coast to live, you should look at La Jolla, before you decide where to live. I think it is a much better place than Laguna in every possible way. It is dear for a small town, but it has a perfect climate in both winter and summer, the finest coastline on the Pacific side of the country, no billboards or concessions or beachfront shacks, an air of cool decency and good manners that is almost startling in California. It has a few writers, not too many, no Bohemian atmosphere (but they will let you take a drink). It has fine public tennis courts and a nice gang of people who play good, but not too good, tennis. It has good schools, including a very fine private girls school, and a hospital, and is one of the most prosperous looking places you ever laid eyes on. I'm not being paid by the Chamber of Commerce either. I simply feel that La Jolla has that intangible air of good breeding, which one imagines may still exist in New England, but which certainly does not exist any more in or around Los Angeles. In theory one may not value very much that quality. One may like a free and easy neighborhood where they smash the empty bottles on the sidewalk on Saturday night. But in practice it's very comfortable. I expect to go back there in the fall, because whatever is the matter with me, climate seems to make very little difference, and I hate these poor man's towns. My idea of perfection would be a home in La Jolla and a very good cabin at Big Bear Lake, not too close to Pine Knot. Maybe I'll have them before my joints begin to creak very badly.

> *Letter to Erle Stanley Gardner,*
> *creator of Perry Mason and other fictional detectives, 5 May 1939. An*
> *ex-lawyer, Gardner had also begun his writing career under Shaw. A*
> *larger-than-life character who had been expelled from school for punching a*
> *teacher, he had also written to Chandler to congratulate him on* The Big
> Sleep. *The two men were to remain correspondents for many years.*
> *Though he was never to achieve the literary recognition of Hammett or*
> *Chandler, Gardner's countless novels (he once claimed to have written one*
> *in three days) have outsold them both — to date they have sold 300 million*
> *copies worldwide.*

When we were talking about the old *Action Detective* magazine I forgot to tell you that I learned to write a novelette on one of yours about a man named Rex Kane, who was an alter ego of Ed Jenkins and got mixed up with some flowery dame in a hilltop house in Hollywood who was running an anti-blackmail organization. You wouldn't remember. It's probably in your file No. 54276–84. The idea, probably not at all original to me, was so good that I tried to work it out on another tyro later on, but he couldn't see the point of putting the effort into something he knew he couldn't sell, preferring to put the effort into nineteen things he thought he could sell and couldn't. I simply made an extremely detailed synopsis of your story and from that rewrote it and then compared what I had with yours, and then went back and rewrote it some more, and so on. It looked pretty good. Incidentally, I found out that the trickiest part of your technique was the ability to put over situations which verged on the implausible but which in the reading seemed quite real. I hope you understand that I mean this as a compliment. I have never come even near to doing it myself. Dumas had this quality in a very strong degree. Also Dickens. It's probably the fundamental of all rapid work, because naturally rapid work has a large measure of improvisation, and to make an improvised scene seem inevitable is quite a trick. At least I think so.

And here I am at 2.40 a.m. writing about technique, in spite of a strong conviction that the moment a man begins to talk about technique, that's proof he is fresh out of ideas.

Letter to Blanche Knopf,
wife and assistant to Alfred Knopf, 23 August 1939. The Nazis had just invaded Poland, making the spectre of a Second World War a suddenly real one.

The effort to keep my mind off the war has reduced me to the mental age of seven. The things by which we live are the distant flashes of insect wings in a clouded sunlight. But –

I enjoyed meeting you so much. There is a touch of the desert about everything in California, and about the minds of the people who live here. During the years when I hated the place I couldn't get away, and now that I have grown to need the harsh smell of the sage I still feel rather out of place here. But my wife is a New Yorker, and that 95 with unlimited humidity doesn't appeal much either.

If I could write another 12,000 words I should have a draft of a book finished. I know what to write, but I have momentarily mislaid the urge. However, by the end of September, as you said, there should be something for you to wrinkle your very polite nose at. It's rather a mixed up mess that will run 75,000 words but I'll likely cut it at least 5000 and perhaps more. It will take me a month to shape it up. The title, if you should happen to approve, is *The Second Murderer*. Please refer to *King Richard III*, Act I, Scene IV.

SECOND MURDERER: What, shall we stab him when he sleeps?
FIRST MURDERER: No: then he will say 'twas done cowardly
  when he wakes . . .
How dost thou feel thyself now?
SECOND MURDERER: 'Faith, some certain dregs of conscience
  are yet within me.

However the joker is that the second murderer is −?

Sanders has been impressing on me the dire necessity of so contriving a detective story that it might be serialized. This is only horse sense, even though good serials seldom make good novels. I do not think this particular opus is the one he is looking for. In fact, I'm very sure of it. I'm not sure anyone is looking for it, but there's a law against burning trash up here during the fire hazard.

The Big Sleep, *and its hero Philip Marlowe, had been much thought of by Alfred Knopf (who had taken out the front page of* Publisher's Weekly *to advertise his new signing) but largely ignored by the critics, who were to take four novels before recognizing Chandler's literary worth. While continuing his magazine work, and his second novel, he and Cissy had moved out of the cramped Santa Monica apartment. Sick of the city, they were living in a series of rented homes around Los Angeles.*

> *Letter to George Harmon Coxe,*
> *17 October 1939. The 'Post' referred to by Chandler is the* Saturday
> Evening Post, *a glossy and high-paying weekly. The story Chandler
> sold to the* Post *is called 'I'll Be Waiting'. When he talks of England,
> and the comments made about the country by a Margaret Halsey, he is
> referring to a popular travel writer of the time, and author of a book called*
> With Malice to Some.

I have never made any money out of writing. I work too slowly, throw away too much, and what I write that sells is not at all the sort of thing I really want to write. I often envy these lads whose minds are tuned to the sort of story the slick magazines like − so that they really think it is good. I can't get around to that point of view. I sold a story to the *Post* recently, but I wrote it principally because Sanders pestered me. I didn't think much of the story when I wrote it – I felt that it was artificial, untrue and emotionally dishonest like all slick fiction. Sanders didn't seem to think much of it either. However he sold it. I still don't know whether it is any good. When I read it in print I thought it was, but print can be so deceiving. On the other hand one of my oldest friends took the trouble to write me two pages telling me how lousy it was. I suppose you have had the same experience. Whatever you do you get smacked in the face and usually from an unprotected angle.

Is your house built and are you in it? How are you getting along? I suppose if I read the right magazines, I should know. I should like to come east very much and find somewhere to live there that is not too hot and full of mosquitos (or mosquitoes) in summer and not too damn cold in winter. Is there such a place, where a poor man can live? I'm sick of California and the kind of people it breeds. Of course I like La Jolla, but La Jolla is only a sort of escape from reality. It's not typical. Anyhow, it's not in the least a matter of how good California is or how intransigent I am. If after twenty years I still fail to like the place, it seems that the case is hopeless. My wife came from New York. She likes California except during the hot months, but I think she agrees with me that the percentage of phonies in the population is increasing. No doubt in years, or centuries to come, this will be the center of civilization, if there is any left, but the melting-pot stage bores me horribly. I like people with manners, grace, some social intuition, an education slightly above the *Reader's Digest* fan, people whose pride of living does not express itself in their kitchen gadgets and their automobiles. I distrust Jews, although I admit that the really nice Jew is probably the salt of the earth. I don't like people who can't sit for half an hour without a glass in their hands, although apart from that I think I should prefer an amiable drunk to Henry Ford. I like a conservative atmosphere, a sense of the past. I like everything that Americans of past generations used to go and look for in Europe, but at the same time I don't want to be bound by the rules. It all seems like asking a bit too much, now that I've written it. I like all the things about England which Margaret Halsey liked and many of the things she didn't like, but that is largely because I was brought up there and English manners don't intimidate me. But I don't like Margaret Halsey, or any writer for whom a laborious and fizzled wisecrack is better than a simple truth.

Let's hear your news

Letter to George Harmon Coxe,
19 December 1939. Chandler notices similarities between the plot-lines of Erle Stanley Gardner and a new writer called A. A. Fair; as it turned out, Fair was in fact a pseudonym being used by Gardner, a point Chandler would later realize. In his mention of La Jolla Beach Club, and the tennis courts there, it is worth pointing out that Chandler had objected to the club's refusal to accept Jewish members and himself played on the public courts. Max Miller was a writer who lived in La Jolla, and an occasional drinking partner of Chandler.

Thanks for your nice meaty letter of October 30th which I hasten to answer with my usual headlong dash for the basket. Also for the photo of your house. It must be nice to have a home. We haven't had one in so long that I look back with a touch of nostalgia to any place we have stayed in as long as six months. I don't think we shall be here long either. Too dear, too damp, too elderly, a nice place, as a visitor remarked this afternoon, for old people and their parents.

If you still have that spare copy of your last book but one I'm hoping you are still feeling generous about it. The stock in the local library is out anyway. You're not represented. But so are not a lot of other people who should be, and so are represented some mighty feeble gestures at detective fiction. What do you make of a place that has one book by Hemingway, nothing by Faulkner, or Hammett, two pieces of oh-so-irritating wise guy crap by one Kurt Steel, everything by one J. S. Fletcher, a British brother who is far far duller than even a British brother has any right to be, nothing by Coxe, Nebel, Whitfield, or anybody you would think of as at all representative. And my god no Gardner, yet a book called *The Bigger They Come* by A. A. Fair which copies the Gardner technique exactly and even swiped Gardner's idea of how Ed Jenkins couldn't be extradited.

I had to throw my second book away, so that leaves me with nothing to show for the last six months and possibly nothing to eat for the next six. But it also leaves the world a far far better place to live in than if I had not thrown it away.

The literary colony here has undergone a few modifications since we were here last year. That is, those of the boys who are making any money are now playing their tennis at the Beach Club. The old caste system at its dirty work again. I don't think the beach club is very expensive, but a few bucks off his whisky ration plays hell with a writer's inspiration. Max Miller still frequents the public courts. He is a tall angular sourpuss with motheaten hair and very surly manners and a habit of swearing under his breath at himself and out loud at his partner. He is a splendid example of the good rule, Never Meet a Writer if You Liked his Book. There is also a dick pulp writer who writes under the name of Dale or something or other – I daresay I could find out. Maybe it's Dale Carnegie. This one has the shoulders of a weight-lifter and is very temperamental, throwing rackets and making tragic gestures at the sky, both arms extended and a look of agony on his face.

Letter to Blanche Knopf,
17 January 1940.

Terribly sorry to be so dilatory in getting out some work for you. I have had bad luck, bad health and a bad disposition for a long time. I finally did get a very rough draft done but was not at all pleased with it and had to put it aside for a while, in the hope of later discovering whether it was just plain lousy or whether it was a distorted point of view that made me think so. However I am a bit cheered up about it (in absentia) as my researches have convinced me that just plain lousy is the normal temperature of the detective story.

24

The troubles of advancing age drove me away from La Jolla. I actually developed a rheumatic right arm. We have not yet found a place to live but hope to soon and when there is a little peace in a world which knows no peace – all I ask is a quiet corner and deaf and dumb neighbors – I'll get at this thing again. You couldn't do anything with it now anyway, I suppose.

Letter to Blanche Knopf,
14 June 1940.

Sorry I haven't any snapshots to send you yet. I don't know how much time there is. My wife will try to take some, a very agonizing process for both of us, since she is very particular and I am very badly behaved. Commercial photos are no good. I am reaching the age where it takes an artistic touch to make anything of me. The fellows who have this want too much money, and I doubt the importance of the cause. While I am compelled by weight of opinion, some of it expert, some frankly prejudiced, to admit being one of the handsomest men of my generation, I also have to concede that this generation is now a little seedy, and I with it.

The last time no page proofs were sent to me. Your Mr Jacobs with whom I wrangled about this and that felt it was not necessary. I guess it wasn't. I never thought it was. As the book finally appeared there were, I think, two slight typographical errors, which should be a very low average for this kind of book. I certainly don't want to read two sets of page proofs, if I don't have to. Nor do I want the set of galley proofs as finally corrected which they sent me. It seems to be a custom, but I regret to say I burned them. Too heavy to carry in my hip pocket.

One thing I should like and that is a few changes in the natty biographical sketch on the jacket, if it is to be repeated. I haven't a copy of the book here, having lent my last copy to a friend who has so far failed to return it. From memory I recall three things I didn't like, one of which was my own fault, the second a misunderstanding, the third a use of the expression 'checkered career' which to me has a pejorative connotation. I used the phrase 'tax expert'.

The third point was that your promotion man seemed to get the impression that Dulwich College was a university. It is, in fact, one of the larger English Public Schools, not ranking with Eton, Harrow, Charterhouse, or Marlborough, but certainly ranking ahead of many of those which *Life* made a fuss over in its last issue. Incidentally, the editors of *Life* seem entirely unaware that a School Tie and an Old School Tie are entirely different things. But I daresay these pathetic relics of a lost world are no longer worth accuracy.

Fourth point, and one I'm sensitive on, but one which is difficult to make other Americans understand. I am not an Irish-American in the sense commonly understood. I am of Quaker descent on both sides. The Irish family my mother belonged to had not a single Catholic relative or connection, even by marriage. Furthermore the professional classes in Southern Ireland are and always have been largely non-Catholic. Those few Irish patriots who have had brains as well as spite have also been non-Catholics. I should not like to say that in Ireland Catholicism reached its all-time low of ignorance, dirt and general degradation of the priesthood, but in my boyhood it was bad enough. It does the Irish great credit that out of this flannel-mouthed mob of petty liars and drunkards there has come no real persecution of the non-Catholic elements.

Letter to George Harmon Coxe,
27 June 1940. In referring to his forthcoming second novel, Chandler mentions the resistance shown by Alfred and Blanche Knopf to Farewell, My Lovely *as a title.*

Your letter sounds rather gloomy. If so, forget it. The English Channel, even at its narrowest point, is worth fifty Maginot lines, and the English troops are at least equal to the Germans and the British colonials are far better. The job of landing in England enough shock troops, tanks and guns to overrun the country is probably a military possibility, but it is infinitely more difficult than anything the Nazis have yet attempted. Probably Hitler would rather have destroyed or captured the British army than anything else in the world, and he had all the cards.

As for bombing, it will be bad, but it will work both ways. If Hitler uses gas on England, it will be used on Germany. If he bombs London, Berlin will be bombed. And the British night bombers are better than the Germans, because the British have made a speciality of night bombing for twenty-five years. And on top of all this the English civilian population is the least hysterical in the world. They can take an awful pounding and still keep on planting lobelias.

On your recommendation and that alone I read Agatha Christie's *And Then There Were None*, and after reading it I wrote an analysis of it, because it was blurbed as the perfect crime story, incapable of dishonesty by reason of the way it was constructed. As entertainment I like the first half and the opening, in particular. The second half got pallid. But as an honest crime story, honest in the sense that the reader is given a square deal and the motivation and mechanisms of the murders are sound – it is bunk. The fundamental conception of the book in particular annoyed me. Here is a judge, a jurist, and this man condemns to death and murders a group of people on nothing but hearsay evidence. In no case did he have a shred of proof that any one of them had actually committed murder. In every case it was merely someone's opinion. But proof, even absolute inner conviction, simply did not exist. Some of these people admit their crimes, but this is all after the murders were planned, the judgement entered, the sentence pronounced. In other words it is as complete and shameless a bamboozling of the reader as ever was perpetrated. And I won't go into the mechanism of the crimes, most of which were predicated on pure chance, and some actually impossible. They also show an abysmal ignorance of lethal drugs and their action. But I'm very glad I read the book because it finally and for all time settled a question in my mind that had at least some lingering doubt attached to it. Whether it is possible to write a strictly honest mystery of the classic type. It isn't. To get the complication you fake the clues, the timing, the play of coincidence, assume certainties where only 50 per cent chances exist at most. To get the surprise murderer you fake character, which hits me hardest of all, because I have a sense of character. If people want to play this game, it's all right by me. But for Christ's sake let's not talk about honest mysteries. They don't exist.

Time out while I take a long breath.

The title of my book is not *The Second Murderer*, and that was not the title I had in mind when I was talking to you. I used that for a while as a working title, but I didn't like it, although Mrs Knopf did. I didn't know it had been announced under that name. When I turned the manuscript in they howled like hell about the title, which is not at all a mystery title, but they gave in. We'll see. I think the title is an asset. They think it is a liability. One of us has to be wrong. I suppose, since they are in the business, it should be I. On the other hand I have never had any great respect for the ability of editors, publishers, play and picture producers to guess what the public will like. The record is all against them. I have always tried to put myself in the shoes of the ultimate consumer, the reader, and ignore the middleman. I have assumed that there exists in the country people of education and some educated by life, who like what I like. Of course the real trouble is that you can be read by an enormous number of people who don't buy any books. My book is supposed to come out in August. The proofs were a bloody mess. I've just finished them and don't feel at all that they are a clean job yet.

All the best,
Ray

Letter to Blanche Knopf,
9 October 1940. Despite Knopf's efforts, Chandler's second novel had
again been largely ignored by the critics. Knopf was now rather bitterly
putting this down to the title.

Thanks for yours of October 1st which only just caught up with me. I am terribly sorry about the title and all that, and because the advance sales disappointed us, but you must remember that I didn't refuse to change the title, I just couldn't think of another one, you gave me no time at all, and although I said I liked the title, that should not have made you go against your business judgement. Everyone I know likes the title very much, but of course they are not in the trade. And I still think *Zounds, He Dies* was a good title. If I had had some of the time the book was being prepared, I'm sure I could have come up with something that would have satisfied you. But you caught me off base and got me rattled.

Personally, and in this I am borne out by one professional opinion, I think the handicap of the title will be only temporary and that if the sales do not do anything, it will really be for some other cause. For instance, the war. A woman out here who runs a string of rental libraries in and around Hollywood told a friend of mine that one of her branches had ten copies of the book out and that she hardly ever bought more than two copies of a mystery story. She said she thought this was in part due to a 'very marvellous' review in the *Hollywood Citizen-News* of Sept 21st. I hope you have seen this. Evidently they jumped the gun on the publication date. Of course it would have only a local influence, but the mere fact that a critic who confessedly does not like mystery stories and thinks they are mostly tripe should take this book seriously as a piece of writing is worth an awful lot to me. Because I am not innately a hack writer.

Syd Sanders sent me a cut of your advertisement in *The New York Times*. I don't see how you can afford it. If that doesn't start something, what's the use?

Letter to George Harmon Coxe,
5 November 1940.

Funny thing civilization. It promises so much and all it delivers is mass production of shoddy merchandise and shoddy people.

Letter to Erle Stanley Gardner,
1 February 1941. 'The streps' means streptococcus, a bacterial infection.

Good God, we have moved again.
Living, if you call it that, in a big apartment house in Santa

Monica, brand new and all that, I longed for your ranch. I longed for some place where I could go out at night and listen and hear the grass growing. But of course it wouldn't do for us, just the two of us, even if I had the price of a piece of virgin foothill. It's better over here, quiet and a house in a nice garden. But they are just beginning to build a house across the way. I shan't mind it as much as the good neighbors bouncing on the bed springs over at the apartment house.

Awfully sorry to hear you had been sick. I know what the streps can do to a person. Sulfanilimide seems to be able to cure anything but flat brain, which is what I suffer from.

Regards to your gang

Going to ground for a year, in which time he wrote hardly any letters, Chandler worked on a third novel. He was starting to grow dispirited with his lack of success.

Letter to Blanche Knopf,
15 March 1942.

Your letter, kind and charming as always, reaches me at a very bad time. I'm afraid the book is not going to be any good to you. No action, no likeable characters, no nothing. The detective does nothing. I understand that it is being typed, which seems like a waste of money, and will be submitted to you, and I'm not sure that that is a good idea, but it is out of my hands. At least I felt that you should be relieved of any necessity of being kind to me in a situation where kindness is probably not of any use. About all I can say by way of extenuation is that I tried my best and seemed to have to get the thing out of my system. I suppose I would have kept tinkering at it indefinitely otherwise.

The thing that rather gets me down is that when I write something that is tough and fast and full of mayhem and murder, I get panned for being tough and fast and full of mayhem and murder, and then when I try to tone down a bit and develop the mental and emotional side of a situation, I get panned for leaving out what I was panned for putting in the first time. The reader expects thus and thus of Chandler because he did it before, but when he did it before he was informed that it might have been much better if he hadn't.

However all this is rather vain now. From now on, if I make mistakes, as no doubt I shall, they will not be made in a futile attempt to avoid making mistakes.

Most sincerely,
Raymond Chandler

Letter to Alfred Knopf,
16 July 1942. The third book was published under the title The High Window.

I think the book is a very nice job indeed. I particularly like the type, which being smaller and yet very clear, keeps the page from looking crowded. The jacket also seems to be very effective. My wife does not like the photo on the back. All the photos I sent you were bad, and this is perhaps about the best, except the very first one, which no longer looks like me. I was reading in an English book the other day and noticed the remark, 'the kind of squit who has his picture on the dust cover of his book', or something like that. I feel a good deal like that myself. It is the custom in the country, of course, but most writers are such horrible-looking people that their faces destroy something which perhaps wanted to like them. Perhaps I am oversensitive, but I have several times been so repelled by such faces that I have not been able to read the books without the face coming between. Especially these fat crowlike middle-aged women's faces.

Letter to Blanche Knopf,
22 October 1942. The High Window, *yet again, was ignored by the reviewers.*

Thank you very much for writing to me about the sales of my last story, and many thanks also for your kind invitation to lunch. But alas, I'm down here in the desert 130 miles from Beverly Hills and I'm afraid I simply can't make it this time. I'm trying to bake out a sinus condition which has been weakening me for years. Don't expect any luck, but felt it had to be tried. I hope you and Mr Knopf are well and are bearing up under the many cares of these times.

So sorry you are feeling badly about the sales of *The High Window*. Last time you were out here you told me 4000 copies was the ceiling on a mystery. Either you were just saying that to comfort a broken heart or you are now repining for nothing at all. Why should it sell any more? And why should you spend so much advertising, and such very demanding advertising? I don't know anything about promotion, but when Mr Knopf was out here he gave me figures on what had been spent advertising *FML*, and to me they seemed very high. I said: 'Can you afford it?' He said: 'No.' But you keep on doing it. Why? *The High Window* was not the striking and original job of work that could be promoted to anything of consequence. Some people liked it better than my other efforts, some people liked it much less. But nobody went into any screaming fits either way. I'm not disappointed in the sales. I think it did well to get by at all. I am sure Sanders thinks so. I hope the next will be livelier and better and faster, because, as you know very well, it is the pace that counts, not the logic or the plausibility or the style. I have just been reading a book called *Phantom Lady*, by William Irish, whoever that is. It has one of those artificial trick plots and is full of small but excessive demands on the Goddess of Chance, but it is a swell job of writing, one that gives everything to every character, every scene, and never, like so many of our overrated novelists, just flushes the highlights and then gets scared and runs. I happen to admire this kind of writing very much. I haven't seen the book advertised anywhere and such reviews as I have seen of it show a complete unawareness of the technical merits of the book. So what the hell.

But as I said I do hope the next one will be better and that one of these days I shall turn one out that will have that fresh and sudden touch that will click. Most of all perhaps, in my rather sensitive mind, I hope the day will come when I won't have to ride around on Hammett and James Cain, like an organ grinder's monkey. Hammett is all right. I give him everything. There were a lot of things he could not do, but what he did he did superbly. But James Cain – faugh! Everything he touches smells like a billygoat. He is every kind of writer I detest, a *faux naif*, a Proust in greasy overalls, a dirty little boy with a piece of chalk and a board fence and nobody looking. Such people are the offal to literature, not because they write about dirty things, but because they do it in a dirty way. Nothing hard and clean and cold and ventilated. A brothel with a smell of cheap scent in the front parlor and bucket of slops at the back door. Do I, for God's sake, sound like that? Hemingway with his eternal sleeping bag got to be pretty damn tiresome, but at least Hemingway sees it all, not just flies on the garbage can.

Heigho. I think I'll write an English detective story, one about Superintendent Jones and the two elderly sisters in the thatched cottage, something with Latin in it and music and period furniture and a gentleman's gentleman: above all one of those books where everybody goes for nice long walks.

Letter to Alfred Knopf,
8 February 1943.

Thanks for yours of Jan 14th, and it was friendly, understanding and welcome, as always. Thank you also for the two-bit edition of *The Big Sleep*. I looked into it and found it both much better and much worse than I had expected – or than I remembered. I have been so belabored with tags like tough, hardboiled, etc., that it is almost a shock to discover occasional signs of almost normal sensitivity in the writing. On the other hand I sure did run the similes into the ground.

William Irish is a man named Cornell Woolrich, an author under his own name, and one of the oldest hands there are at the pulp detective business. He is known in the trade as an idea writer, liking the tour de force, and not much of a character man. I think his stuff is very readable, but leaves no warmth behind it.

No, I don't think the sinus condition is clearing up. This place bores me. But I've just about been talked into sticking out the mountains and the desert for another year. After that to hell with the climate, let's meet a few people. We have a one-store town here, and the meat situation would make you scream. On Wednesday morning the guy opens at 7 A.M. and all the desert rats are there waiting for him to give out numbered [rationing] tickets. Anybody who delays long enough to wash his face is automatically classed as parasitic and gets a high number, if he gets one at all. On Thursday at 10 the inhabitants bring their bronchitis and halitosis into the store and park in front of the meat counter and the numbers are coon-shouted. When we, having a very late number, kick our way up to the collapsed hunk of hamburger we are greeted with a nervous smile that suggests a deacon caught with his hand in the collection plate, and we leave bearing off enough meat for the cat. This happens once a week and that is all that happens, in the way of meat.

Of course we got to Palm Springs. If we didn't, I should not be writing this letter. I should be out in the desert trying to dig up a dead gopher. We happened on a rib roast a couple of weeks back, just walked in and said hello, and there the damn thing was. We ate for six nights running, behind drawn curtains, chewing quietly, so the neighbors wouldn't hear.

There are a bunch of guys in Washington, high-minded and pure, but once in a while I hunger for a touch of dirty Irish politics.

I hope to get a book out fairly soon. I am trying to think up a good title for you to want me to change.

Despite his restlessness, Chandler was growing more and more intrigued by the mechanics of writing and storytelling. There was also some glimmer of turning luck for him, from England. His first two novels had been published in Britain by Hamish Hamilton, and although he had been similarly ignored there by the critics, a significant fan base (including some in high literary circles) had started to emerge. In recognition of this, The High Window *had been reviewed prominently by* The Sunday Times. *His British sales were now matching his American ones.*

Chandler had started assembling some of his thoughts about writing for his own reference. From this early period, they include the following.

Notes (Very Brief Please) on English and American Style

The merits of American style are less numerous than its defects and annoyances, but they are more powerful.

It is a fluid language, like Shakespearean English, and easily takes in new words, new meanings for old words, and borrows at will and at ease from the usages of other languages, for example, the German free compounding of words and the use of noun or adjective as verb; the French simplification of grammar, the use of one, he, etc.

Its overtones and undertones are not stylized into a social conventional kind of subtlety which is in effect a class language. If they exist at all, they have a real impact.

It is more alive to *clichés*. Consider the appalling, because apparently unconscious, use of *clichés* by as good a writer as Maugham in *The Summing Up*, the deadly repetition of pet words until they almost make you scream. And the pet words are always little half-archaic words like *jejune* and *umbrage* and *vouchsafe*, none of which the average educated person could even define correctly.

Its impact is sensational rather than intellectual. It expresses things experienced rather than ideas.

It is a mass language only in the same sense that its baseball slang is born of baseball players. That is, it is a language which is being molded by writers to do delicate things and yet be within the grasp of superficially educated people. It is not a natural growth, much as its proletarian writers would like to think so. But compared with it at its best, English has reached the Alexandrian stage of formalism and decay.

It has Disadvantages.

It overworks its catchphrases until they not merely become meaningless play talk, like English catchphrases, but sickening, like overworked popular songs.

Its slang, being invented by writers and palmed off on simple hoodlums and ballplayers, often has a phony sound, even when fresh.

The language has no awareness of the continuing stream of culture. This may or may not be due to the collapse of classical education and it may or may not happen also in English. It is certainly due to a lack of the historical sense and to shoddy education, because American is an ill-at-ease language, without manner or self-control.

It has too great a fondness for the *faux naif*, by which I mean the use of a style such as might be spoken by a very limited sort of mind. In the hands of a genius like Hemingway this may be effective, but only by subtly evading the terms of the contract, that is, by an artistic use of the telling detail which the speaker never would have noted. When not used by a genius it is as flat as a Rotarian speech.

The last noted item is very probably the result of the submerged but still very strong homespun revolt against English cultural superiority. 'We're just as good as they are, even if we don't talk good grammar.' This attitude is based on complete ignorance of the English people as a mass. Very few of them talk good grammar. Those that do probably speak more correctly than the same type of American, but the homespun Englishman uses as much bad grammar as the American, some of it being as old as *Piers Ploughman*, but still bad grammar. But you don't hear English professional men making elementary mistakes in the use of their own language. You do hear that constantly in America. Of course anyone who likes can put up an argument against any other person's ideas of correctness. Naturally this is historical up to a point and contemporary up to a point. There must be some compromise, or we should all be Alexandrians or boors. But roughly and ordinarily and plainly speaking, you hear American doctors and lawyers and schoolmasters talking in such a way that it is very clear they have no real understanding of their own language and its good or bad form. I'm not referring to the deliberate use of slang and colloquialisms; I'm referring to the pathetic attempts of such people to speak with unwonted correctness and horribly failing.

You don't hear this sort of collapse of grammar in England among the same kind of people.

It's fairly obvious that American education is a cultural flop. Americans are not a well-educated people culturally, and their vocational education often has to be learned all over again after they leave school and college. On the other hand they have open quick minds and if their education has little sharp positive value, it has not the stultifying effects of a more rigid training. Such tradition as they have in the use of their language is derived from English tradition, and there is just enough resentment about this to cause perverse use of ungrammaticalities – 'just to show'em'.

Americans, having the most complex civilization the world has seen, still like to think of themselves as plain people. In other words they like to think the comic-strip artist is a better draftsman than Leonardo – just because he is a comic-strip artist and the comic strip is for plain people.

American style has no cadence. Without cadence a style has no harmonics. It is like a flute playing solo, an incomplete thing, very dextrous or very stupid as the case may be, but still an incomplete thing.

Since political power still dominates culture, American will dominate English for a long time to come. English, being on the defensive, is static and cannot contribute anything but a sort of waspish criticism of forms and manners. America is a land of mass production which has only just reached the concept of quality. Its style is utilitarian and essentially vulgar. Why then can it produce great writing or, at any rate, writing as great as this age is likely to produce? The answer is, it can't. All the best American writing has been done by men who are, or at some time were, cosmopolitans. They found here a certain freedom of expression, a certain richness of vocabulary, a certain wideness of interest. But they had to have European taste to use the material.

Final note – out of order – the tone quality of English speech is usually overlooked. This tone quality is infinitely variable and contributes infinite meaning. The American voice is flat, toneless, and tiresome. The English tone quality makes a thinner vocabulary and a more formalized use of language capable of infinite meanings. Its tones are of course read into written speech by association. This makes good English a class language, and that is its fatal defect. The English writer is a gentleman (or not a gentleman) first and a writer second.

Having completed a fourth Marlowe book, The Lady in the Lake, *at the start of 1943, Chandler's enthusiasm for the detective format was beginning to wane. The thought of starting on a fifth book did not much excite him, nor did writing for the pulps. He still had next to no money, and he was fed up with his nomadism, as well as his intense reclusivity. It was in this lull that Chandler received a fateful phone call from Los Angeles. Paramount Studios were searching for someone to adapt James Cain's novel* Double Indemnity, *and a producer called Joe Sistrom had happened to read and like a cheap copy of* The High Window. *He rang Chandler and asked him if he would be interested in the job. Chandler drove over to the studio and met with Sistrom and the film's director Billy Wilder. The meeting sparked a four-year stint in Hollywood which would turn Chandler quite quickly into a rich and famous man.*

Act III (1944–1946)

Throughout his time in Hollywood, and despite returning to full-scale drinking while there, Chandler remained a private man, eschewing the studio party scene. Most of his new intimacies continued to be forged in late-night letter-writing, at his rented house on Drexel Avenue, after Cissy – now in her seventies – had fallen asleep.

The adaptation of Double Indemnity, *Chandler's first screenwriting project, proved a box-office and critical success, and Paramount decided to hire their new find as a contract writer, resurrecting below-standard scripts for them. As his stock quickly rose in Hollywood, and as Warner Brothers announced its plans to make an A-movie adaptation of his first novel,* The Big Sleep, *starring Humphrey Bogart, Chandler became drawn further into Hollywood. It was to be a brief and intense relationship.*

Two new names began to feature in the correspondence of this time. Charles Morton was an early fan of Chandler's Marlowe books and editor of the intellectual East Coast journal Atlantic Monthly, *a magazine he was to persuade Chandler to contribute to occasionally. James Sandoe was also a Chandler fan, a crime book reviewer, and a university librarian in Colorado.*

Letter to James Sandoe,
26 January 1944.

What you say about me and Cain is very nice. It has always irritated me to be compared with Cain. My publisher thought it was a smart idea because he had a great success with *The Postman Always Rings Twice*, but whatever I have or lack as a writer I'm not in the least like Cain. Cain is a writer of the *faux naif* type, which I particularly dislike.

You are certainly not without company in your wish that 'something could be done about the disadvantages of the redlight segregation of detective stories from "novels" by the reviews'. Once in a long while a detective story writer is treated as a writer, but very seldom. However, I think there are a few very good reasons why this is so. For example: (a) Most detective stories are very badly written. (b) Their principal sale is to rental libraries which depend on a commercial reading service and pay no attention to reviews. (c) I believe the detective story is marketed wrong. It is absurd to expect people to pay any more for it than they would for a movie. (d) The detective or mystery story as an art form has been so thoroughly explored that the real problem for a writer now is to avoid writing a mystery story while appearing to do so. However, none of these reasons, valid or invalid as they may be, changes the essential irritation to the writer, which is the knowledge that however well and expertly he writes a mystery story, it will be treated in one paragraph while a column and a half of respectful attention will be given to any fourth-rate, ill-constructed, mock-serious account of the life of a bunch of cotton pickers in the deep south. The French are the only people I know of who think about writing as writing. The Anglo-Saxons think first of the subject matter, and second, if at all, of the quality.

Letter to James M. Cain,
20 March 1944. Mildred Pierce was another book by Cain, soon to be made into a film by Warner Brothers. Chandler would not work on the project.

It was very kind of you to send me an inscribed copy of your book and I'm very grateful to you. We have been down in the desert for a month, with poor luck in weather. I don't offer that as an excuse for not writing before, the fact being that I was so completely pooped after nine months at Paramount that I couldn't even make myself write a letter. Just sat and stared morosely out of the window at the sand dunes.

Very glad to hear about Warners' *Mildred Pierce*. It seems I may have a chance to work on it for them, but Paramount was not too keen about loaning me. Everybody who has seen *Double Indemnity* likes it (everybody that has talked to me, at least). The feeling is that it is a pretty fine picture and for once an emotionally integrated story has got on the screen in the mood in which it was written. I don't think any of the changes we made were in conflict with your basic conception. In fact, you would have had to make them yourself. I do not doubt that some of them might have been made better, but they had to be made. The emotional integration is due to the fact that the three guys who worked on the job did not at any time disagree about what they had wanted to achieve, but only on how to do it.

A curious matter I'd like to call to your attention – although you have probably been all through it with yourself – is your dialogue. Nothing could be more natural and easy and to the point on paper, and yet it doesn't quite play. We tried it out by having a couple of actors do a scene right out of the book. It had a sort of remote effect that I was at a loss to understand. It came to me then that the effect of your written dialogue is only partly sound and sense. The rest of the effect is the appearance on the page. These unevenly shaped hunks of quick-moving speech hit the eye with a sort of explosive effect. You read the stuff in batches, not in individual speech and counterspeech. On the screen this is all lost, and the essential mildness of the phrasing shows up as lacking in sharpness. They tell me that is the difference between photographic dialogue and written dialogue. For the screen everything has to be sharpened and pointed and wherever possible elided. But of course you know far more about it than I do.

I hope you get as good a script of *Mildred Pierce*. You don't need one quite so sharp. Are you working on it yourself?

Letter to Charles Morton,
12 October 1944.

The other day I thought of your suggestion for an article of studied insult about the Bay City (Santa Monica) police. A couple of D.A.'s investigators got a tip about a gambling hell in Ocean Park, a sleazy adjunct to Santa Monica. They went down there and picked up a couple of Santa Monica cops on the way, telling them they were going to kick in a box, but not telling them where it was. The cops went along with the natural reluctance of good cops to enforce the law against a paying customer, and when they found out where the place was, they mumbled brokenly: 'We'd ought to talk to Captain Brown about this before we do it, boys. Captain Brown ain't going to like this.' The D.A.'s men urged them heartlessly forward into the chip and bone parlor, several alleged gamblers were tossed into the sneezer and the equipment seized for evidence (a truckload of it) was stored in lockers at a local police headquarters. When the D.A.'s boys came back next morning to go over it everything had disappeared but a few handfuls of white poker chips. The locks had not been tampered with, and no trace could be found of the truck or the driver. The flatfeet shook their grizzled polls in bewilderment and the investigators went back to town to hand the Jury the story. Nothing will come of it. Nothing ever does. Do you wonder I love Bay City? Alas that its gambling ships are no more. The present governor of California won his office by disposing of them. Others had tried (or pretended to) for years and years. But there was always the legal argument as to whether the 12-mile limit should be measured from this place or that. Warren solved it very simply, and no doubt quite illegally. He commandeered enough boats and deputies to surround the ships and keep anyone from leaving them or reaching them. Then he just stayed there until they gave up.

A real clinical study of such a town would be fascinating reading.

Chandler wrote an article for Morton that autumn about detective writing, published that December in Morton's magazine under the title 'The Simple Art of Murder'.

Hammett took murder out of the Venetian vase and dropped it into the alley; it doesn't have to stay there for ever, but it was a good idea . . . Hammett gave murder back to the kind of people who do it for a reason, not just to provide a corpse; and with the means at hand, not with handwrought duelling pistols, curare and tropical fish. He put these people down on paper as they are, and he made them talk and think in the language they customarily used for these purposes . . . He was spare, frugal, hardboiled, but he did over and over again what only the best writers can ever do at all. He wrote scenes that seemed never to have been written before . . .

Letter to Charles Morton,
20 November 1944. 'Ak-Sar-Ben', referred to in the letter by Chandler,
was a populist movement that had flourished in the Nebraska of his
childhood, Ak-Sar-Ben being Nebraska spelt backwards. 'Bryan' was
Senator William Jennings Bryan, who was nominated as the Democratic
presidential candidate in the 1890s (he lost) and who later in his life
reappeared as counsel for the prosecution in the famous 'monkey trial'
against a Tennessee schoolteacher who had taught the theory of evolution
to his pupils.

Perhaps I ought to live in Boston. The civilized intelligence is pretty rare out west. This sounds like a snobbish thing to say, but I have lived here a long time and met very few people who were not half-baked in one way or another. Hollywood is full of very clever people, some of them rather more than clever, but the hard, glossy patina of Hollywood and New York smartness depresses me. You meet the bright people who have written something successful and have arrived and are very damn conscious of the fact. You meet lively young men who are really keen on making good pictures, if it is at all possible. But you do not meet the quiet, restrained, well-bred and inconspicuously intelligent kind of mind that is fairly common in England and I imagine also in New England. At least I hope so.

One of these days I'll write you something about myself. In the meantime things are not going too well. P. Marlowe is acting up, I have had many interruptions, and also a long-drawn-out wrangle with Paramount about a contract. I wish I had one of these facile plotting brains, like Erle Gardner or somebody. I have good ideas for about four books, but the labor of shaping them into plots appals me.

There was a time when I should have adored your kind of job, but would have been incapable of handling it. I never really had a great urge to write fiction, which is becoming more and more of a pseudo-art. (There's an article in that idea.) But you guys have an obligation too. That is, to avoid pompously bad writing and the kind of dulness that comes from letting flatulent asses pontificate about things they know no more about than the next man, if as much. There is a (to me) shocking example of this in the November *Harper's*, called 'Salute to the Literateurs'. Consider:

'For writers are people of peculiar sensitivity to the winds of doctrine which blow with especial violence in a time of rapid change – some more so than others, but none, except the outright hacks, completely immune.'

I regard that sentence as a disgrace to English prose. It says nothing and says it ponderously, in a clichéd manner, and without syntax. The 'some' obviously, by the sense, refers to writers, but just as obviously by the construction refers to 'winds of doctrine'. (Can't we leave phrases like that to Somerset Maugham?) How outright is a hack? And how completely immune is immune. Phooey. I continue:

'They react this way and that; they resist the currents and run with them: and while some produce works of little value in literary or any other terms, others of greater ability and substance, and therefore of greater importance, exhibit the same tendencies in writings of a high degree of excellence.'

Is there anything said here that could not be said better with a simple after-dinner belch? A little later he says:

'When the present war was in the making the most indicative scratchings on the literary seismograph were in red.'

44

When I showed that to my little seismograph he began to indicate four letter words in a very nasty shade of brownish-purple and had to be shut up in a dark room.

'Most indicative', 'literature seismograph [sic]', 'run with the current', two thousand years of Christianity and this is what we get in a literary magazine. Shame on you fellows!

I had an uncle in Omaha who was a minor politician – crooked, if I am any judge of character. I've been there a time or two. As a very small boy I used to be sent to spend part of summer at Plattsmouth. I remember the oak trees and the high wooden sidewalks beside the dirt roads and the heat and the fireflies and walking-sticks and a lot of strange insects and the gathering of wild grapes in the fall to make wine and the dead cattle and once in a while a dead man floating down the muddy river and the dandy little three-hole privy behind the house. I remember Ak-Sar-Ben and the days when they were still trying to elect Bryan. I remember the rocking chairs on the edge of the sidewalk in a solid row outside the hotel and the tobacco spit all over the place. And I remember a trial run on a mail car with a machine my uncle invented to take on mail without stopping, but somebody beat him out of it and he never got a dime. After that I went to England and was raised on Latin and Greek, like yourself.

Letter to Charles Morton,
18 December 1944.

I cannot complete my piece about screenwriters and screenwriting for the simple reason that I have no honesty about it. I may wake up with a different notion, but you cannot bully me into sending you something I am so deadly unsure about. There are points like these to make, but when you make them you get in a mess. E.g., 1. There is no mature art of the screenplay, and by mature I don't mean intellectual or postgraduate or intelligentsia-little magazine writing. I mean an art which knows what it is doing and has the techniques necessary to do it. 2. An adult, that is dirty or plain-spoken art of the screen, could exist at any moment the Hays Office and the local censorship boards would let it, but it would be no more *mature* than *Going My Way* is. 3. There is no available body of screenplay literature, because it belongs to the studios, not to the writers, and they won't show it. For instance, I tried to borrow a script of *The Maltese Falcon* from Warners; they would not lend it to me. All the writer can do is look at pictures. If he is working in a studio, he can get the scripts of that studio, but his time is not his own. He can make no leisurely study and reconstruction of the problems. 4. There is no teaching in the art of the screenplay because there is nothing to teach; if you do not know how pictures are made, you cannot possibly know how to write them. No outsider knows that, and no writer could be bothered, unless he was an out-of-work or manqué writer. 5. The screenplay as it exists is the result of a bitter and prolonged struggle between the writer (or writers) and the people whose aim is to exploit his talent without giving it the freedom to be a talent. 6. It is only a little over 3 years since the major (and only this very year the minor) studios were forced after prolonged and bitter struggle to agree to treat the writer with a reasonable standard of business ethics. In this struggle the writers were not really fighting the motion picture industry at all; they were fighting those powerful elements in it that had hitherto glommed off all the glory and prestige and who could only continue to do so by selling themselves to the world as the makers of pictures. This struggle is still going on, and the writers are winning it, and they are winning it in the wrong way: by becoming producers and directors, that is, by becoming showmen instead of creative artists. This will do nothing for the art of the screenplay and will actually harm those writers who are temperamentally unfitted for showmanship (and this will include always the best of them). 7. The writer is still very far from winning the right to create a screenplay without interference from his studio. Why? because he does not know how, and it is to the interest of the producers and directors to prevent him from learning how. If even a quarter of the *highly-paid* screenwriters of Hollywood (leaving out all the people who work on program pictures) could produce a completely integrated and thoroughly photographable screenplay, with only the amount of interference and discussion necessary to protect the studio's investment in actors and freedom from libel and censorship troubles, then the producer would become a business co-ordinator and the director would become the interpreter of a completed work, instead of, as at present, the maker of the picture. They will fight to the death against it.

I have a three year contract with Paramount, for 26 weeks work a year, at a vast sum of money (by my standards). Nothing of the above would give particular offense to the studio, but much of it would be deeply resented by many individuals and would involve me in constant arguments which would wear me out. But there is still more to be said, and it is worse yet. A system like this, prolonged over a long period of time, produces a class of kept writers without initiative, independence or fighting spirit; they exist only by conforming to Hollywood standards, but they can produce art only by defying them. Few, very few, of them are capable of earning a living as independent writers, but you will always have to have them, because you will never find enough talent in all Hollywood to make more than one tenth of its pictures even fairly good. Granted that there are too many made; they are going to be made, or the theaters will be dark. Enormous vested interests and the livelihoods of countless thousands of people are involved. Granted again that ninety per cent of Hollywood's pictures are not really worth making; I say that ninety per cent of the books and plays and short stories they were made from are not worth seeing or reading, by the same standards. And you and I know those standards are not going to change in our time.

Yet a writer, like me, who has little experience in Hollywood, and presumes to discuss the writers of Hollywood, must either lie, or say that they are largely over-dressed, overpaid, servile and incompetent hacks. All progress in the art of the screenplay depends on a very few people who are in a position (and have the temperament and toughness) to fight for excellence. Hollywood loves them for it and is only too anxious to reward them by making them something else than writers. Hollywood's attitude to writers is necessarily conditioned by the mass of its writers, not by the few who have what it calls integrity. It loves the word, having so little of the quality. Yet it is not fair for me to say in print that the writers of Hollywood are what they are; they have a guild and it may be that in so large an industry they must fight as a group; it is obvious that I have done nothing to help them achieve what they have achieved, and am not likely to, except indirectly, by helping to get out a few pictures a bit above the ruck. It is not even fair to call them overpaid; because other writers as a group are shockingly underpaid; Hollywood is the only industry in the world that pays its workers the kind of money only capitalists and big executives make in other industries. If it is something less than ideal, it is the only industry that even tries for idealism; if it makes bad art, no other makes any art, except as a by-product of money-making. If it makes money out of poor pictures, it could make more money out of good ones, and it knows it and tries to make them. There is simply not enough talent in the world to do it with, on any such scale. Its pictures cost too much and therefore must be safe and bring in big returns; but why do they cost too much? Because it pays the people who do the work, not the people who cut coupons. If it drains off all the writing talent in the world and then proceeds to destroy it by the way it treats it, then why is it able to drain off that talent? Because it knows how to pay for talent. The man who publishes my books has made more out of me than I have out of him, and he has not made it by selling the books, but by cutting himself in on radio and motion picture and reprint rights, which did not cost him a cent. Did he venture anything on the books? Of course not, not a dime. He was insured against loss by the rental libraries. He does not even know how to sell my kind of books, or how to promote them or how to get them reviewed. He just sits there and waits for something to happen, and when it happens, he rubs his hands and cuts himself a nice fat slice of it. But Hollywood pays me a large salary merely to try to write something it can perhaps use. And when I write something that pays, then it tears up my contract and writes a better one. I cannot despise an industry that does this.

I have a story in mind which I hope to do before I die; it will have almost no surface toughness at all, but the go to hell attitude, which is no pose with me, is likely to appear in it all the same.

My doubtfully honest uncle's (by marriage only) name was Ernest Fitt, and he was a boiler inspector or something, at least in name. He is dead now. I remember him very well. He used to come home in the evening (in the Plattsmouth period) put the paper on the music rack and improvise while he read it. I have read somewhere that Harold Bauer used to play his programmes through while reading a paper, but I always thought him a dull pianist, so it didn't surprise me. My uncle had talent, but no musical education. He had a brother who was an amazing character. He had been a bank clerk or manager in a bank in Waterford, Ireland (where all my mother's people come from but none of them were Catholics) and had embezzled money. He cleaned out the till one Saturday and, with the help of the Masons, escaped the police net to the continent of Europe. In some hotel in Germany his money was stolen, or most of it. When I knew him, long after, he was an extremely respectable old party, always immaculately dressed, and of an incredible parsimony. He once invited me to dinner. After the dinner he leaned over and in a confidential whisper said: 'We'll each pay for our own.' Not a drop of Scotch blood anywhere either. Pure middle-class Protestant Irish. I have a great many Irish relatives, some poor, some not poor, and all Protestants and some of them Sinn Feiners and some entirely pro-British . . . People over here don't understand the Irish at all. A third of the population of Eire is Protestant, and it is by far the best educated and most influential third. Almost all the great Irish rebels were Protestants, and the whole tone of their present nation is Calvinistic rather than Catholic. I grew up with a terrible contempt for Catholics, and I have trouble with it even now. My uncle's snob housekeeper wouldn't have a Catholic servant in the house, although they were probably much better than the trash she did have. What a world!

The rather amusing development in my uncle's case was that he took unto himself a Jewish mistress in London, raised her son, had two illegitimate children himself, and then married her. *But he never took her to Ireland!* I could make a book about these people, but I am too much of an Irishman myself ever to tell the truth about them.

Well, Hollywood is funny too. They had a contract with me and no story for me to work on. So I cooked up an idea and went in and told it to them and they rubbed their hands and said lovely, when do we start? But when my agent enquired what they proposed to pay for the idea, they tore their clothing into shreds and heaped ashes on their heads. It took several weeks of bitter wrangling to get them to see the light. I don't care anything about the money, I just like to fight. I'm a tired old man, but it takes more than a motion picture studio to push me around.

Letter to Dale Warren,
publicity director of the Houghton Mifflin publishing firm, 7 January
1945. Chandler's relationship with Alfred Knopf had soured during his
time in Hollywood, following a plagiarism incident. It had been brought to
the attention of Chandler, by a fan, that the crime writer James Hadley
Chase was lifting whole passages of Chandler's old fiction, most blatantly
in a book called No Orchids for Miss Blandish. *Chandler had*
contacted both his British and American publishers. While Hamish
Hamilton had forced Chase to write an apology in the British trade press,
Knopf – under advice from his attorney – had decided not to press the
matter. Annoyed, Chandler had moved to Houghton Mifflin. To
enhance the fresh slate, he was about to take the opportunity to change
agents, leaving Sydney Sanders for the New York firm Brandt &
Brandt.

I wrote melodrama because when I looked around me it was the only kind of writing I saw that was relatively honest and yet was not trying to put over somebody's party line. So now there are guys talking about prose and other guys telling me I have a social conscience. P. Marlowe has as much social conscience as a horse.

He has a personal conscience, which is an entirely different matter. There are people who think I dwell on the ugly side of life. God help them! If they had any idea how little I have told them about it! P. Marlowe doesn't give a damn who is president; neither do I, because I know he will be a politician. There was even a bird who informed me I could write a good proletarian novel; in my limited world there is no such animal, and if there were, I am the last mind in the world to like it, being by tradition and long study a complete snob. P. Marlowe and I do not despise the upper classes because they take baths and have money; we despise them because they are phony. And so on. And now I see ahead of me either an acute self-consciousness about simple things which I never had any idea of explaining, or a need to explain them at length, and with fury, in the very lingo I had been trying to forget. Because that is the only lingo people who can understand explanations of the sort will accept them in.

I have a letter from a lady in Caracas, Venezuela, who asks me if I would like to be her friend when she comes to New York. It has a faint suggestion about it of another letter I had once from a girl in Seattle who said that she was interested in music and sex, and gave me the impression that, if I was pressed for time, I need not even bother to bring my own pyjamas.

Letter to Hamish 'Jamie' Hamilton,
Chandler's British publisher, 11 January 1945. Chandler quotes a recent
letter from Hamilton, whom he has never met.

'I gather that he is a very big shot in Hollywood these days, and might resent advice, whoever the sender may be and however good his intentions.' That really cuts me to the quick. I am not a big shot in Hollywood or anywhere else and have no desire to be. I am, on the contrary, extremely allergic to big shots of all types wherever found, and lose no opportunity to insult them whenever I get the chance. Furthermore, I love advice and if I very seldom take it, on the subject of writing, that is only because I have received practically none except from my agent, Sydney Sanders, and he has rather concentrated on trying to make me write stuff for what we call the slick magazines over here. That is, the big shiny paper national weeklies and monthlies which cater principally to the taste of women. I have always felt myself entirely unfitted for this kind of writing. I much prefer Hollywood, with all its disadvantages.

Why not try me with a little advice some time? I am sure I should treat yours with the greatest respect and should, in any case, like to hear from you.

Letter to Charles Morton,
15 January 1945. Chandler had just signed another contract to work for Paramount, working on an original screenplay. 'HJ' is Henry James.

Yes, I know damn well that Harry Fitt was one of the clan of Limerick. I didn't know that he drank, but liquor was a family vice. Those who escaped it either turned religious or went in for white duck pants, like my Uncle Gus. Harry, your father's hired hand, must have been a cousin of my uncle. He was no near relation and I hardly know him, but when I read your letter I recalled that there was a Harry Fitt, that he lived in Omaha and that he worked in a hardware store. Since I was fresh out from England at the time and a hardware store was 'trade' I could hardly be expected to get on terms of anything like familiarity with him. Boy! Two stengahs, chop chop!

I am back at the grind and you might as leave write me there for a while. It makes no difference. (Perhaps you won't be writing to me any more at all.) In less than two weeks I wrote an original story of 90 pages like this. All dictated and never looked at until finished. It was an experiment and for a guy subject from early childhood to plot-constipation, it was rather a revelation. Some of the stuff is good, some very much not. But I don't see why the method could not be adapted to novel writing, at least by me. Improvise the story as well as you can, in as much detail or as little as the mood seems to suggest, write dialogue or leave it out, but cover the movement, the characters and bring the thing to life. I begin to realize the great number of stories that are lost by us rather meticulous boys simply because we permit our minds to freeze on the faults rather than let them work for a while without the critical overseer sniping at everything that is not perfect. I can see where a special vice might also come out of this kind of writing; in fact two: the strange delusion that something on paper has a meaning because it is written. (My revered HJ rather went to pieces a bit when he began to dictate.) Also, the tendency to worship production for its own sake. (Gardner suffers badly from this: but God never had any idea of making him a writer anyway. Edgar Wallace ditto. But Dumas Père might really have missed something by grinding the stuff out of the sausage machine.)

Had a nice letter from Dale Warren, but I wish people would stop writing letters about the neglected works of Raymond Chandler. I am so little neglected that I am often actually embarrassed by too much attention.

Letter to Charles Morton,
21 January 1945.

I have one complaint to make, and it is an old one – the cold silence and the stalling that goes on when something comes in that is not right or is not timely. This I resent and always shall. It does not take weeks to tell a man (by pony express) that his piece is wrong when he can be told in a matter of days that it is right. Editors do not make enemies by rejecting manuscripts, but by the way they do it, by the change of atmosphere, the delay, the impersonal note that creeps in. I am a hater of power and of trading, and yet I live in a world where I have to trade brutally and exploit every item of power I may possess. But in dealing with the *Atlantic*, there is none of this. I do not write for you for money or for prestige, but for love, the strange lingering love of a world wherein men may think in cool subtleties and talk in the language of almost forgotten cultures. I like that world.

Letter to Jamie Hamilton,
26 February 1945.

It was nice to hear from you and to be writing to you. I suppose agents are necessary to a writer because the writer, living a more or less secluded life as a rule, cannot possibly know what is going on in the literary world, what he ought to get for his material, and on what sort of conditions he should sell it. But I think the agent's function ends there. The moment he tries to influence a writer in his work, the agent just makes a nuisance of himself.

Letter to Charles Morton,
19 March 1945.

A man named Inkstead took some pictures of me for *Harper's Bazaar* a while ago (I never quite found out why) and one of me holding my secretary in my lap came out very well indeed. When I get the dozen I have ordered I'll send you one. The secretary, I should perhaps add, is a black Persian cat, 14 years old, and I call her that because she has been around me ever since I began to write, usually sitting on the paper I wanted to use or the copy I wanted to revise, sometimes leaping up against the typewriter and sometimes just quietly gazing out of the window from a corner of the desk, as much as to say, 'The stuff you're doing's a waste of my time, bud.' Her name is Taki (it was originally Take, but we got tired of explaining that this was a Japanese word meaning bamboo and should be pronounced in two syllables), and she has a memory like no elephant ever even tried to have. She is usually politely remote, but once in a while will get an argumentative spell and talk back for ten minutes at a time. I wish I knew what she is trying to say to them, but I suspect it all adds up to a very sarcastic version of 'You can do better.' I've been a cat lover all my life (have nothing against dogs except that they need such a lot of entertaining) and have never quite been able to understand them. Taki is a completely poised animal and always knows who likes cats, never goes near anybody that doesn't, always walks straight up to anyone, however lately arrived and completely unknown to her, who really does. She doesn't spend a great deal of time with them, however, just takes a moderate amount of petting and strolls off. She has another curious trick (which may or may not be rare) of never killing anything. She brings 'em back alive and lets you take them away from her. She has brought into the house at various times such things as a dove, a blue parakeet, and a large butterfly. The butterfly and the parakeet were entirely unharmed and carried on just as though nothing had happened. The dove gave her a little trouble, apparently not wanting to be carried around, and had a small spot of blood on its breast. But we took it to a bird man and it was all right very soon. Just a bit humiliated. Mice bore her, but she catches them if they insist and then I have to kill them. She has a sort of tired interest in gophers, and will watch a gopher hole with some attention, but gophers bite and after all who the hell wants a gopher anyway? So she just pretends she might catch one, if she felt like it.

She goes with us wherever we go journeying, remembers all the places she has been to before and is usually quite at home anywhere. One or two places have got her – I don't know why. She just wouldn't settle down in them. After a while we know enough to take the hint. Chances are there was an axe murder there once and we're much better somewhere else. The guy might come back. Sometimes she looks at me with a rather peculiar expression (she is the only cat I know who will look you straight in the eye) and I have a suspicion that she is keeping a diary, because the expression seems to be saying: 'Brother, you think you're pretty good most of the time, don't you? I wonder how you'd feel if I decided to publish some of the stuff I've been putting down at odd moments.' At certain times she has a trick of holding one paw up loosely and looking at in a speculative manner. My wife thinks she is suggesting we get her a wrist watch; she doesn't need it for any practical reason – she can tell the time better than I can – but after all you gotta have some jewelry.

I don't know why I'm writing all this. It must be I couldn't think of anything else, or – this is where it gets creepy – am I really writing it at all? Could it be that – no, it must be me. Say it's me. I'm scared.

P.S. Am working on a screen treatment of *The Lady in the Lake* for MGM. It bores me stiff. The last time I'll ever do a screenplay of a book I wrote myself. Just turning over dry bones.

> *Letter to Charles Morton,*
> *13 October 1945. Chandler was writing from Big Bear Lake, a mountain resort he and Cissy often used to escape the Angelino inferno. 'La Hellman' refers to Lillian Hellman, the New York playwright and long-term companion of Dashiell Hammett.*

As to talking about Hammett in the past tense, I did myself in that essay. I hope he is not to be so spoken of. As far as I know he is alive and well, but he has gone so long without writing – unless you count a couple of screenplay jobs which, rumor says, La Hellman really did for him that I wonder. He was one of the many guys who couldn't take Hollywood without trying to push God out of the high seat. I recall an incident reported to me when Hammett was occupying a suite at the Beverly-Wilshire. A party wished to make him a proposition and called late of a morning, was admitted by Hammett's houseboy to a living room, and after a very long wait, an inner door opened and the great man appeared in it, clad in an expensive lounging robe (no doubt with his initials on the pocket) with a scarf draped tastefully around his neck. He stood in silence as the man expounded. At the end he said politely: 'No.' He turned and withdrew, the door closed, the houseboy ushered the gent out, and the silence fell, interrupted only by the gurgling of a Scotch from an inner room. If you ever saw Hammett, you will realize the dignity and pathos of this little scene. He is a very distinguished-looking guy, and I imagine he could say 'no' without perceptible trace of a Brooklyn accent. I liked him very much and he was an amazingly competent drunk, which, having a poor head for liquor, I seem always to admire. It was a great pity that he stopped writing. I've never known why. I suppose he may have come to the end of his resources in a certain style and have lacked the intellectual depth to compensate for that by trying something else. But I'm not sure. I think the man has been both overrated and underrated. Your friend Dale Warren recently read *The Maltese Falcon*, for the first time too, and saw little in it. But I have read so much of this kind of writing that the gulf between Hammett and the merely tough boys seems to me vast. Old Joe Shaw may have put his finger on the trouble when he said Hammett never really cared for any of his characters.

I don't know whether this is a relaxed letter or not. I do begin to feel a little easing of the strain. This place is 7000 feet up, on the edge of a lake 20 miles long. It is no longer unspoiled nature, but it still has its points. The air is thin and dry like the desert (the Mojave is just down the hill to the east) and at this time of year it is very quiet, warm in the daytime and rather cold at night. We have had a fire before evening only once. There is nothing to do and I do it. We go out in the woods and I chop knots out of fallen trees and break up a few stumps of ironwood or mountain mahogany, a very hard reddish wood that burns like coal. I try to keep work out of my head, but can't quite do that. I had a bad time with MGM, very bad. Not their fault, they were very nice to me. After the first two days I worked entirely at home, which is against their rules but they made an exception. The trouble was that I was already too fed up to do a good job on any script; that I did not like working on a story of my own, being stale on it long since; and that I assumed in the beginning that a preliminary script would be all they could expect, since they take a very long time making their pictures. I found out as I began to send it in that they were regarding it as a shooting script (subject to cutting) and didn't want any other writer on it. That put the heat on me and I began to get nervous. MGM never had a script in 13 weeks since the company was organized, and here they were talking about going into production in November. Towards the end when I realized that I was getting more mechanical every day I tried to explain to them that they were making a mistake, that this work was full of loose ends and tired attitudes, and that if they really wanted to start shooting that soon, they needed a writer with some enthusiasm. No soap.

Letter to Charles Morton,
12 December 1945. Chandler had written a piece about screenwriting for
the Atlantic Monthly. *Beirne Lay was the author of a book called*
Twelve O'Clock High, *and Studs Lonigan was the pseudonym of the*
writer James T. Farrell. Jules Romains was a well-reputed French poet
and dramatist. J. P. Marquand, also referred to in this letter, was a writer
considered a great by many serious New York critics of the time, but who
Chandler – correctly, as it turned out – predicted would be soon forgotten.
Wolcott Gibbs and Edmund Wilson were both New York critics.

I noticed that (unlike the *Post*) you did not open my fan mail. There wasn't much, but there was a very charming letter from Beirne Lay and also one from Studs Lonigan which I have still to answer. He thinks I didn't go far enough, that I should have co-ordinated Hollywood with the special problems of the time. That's the worst of these deep thinkers. They can't let you speak your piece, then put your hat on and go home. Everything to them is just a chapter in the unfolding of the human struggle for decent expression, or like another volume from Jules Romains. Of course they're right in a way, more right than Wolcott Gibbs, for example, who seems to take the view, intellectually unsound, that an art which is practiced badly is simply a bad art and the view, socially and factually unsound, that a man is of necessity more intelligent than his cook. I liked his piece because I like the way he says things; I like but do not crave to practice the somewhat arctic style of the *New Yorker*. It has made *New Yorker* writers out of too many people who might have been their own writers. But I should somehow like to ask Wolcott whether he really believes the medium which has produced *The Last Laugh, Variety, M., Mayerling, Night Must Fall, Intolerance, The Little Foxes* (screen version), *The More the Merrier,* etc. etc. is really inferior to the medium which has produced *Dear Ruth, The Voice of the Turtle, Mrs Tanqueray's Past, The Lion and the Mouse, Oklahoma, Dear Brutus, Getting Married,* etc. etc. And if he agrees that it is not, I should further like to ask him whether criticism has any function whatsoever in the development and self-education of an art; because if it has, all he is really saying is that he does not want to review pictures because they are bad and bore him, whereas he does want to review plays because they are good and do not bore him. That may be his privilege but it is certainly not a critical opinion.

. . . I am still a bit dizzy from some remarks your pal Dale Warren made about *The Maltese Falcon*, which he apparently regards as quite inferior to *The Leavenworth Case*. (Read it for laughs, if you haven't.) I reread the *Falcon* not long ago, and I give up. Somebody in this room has lost a straitjacket. It must be me. Frankly, I can conceive of better writing than the *Falcon*, and a more tender and warm attitude to life, and a more flowery ending; but by God, if you can show me twenty books written approximately 20 years back that have as much guts and life now, I'll eat them between slices of Edmund Wilson's head. Really I'm beginning to wonder quite seriously whether anybody knows what writing is anymore, whether they haven't got the whole bloody business so completely mixed up with the subject matter and significance and who's going to win the peace and what they gave him for the screen rights and if you're not a molecular physicist, you're illiterate, and so on, that there simply isn't anybody around who can read a book and say that the guy knew how to write or didn't. Even poor old Edmund Wilson, who writes as if he had a loose upper plate, dirtied his pants in the *New Yorker* a few short weeks ago in reviewing Marquand's last book. He wrote: 'A novel by Sinclair Lewis, however much it may be open to objection, is at least a book by a writer – that is, a work of the imagination that imposes its atmosphere, a creation that shows the color and modelling of a particular artist's hand.' Is that all a good writer has to do? Hell, I always thought it was, but hell I didn't know Wilson knew it.

Can I do a piece for you entitled 'The Insignificance of Significance', in which I will demonstrate in my usual whorehouse style that it doesn't matter a damn what a novel is about, that the only fiction of any moment in any age is that which does magic with words, and that the subject matter is merely the springboard for the writer's imagination; that the art of fiction, if it can any longer be called that, has grown from nothing to an artificial synthesis in a mere matter of 300 years, and has now reached such a degree of mechanical perfection that the only way you can tell the novelists apart is by whether they write about miners in Butte, coolies in China, Jews in the Bronx, or stockbrokers on Long Island, or whatever it is; that all the women and most of the men write exactly the same, or at least choose one of half a dozen thoroughly standardized procedures; and that in spite of certain inevitable slight differences (very slight indeed on the long view) the whole damn business could be turned out by a machine just as well, and will be almost any day now; and that the only writers left who have anything to say are those who write about practically nothing and monkey around with odd ways of doing it?

I think you're all crazy. I'm going into the motion picture business.

Letter to Jamie Hamilton,
9 January 1946.

I am out on strike at Paramount – a one man strike. That is to say I refuse to perform under my contract and so far they refuse to cancel it. There is much talk of money, but that is a smoke screen. Beyond a certain point money merely means complication. You have the bother and expense of handling it and protecting it and you do not have the spending of it. Fundamentally the issue is freedom. I have only a limited number of useful years left and I do not want to use any of them up destroying what talent I have. It is possible to make good pictures – within limits – but to do it you have to work with good people. They exist in Hollywood, but they are scattered and at the moment none of them is available to me at Paramount. The studio is now under the control of a man whose attitude to picture-making is that if you own 1600 theatres, all you have to do is grind out the product as quickly and economically as possible. I cannot do anything in that atmosphere except spend time and collect a salary. It's not good enough. The last picture I did there nearly killed me. The producer was in the doghouse – he has since left – and the director was a stale old hack who had been directing for thirty years without once achieving any real distinction. Obviously he never could. So here was I a mere writer and a tired one at that screaming at the front office to protect the producer and actually going on the set to direct scenes – I know nothing about directing – in order that the whole project might be saved from going down the drain. Well, it was saved. As pictures go it is pretty lively. No classic, but no dud either. But at what a price! And then I had to go to MGM to work on *The Lady in the Lake*, which bored me so enormously that I practically rewrote the story in order to have something fresh to look at. I didn't finish it, and it is probably all bitched up by now (or perhaps I bitched it up), but after that one was over I had to be hit on the head with a baseball bat to make me get out of a chair.

I am doing a Marlowe story and frankly I wish it were better. In fact, except for practical reasons I'd like to forget all about Mr Marlowe for several years. But I have to keep him alive somehow. There are radio programs in the offing and other low ways of making money.

Letter to Miss Aron,
11 January 1946. The book being referred to is The High Window,
which features a Jewish coin-collector called Morningstar.

Dear Miss Aron:

I hope I address you correctly. I assume that you would have indicated, if it had been 'Mrs'. I thank you for your letter of November 30th and I quite agree that it deserves an answer. But I'm afraid I can't make a very good one, for the reason that I don't know what it is all about. I might say that I have received about a dozen letters on this subject, ranging from the pathological-vituperative to the courteous (of which yours is the only true example).

This book was published in 1942. It has been for sale and in rental libraries for quite a long time. Apparently the outburst is due to the .25 [cent] edition. I had heard no previous whisper of complaint. I have many Jewish friends. I even have Jewish relatives. My publisher is a Jew. Are you one of those who object to that word? If so, what would you like me to substitute? I am not being sarcastic. Also, all the letters have come from the east. Out here the Jews seem to be in a fair way to losing their inferiority complex. At least my doctor thinks so. He is a Jew also.

You say why don't I introduce a character as a 'thin-blooded Roman Catholic or a rugged Episcopalian'? Simply, my dear, because religion has nothing to do with it. You may happen to be an orthodox Hebrew, but there are Roman Catholic Jews and Christian Scientist Jews and Jews with no religion at all, and Jews – very, very many – who are Hebrews just once a year, on the Day of Atonement. I call a character a Jew for purely intellectual reasons occasionally, since there is, except on the most exalted levels of personality, a Jewish way of thought too.

The Jew is a type and I like types, that being so far as I have gone. He is of course many types, some recognizable a block away, some only on more intimate study, some hardly at all. I know there are Jewish people whom even Jews cannot pick out. I have had two secretaries who told me that, being both Jewish girls. There is a tone of voice, there is a certain eye, there is a coloring. It is not, dear lady, a matter of noses.

You are kind enough not to accuse me of anti-semitism. I am grateful for that since I am horribly tired of the whole subject. And at the same time I am terribly sorry for these tormented minds which cannot leave it alone, which worry it and keep it sore. A writer in the *Saturday Review of Literature* lately said that what the Jews demand is not the right to have geniuses, but the right to have scoundrels. I agree. And I demand the right to call a character named Weinstein a thief without being accused of calling all Jews thieves.

Let me in all kindness say one final word. You are yourself not the type, but if among your friends there is an impulse to go on an anti-semitic witch hunt, let them look for their enemies not among those who call a Jew a Jew, who put Jewish characters in their books because there are many Jews in their lives and all interesting and all different and some noble and some rather nasty – like other people – but let them look for their enemies among the brutes (whom they can easily recognize) and among the snobs who do not speak of Jews at all.

You are safe and more than safe with outspoken people like me.

Letter to Alfred Knopf,
12 January 1946. Though no longer Chandler's publisher, Knopf had
buried the hatchet with Chandler, and was to remain in touch for the rest
of Chandler's life. Knopf had written in response to reading Chandler's
article in the Atlantic *about screenwriting.*

One of the troubles is that it seems quite impossible in Hollywood to convince anyone that a man would turn his back on a whopping salary – whopping by the standards of normal living – for any reason but a tactical manoeuvre through which he hopes to acquire a still more whopping salary. What I want is something quite different: a freedom from datelines and unnatural pressures, and a right to find and work with those few people in Hollywood whose purpose is to make the best pictures possible within the limitations of a popular art, not merely to repeat the old and vulgar formulae. And only a little of that.

The ethics of this industry may be judged by the fact that late last night a very important independent producer called me up and asked me to do a screenplay of one of the most advertised projects of the year, do it on the quiet, secretly, with full knowledge that it would be a violation of my contract. That meant nothing to him; it never occurred to him that he was insulting me. Perhaps, in spite of my faults, I still have a sense of honor. I may quarrel, but at least I put the point at issue down on the table in front of me. I am perfectly willing to let them examine my sleeves for hidden cards. But I don't think they really want to. They would be horrified to find them empty. They do not like to deal with honest men.

From the beginning, from the first pulp story, it was always with me a question (first of course of how to write a story at all) of putting into the stuff something they would not shy off from, perhaps even not know was there as a conscious realization, but which would somehow distill through their minds and leave an afterglow. A man with a realistic habit of thought can no longer write for intellectuals. There are too few of them and they are too specious. Neither can he deliberately write for people he despises, or for the slick magazines (Hollywood is less degrading than that), or for money alone. There must be idealism but there must also be contempt. This kind of talk may seem a little ridiculous coming from me. It is possibly that like Max Beerbohm I was born half a century too late, and that I too belong to an age of grace. I could so easily have become everything our world has no use for. So I wrote for the *Black Mask*. What a wry joke.

No doubt I have learned a lot from Hollywood. Please do not think I completely despise it, because I don't. The best proof of that may be that every producer I have worked for I would work for again, and every one of them, in spite of my tantrums, would be glad to have me. But the overall picture, as the boys say, is of a degraded community whose idealism even is largely fake. The pretentiousness, the bogus enthusiasm, the constant drinking and drabbing, the incessant squabbling over money, the all-pervasive agent, the strutting of the big shots (and their usually utter incompetence to achieve anything they start out to do), the constant fear of losing all this fairy gold and being the nothing they have really never ceased to be, the snide tricks, the whole damn mess is out of this world. It is a great subject for a novel – probably the greatest still untouched. But how to do it with a level mind, that's the thing that baffles me. It is like one of these South American palace revolutions conducted by officers in comic opera uniforms – only when the thing is over the ragged dead men lie in rows against the wall, and you suddenly know that this is not funny, this is the Roman circus, and damn near the end of civilization.

Letter to Erle Stanley Gardner,
29 January 1946. Chandler was now working steadily on a fifth Marlowe
novel. The cheap editions of all four earlier Marlowes were now selling in
the hundreds of thousands, and Newsweek *had reported in 1945 that*
'Chandlerism, a select cult a year ago, is about to engulf the nation.'

Most of what you write is a complete surprise to me – including the idea that you are a lousy writer . . . As I speak I have two solid rows of Gardners in front of me, and am still trying to shop around to complete the collection. I probably know as much about the essential qualities of good writing as anybody now discussing it. I do not discuss these things professionally for the simple reason that I do not consider it worthwhile. I am not interested in pleasing the intellectuals by writing literary criticism, because literary criticism as an art has in these days too narrow a scope and too limited a public, just as has poetry. I do not believe it is a writer's function to talk to a dead generation of leisured people who once had time to relish the niceties of critical thought. The critics of today are tired Bostonians like Van Wyck Brooks or smart-alecks like Fadiman or honest men confused by the futility of their job, like Edmund Wilson. The reading public is intellectually adolescent at best, and it is obvious that what is called 'significant literature' will only be sold to this public by exactly the same methods as are used to sell it toothpaste, cathartics and automobiles. It is equally obvious that since this public has been taught to read by brute force it will, in between its bouts with the latest 'significant' bestseller, want to read books that are fun and excitement. So like all half-educated publics in all ages it turns with relief to the man who tells a story and nothing else. To say that what this man writes is not literature is just like saying that a book can't be any good if it makes you want to read it. When a book, any sort of book, reaches a certain intensity of artistic performance, it becomes literature. That intensity may be a matter of style, situation, character, emotional tone, or idea, or half a dozen other things. It may also be a perfection of control over the movement of a story similar to the control a great pitcher has over the ball. That is to me what you have more than anything else and more than anyone else. Dumas Père had it. Dickens, allowing for his Victorian muddle, had it; begging your pardon I don't think Edgar Wallace approached it. His stories died all along the line and had to be revived. Yours don't. Every page throws the hook for the next. I call this a kind of genius. I regard myself as a pretty exacting reader; detective stories as such don't mean a thing to me. But it must be obvious that if I have half a dozen unread books beside my chair and one of them is a Perry Mason, and I reach for the Perry Mason and let the others wait, that book must have a quality.

As to me, I am not busy and I am not successful in any important way. I don't get written what I want to write and I get balled up in what I write. I made a lot of money last year, but the government took half of it and expenses took half of the rest. I'm not poor, but neither am I in anything like your condition, or ever will be. My wife has been under the weather with the flu for ten days, but she wants to come down to your place as much as I do. I'm working at home because I refused to report to Paramount and took a suspension. They refused to tear up my contract. A writer has no real chance in pictures unless he is willing to become a producer, and that is too tough for me. The last picture I worked on was just one long row.

Letter to Blanche Knopf,
27 March 1946. Like Gardner, who eventually took to printing his own books, Chandler was outraged at how little he was making on the cheap reprints of his first four novels.

Thanks for your note, and it's always a pleasure to hear from you. I got pretty well into a Marlowe story but ran into a bad spell of flu and have been dragging myself around ever since . . . I don't understand this reprint situation at all. Is it right that a sale of a million copies of a two-bit reprint should bring the man who created the material sold a matter of $7500? This needs an answer. I do not think it is right. I think the author on all reprints should have a minimum royalty of ten per cent of the retail price. Anything less has me wondering what goes on. No wonder writers accept the conditions of Hollywood and say to hell with bookwriting. Leave it to the women. It's all mechanics and promotion anyway.

But don't take me too seriously. I am becoming a pretty sour kind of citizen. Even Hemingway has let me down. I've been rereading a lot of his stuff. I would have said here is one guy who writes like himself, and I would have been right, but not the way I meant it. Ninety per cent of it is the goddamndest self-imitation. He never really wrote but one story. All the rest is the same thing in different places – or without different parts. And his eternal preoccupation with what goes on between the sheets becomes rather nauseating in the end. One reaches a time of life when limericks written on the walls of comfort stations are not just obscene, they are horribly dull. This man has only one subject and he makes that ridiculous. I suppose the man's epitaph, if he had the choosing of it, would be: Here Lies A Man Who Was Bloody Good in Bed. Too Bad He's Alone Here. But the point is I begin to doubt whether he ever was. You don't have to work so hard at things you are really good at – or do you?

Letter to Jamie Hamilton,
30 May 1946.

When and if you see *The Big Sleep* (the first half of it anyhow), you will realize what can be done with this sort of story by a director with the gift of atmosphere and the requisite touch of hidden sadism. Bogart, of course, is also so much better than any other tough-guy actor that he makes bums of the Ladds and the Powells. As we say here, Bogart can be tough without a gun. Also he has a sense of humor that contains that grating undertone of contempt. Ladd is hard, bitter and occasionally charming, but he is after all a small boy's idea of a tough guy. Bogart is the genuine article. Like Edward G. Robinson when he was younger all he has to do to dominate a scene is to enter it. *The Big Sleep* has had an unfortunate history. The girl who played the nymphy sister was so good she shattered Miss Bacall completely. So they cut the picture in such a way that all her best scenes were left out except one. The result made nonsense and Howard Hawks threatened to sue to restrain Warners from releasing the picture. After long argument, I hear it, he went back and did a lot of re-shooting. I have not seen the result of this. The picture has not even been trade-shown. But if Hawks got his way, the picture will be the best of its kind. Since I had nothing to do with it, I say this with some faint regret. Well, that's not exactly true because Hawks time after time got dissatisfied with his script and would go back to the book and shoot scenes straight out of it. There was also a wonderful scene he and I planned together in talk. At the end of the picture Bogart and Carmen were caught in Geiger's house by Eddie Mars and his lifetakers. That is Bogart (Marlowe) was trapped there and the girl came along and they let her go in. Bogart knew she was a murderess and he also knew that the first person out of that door would walk into a hail of machine gun bullets. The girl didn't know this. Marlowe also knew that if he sent the girl out to be killed, the gang would take it on the lam, thus saving his own life for the time being. He didn't feel like playing God or saving his skin by letting Carmen leave. Neither did he feel like playing Sir Philip Sydney to save a worthless life. So he put it up to God by tossing a coin. Before he tossed the coin he prayed out loud, in a sort of way. The gist of his prayer was that he, Marlowe, had done the best he knew how and through no fault of his own was put in a position of making a decision God had no right to force him to make. He wanted that decision made by the authority who allowed all this mess to happen. If the coin came down heads, he would let the girl go. He tossed and it came down heads. The girl thought this was some kind of a game to hold her there for the police. She started to leave. At the last moment, as she had her hand on the doorknob, Marlowe weakened and started for her to stop her. She laughed in his face and pulled a gun on him. Then she opened the door an inch or two and you could see she was going to shoot and was thoroughly delighted with the situation. At that moment a burst of machine gun fire walked across the panel of the door and tore her to pieces. The gunmen outside had heard a siren in the distance and panicked and thrown a casual burst through the door just for a visiting card – without expecting to hit anyone. I don't know what happened to this scene. Perhaps the boys wouldn't write it or couldn't. Perhaps Mr Bogart wouldn't play it. You never know in Hollywood. All I know is it would have been a hair-raising thing if well done. I think I'll try it myself sometime.

Letter to Charles Morton,
14 June 1946.

I remember, long ago, when I was doing book-reviews in London, that my first impulse always was to find something smart and nasty to say because that sort of writing is so much easier. In spite of its superficial sophistication, the whole attitude of the *New Yorker* seems to me to have that same touch of under-graduate sarcasm. I find this sort of thing rather juvenile. In fact, heretical as it may seem, I'm beginning to find the *New Yorker* a very dull periodical.

Letter to H. N. Swanson,
Chandler's Hollywood agent, July 1946.

The publishers and others should quit worrying about losing customers to TV. The guy who can sit through a trio of deodorant commercials to look at Flashgun Casey or swallow a flock of beer and loan-shark spiels in order to watch a couple of fourth-rate club fighters rub noses on the ropes is not losing any time from book reading.

Letter to H. N. Swanson,
4 August 1946.

Dear Swanie:
   Thanks for your of July 31st. I imagine everyone ought to meet Samuel Goldwyn this side of paradise. I've heard he feels so good when he stops. But since the whole thing is predicated on my working for him and I ain't gonna, is it worth while? I don't know.

I don't know anything, except that the standard method of working with writers is not for me. I suppose you would regard Dudley Nichols as a great screenplay writer, and I shouldn't deny it. But what is there in his work that is Nichols? Is there anything in *The Bells of St Mary's*, *Scarlet Street* and *Stagecoach* that belongs to one man and one man only? If there is, I can't see it. Perhaps to someone more expert in the business, it would be apparent. To me all three of these pictures, and any others of his you care to mention that I have seen, could have been written by different writers. As far as any individual style is concerned, they are completely anonymous. This is not the kind of work I want to do in pictures. If that is the only kind of work – or something much inferior, technically – I am allowed to do, then I have nothing to contribute. For this reason I will not work for dominating people like Selznick or Goldwyn.

Love
Ray

P.S. La Valencia Hotel, Glencoe 52175 (San Diego) in case of emergency. An emergency would to my mind be a lot of money for nothing.

Chandler having decided to stop studio work and move permanently to La Jolla, the Atlantic Monthly *persuaded him to report on that year's Oscar ceremony for them.*

If you think most motion pictures are bad, which they are (including the foreign), find out from some initiate how they are made, and you will be astonished that any of them could be good. Making a fine motion picture is like painting 'The Laughing Cavalier' in Macy's basement, with a floorwalker to mix your colors for you. Of course most motion pictures are bad. Why wouldn't they be? Apart from its own intrinsic handicaps of excessive cost, hypercritical bluenosed censorship, and the lack of any single-minded controlling force in the making, the motion picture is bad because 90 per cent of its source material is tripe, and the other 10 per cent is a little too virile and plain-spoken for the petty-minded clerics, the elderly ingénues of the women's clubs, and the tender guardians of that godawful mixture of boredom and bad manners known more eloquently as the Impressionable Age.

The point is not whether there are bad motion pictures or even whether the average motion picture is bad, but whether the motion picture is an artistic medium of sufficient dignity and accomplishment to be treated with respect by the people who control its destinies. Those who deride the motion picture usually are satisfied that they have thrown the book at it by declaring it to be a form of mass entertainment. As if that meant anything. Greek drama, which is still considered quite respectable by most intellectuals, was mass entertainment to the Athenian freeman. So, within its economic and topographical limits, was the Elizabethan drama. The great cathedrals of Europe, although not exactly built to while away an afternoon, certainly had an aesthetic and spiritual effect on the ordinary man. Today, if not always, the fugues and chorales of Bach, the symphonies of Mozart, Borodin, and Brahms, the violin concertos of Vivaldi, the piano sonatas of Scarlatti, and a great deal of what was once rather recondite music are mass entertainment by virtue of radio. Not all fools love it, but not all fools love anything more literate than a comic strip. It might reasonably be said that all art at some time and in some manner becomes mass entertainment, and that if it does not it dies and is forgotten.

The motion picture admittedly is faced with too large a mass; it must please too many people and offend too few, the second of these restrictions being infinitely more damaging to it artistically than the first. The people who sneer at the motion picture as an art form are furthermore seldom willing to consider it at its best. They insist upon judging it by the picture they saw last week or yesterday; which is even more absurd (in view of the sheer quantity of production) than to judge literature by last week's ten best-sellers, or the dramatic art by even the best of the current Broadway hits. In a novel you can still say what you like, and the stage is free almost to the point of obscenity, but the motion picture made in Hollywood, if it is to create art at all, must do so within such

71

strangling limitations of subject and treatment that it is a blind wonder it ever achieves any distinction beyond the purely mechanical slickness of a glass and chromium bathroom. If it were merely a transplanted literary or dramatic art, it certainly would not. The hucksters and the bluenoses would between them see to that.

But the motion picture is not a transplanted literary or dramatic art, any more than it is a plastic art. It has elements of all these, but in its essential structure it is much closer to music, in the sense that its finest effects can be independent of precise meaning, that its transitions can be more eloquent than its high-lit scenes, and that its dissolves and camera movements, which cannot be censored, are often far more emotionally effective than its plots, which can. Not only is the motion picture an art, but it is the one entirely new art that has been evolved on this planet for hundreds of years. It is the only art at which we of this generation have any possible chance to greatly excel.

In painting, music and architecture we are not even second-rate by comparison with the best work of the past. In sculpture we are just funny. In prose literature we not only lack style but we lack the educational and historical background to know what style is. Our fiction and drama are adept, empty, often intriguing, and so mechanical that in another fifty years at most they will be produced by machines with rows of push buttons. We have no popular poetry in the grand style, merely delicate or witty or bitter or obscure verses. Our novels are transient propaganda when they are what is called 'significant', and bedtime reading when they are not.

But in the motion picture we possess an art medium whose glories are not all behind us. It has already produced great work, and if, comparatively and proportionately, far too little of that great work has been achieved in Hollywood, I think that is all the more reason why in its annual tribal dance of the stars and the big-shot producers Hollywood should contrive a little quiet awareness of the fact. Of course it won't. I'm just daydreaming.

Show business has always been a little overnoisy, overdressed, overbrash. Actors are threatened people. Before films came along to make them rich they often had need of a desperate gaiety. Some of these qualities prolonged beyond a strict necessity have passed into the Hollywood mores and produced that very exhausting thing, the Hollywood manner, which is a chronic case of spurious excitement over absolutely nothing. Nevertheless, and for once in a lifetime, I have to admit that Academy Awards night is a good show and quite funny in spots, although I'll admire you if you can laugh at all of it.

If you can go past those awful idiot faces on the bleachers outside the theater without a sense of the collapse of the human intelligence; if you can stand the hailstorm of flash bulbs popping at the poor patient actors who, like kings and queens, have never the right to look bored; if you can glance out over this gathered assemblage of what is supposed to be the elite of Hollywood and say to yourself without a sinking feeling, 'In these hands lie the destinies of the only original art the modern world has conceived'; if you can laugh, and you probably will, at the cast-off jokes from the comedians on the stage, stuff that wasn't good enough to use on their radio shows; if you can stand the fake sentimentality and the platitudes of the officials and the mincing elocution of the glamour queens (you ought to hear them with four martinis down the hatch); if you can do all these things with grace and pleasure, and not have a wild and forsaken horror at the thought that most of these people actually take this shoddy performance seriously; and if you can then go out into the night to see half the police force of Los Angeles gathered to protect the golden ones from the mob in the free seats but not from that awful moaning sound they give out, like destiny whistling through a hollow shell; if you can do all these things and still feel next morning that the picture business is worth the attention of one single intelligent, artistic mind, then in the picture business you certainly belong.

Act IV (1946–1954)

In 1946, Raymond Chandler bought a house overlooking the coast at La Jolla, north of San Diego, and tried to complete his fifth Marlowe novel, which he had entitled The Little Sister. *Freed from the strain of studio jobbing, and relishing the peace and quiet, Chandler also returned with fresh vigour to his letter-writing.*

Letter to Dale Warren,
2 October 1946.

I suppose you read a bookseller out here was convicted of selling indecency in Edmund Wilson's *Memoirs of Hectate County*. Very discouraging. The book is indecent enough of course, and in exactly the most inoffensive way – without passion, like a phallus made of dough. Now they are bootlegging the damn thing at $25 a copy. It isn't worth the original . . . Wilson's careful and pedestrian and sometimes rather clever book reviews misguide one into thinking there is something in his head besides mucilage. There isn't.

Having started both the above paragraphs with I – I was taught not to as a schoolboy – let me add that I (we) have moved to La Jolla permanently, or as permanently as anything can be nowadays. If I do any more work in Hollywood, which I probably shall, I can do nine tenths of it here anyway. That is, if I can find a secretary. We live close beside the sounding sea – it's just across the street and down a low cliff – but the Pacific is very sedate. We have a much better home than an out-of-work pulp writer has any right to expect.

The story I am working on seems to me to lack some of the nobler qualities. In addition to which I find it dull. I wonder could I be washed up for good. It's possible. Better men than me have gone to grease in Hollywood.

Letter to Jamie Hamilton,
6 October 1946.

My title may not be very good. It's just the best I can think of without straining. I have peculiar ideas about titles. They should never be obviously provocative, nor say anything about murder. They should be rather indirect and neutral, but the form of words should be a little unusual. I haven't achieved this here. However, as some big publisher once remarked, a good title is the title of a successful book. Offhand, nobody would have thought *The Thin Man* a great title. *The Maltese Falcon* is, because it has rhyme and rhythm and makes the mind ask questions.

Letter to Charles Morton,
5 December 1946.

The only slang that was any use to me in a book was either fresh-minted by Chandler or had stood a reasonable test of time. Anything else is liable to be obsolete by the time you get it into print.

Letter to Charles Morton,
12 December 1946.

I have my pedantic days, my ignorant days, and my don't-give-a-damn days, and I hope my secretary shares my moods.

Letter to Mrs Robert Hogan,
a New Jersey teacher who had written to Chandler asking for advice to give the young, 27 December 1946.

My experience with trying to help people to write has been limited but extremely intensive. I have done everything from giving would-be writers money to live on to plotting and rewriting their stories for them, and so far I have found it to be all waste. The people whom God or nature intended to be writers find their own

75

answers, and those who have to ask are impossible to help. They are merely people who want to be writers.

Letter to Charles Morton,
5 January 1947. The book he refers to, Command Decision, *was by a writer named William Wister Haines. 'Mr Weeks' was the Arts Editor of the* Atlantic.

I wrote you once in a mood of rough sarcasm that the techniques of fiction had become so highly standardized that one of these days a machine would write novels. What bothers me about this book, *Command Decision*, and others like it is that it has everything in the way of skill and perception and wit and honesty a good novel ought to have. It has a subject, something I never had yet; it has a sharp immediate sense of life as it is right now. I'd be hard put to it to say just what it does not have. I'm absolutely sure of that, although I don't expect to sell anyone else on the idea. Your Mr Weeks, who is a much more intelligent man than I am, thinks Marquand is a serious writer. I do not. I think he is a quick and clever journalist. I think he will be utterly forgotten five years after he dies, by all but a few. Is it that these books are written very quickly, in a kind of heat? No answer; so was a lot of literature that has lasted a long time. The time of composition has nothing to do with it; some minds distill much faster than others. Is it that writers of these books are using completely borrowed techniques and consequently do not convey the feeling that they have created, but rather that they have reported? Closer, but still not quite the answer. Undoubtedly we are getting a lot of adept reportage which masquerades as fiction and will go on getting it, but essentially I believe that it is lacking an emotional quality. Even when they deal with death, and they often do, they are not tragic. I suppose that is to be expected. An age which is incapable of poetry is incapable of any kind of literature except that cleverness of a decadence. The boys can say anything, their scenes are almost tiresomely neat, they have all the facts and all the answers, but they are little men who have forgotten how to pray. As the world grows smaller, so the minds of men grow smaller, more compact, and more empty. These are the machine-minders of history.

Letter to Edward Weeks of Atlantic Monthly,
regarding Chandler's article on the Oscar ceremony.

I'm afraid you've thrown me for a loss. I thought 'Juju Worship in Hollywood' was a perfectly good title. I don't see why it has to be linked up with crime and mystery. But you're the Boss. When I wrote about writers this did not occur to you. I've thought of various titles such as *Bank Night in Hollywood, Sutter's Last Stand, The Golden Peepshow, All it Needs is Elephants, The Hot Shot Handicap, Where Vaudeville Went When it Died,* and rot like that. But nothing that smacks you on the kisser. By the way, would you convey my compliments to the purist who reads your proofs and tell him or her that I write in a sort of broken-down patois which is something like the way a Swiss-waiter talks, and that when I split an infinitive, God damn it, I split it so it will remain split, and when I interrupt the velvety smoothness of my more or less literate syntax with a few dozen words of barroom vernacular, this is done with the eyes wide open and the mind relaxed but attentive. The method may not be perfect, but it is all I have. I think your proof reader is kindly attempting to steady me on my feet, but much as I appreciate the solicitude, I am really able to steer a pretty clear course, provided I get both sidewalks and the street in between.

Letter to James Sandoe,
7 February 1947.

The element of suspense in watching two characters gradually approach an inevitable catastrophe simply makes me nervous. I find I cannot read books like this any more.

Not very long ago, I was reading a book called *Man Against Himself*
by the eminent Dr Karl Menninger, who has a lucrative psychiatric
clinic somewhere in Kansas and was, I believe, a Brigadier General
in charge of neuroses in the United States Army. I got about a third
of the way through the book before I became completely convinced
that the whole thing was a fake.

One of my peculiarities and difficulties as a writer is that I won't
discard anything. I have heard that this is unprofessional and that it
is a weakness of the amateur not to be able to tell when his stuff is
not coming off. I can tell that all right, as to the matter in hand, but
I can't overlook the fact that I had a reason, a feeling, for starting
to write it, and I'll be damned if I don't lick it. I have lost months
of time because of this stubborness. However, after working in
Hollywood, where the analysis of plot and motivation is carried on
daily with an utter ruthlessness, I realize that it was always a plot
difficulty that held me up. I simply would not plot far enough
ahead. I'd write something I liked and then I would have a hell of
a time making it fit to the structure. This resulted in some rather
startling oddities of construction, about which I care nothing, being
fundamentally rather uninterested in plot.

Another of my oddities (and this one I believe in absolutely) is
that you never quite know where your story is until you have
written the first draft of it. So I always regard the first draft as raw
material. What seems to be alive in it is what belongs in the story.
Even if the neatness has to be lost, I will still keep whatever has the
effect of getting up on its own feet and marching. A good story
cannot be devised; it has to be distilled. In the long run, however
little you talk about it, the most durable thing in writing is style,
and style is the most valuable investment a writer can make with

his time. It pays off slowly, your agent will sneer at it, your publisher will misunderstand it, and it will take people you never heard of to convince them by slow degrees that the writer who puts his individual mark on the way he writes will always pay off. He can't do it by trying, because the kind of style I am thinking about is a projection of personality and you have to have a personality before you can project it. But granted that you have one, you can only project it on paper by thinking of something else. This is ironical in a way. It is the reason, I suppose, why in a generation of 'made' writers, I still say you can't make a writer. Preoccupation with style will not produce it. No amount of editing and polishing will have any appreciable effect on the flavor of how a man writes. It is a product of the quality of his emotion and perception; it is the ability to transfer these to paper which makes him a writer, in contrast to the great number of people who have just as good emotions and just as keen perceptions, but cannot come within a googol of miles of putting them on paper. I know several made writers. Hollywood, of course, is full of them; their stuff often has an immediate impact of competence and sophistication, but it is hollow underneath, and you never go back to it.

Letter to James Sandoe,
8 March 1947.

I dispute your point about *Pin to see Peepshow* connecting up with *Hamlet*, etc. I think *Hamlet*, *Macbeth*, the great Greek tragedies, *Anna Karenina* and Dostoievsky etc. are quite another matter, not so much because they are better, as because they are not nervous-making in the same sense. There is a great difference (to me at least) between a tragic ending and a miserably unhappy ending. You cannot write tragedy on the level of a suburban novel; you just get misery without the purging of high emotions. And naturally the quality of the emotions is a matter of projection, how it is done, what the total effect of style is. It is not a matter of dealing with heroic-sized people.

Letter to B. D. Zevion,
a publisher who had written to Chandler asking if he might provide a
pre-publication blurb for a book of poems by another colleague from his old
Black Mask *days, 9 March 1947.*

Thank you very much indeed for the Sandberg book. These poems
are curious reading now. When they were first published, apparently
they were blunt and brutal as hell. Now they seem, if anything,
restrained. They have a lot of Whitmanesque blether about man-
child and woman-child etc. which seems curiously strained, like a
pulp writer trying to achieve force by the use of harsh words rather
than harsh things. The 'he latchkeyed his way into the room' sort of
style. Once in a while I find it in my old stories, but don't think I put
it there. Editors took a lot of liberties with me in those days. I have a
couple of letters from Sandberg, very nice ones and very kind. They
are written in the same hopped-up lingo, which I suppose is natural
to him now, but I think originally it was just heavy breathing.

By the way, do you ever read the Bible? I suppose not very often,
but I had occasion to the other night and believe me it is a lesson
in how not to write for the movies. The worst kind of overwriting.
Whole chapters that you could have said in one paragraph. And
the dialogue! I bet you Macmillan's are sore as hell they didn't get
to publish it. They could have made it a best-seller easy. And as for
getting it banned in Boston I don't think they'd even have to grease
the Watch and Ward Committee to put the red light on it.

The really good detective picture has not yet been made, unless by
Hitchcock, and that is a rather different kind of picture. *The Maltese*

Falcon came closest. The reason is that the detective in the picture always has to fall for some girl, whereas the real distinction of the detective's personality is that, as a detective, he falls for nobody. He is the avenging justice, the bringer of order out of chaos, and to make his doing this part of a trite boy-meets-girl story is to make it silly. But in Hollywood you cannot make a picture which is not essentially a love story, that is to say, a story in which sex in paramount.

Letter to Charles Morton,
15 July 1947.

The picture of you I got from Swanson was a great shock to me. I had imagined you as a dry, pawky individual about 45 years old, addicted to a smelly pipe, conservative in dress and appearance, and a little Edwardian or perhaps late-Victorian or earlier. The fact seems to me that you are addicted to violent waistcoats like an English bookmaker, that you like to travel in souped up Fords which can outrun Cadillacs, and that you and your wife toured France on a motorcycle.

Letter to James Sandoe,
10 August 1947.

The *Partisan Review* arrived. It is rather a good magazine of the sort. These clever-clever people are a useful catharsis to the more practical minded writer who, whether he be commercial or not, has usually lived long enough not to take any set of opinions too seriously. As a very young man, when Shaw's beard was still red, I heard him lecture in London on Art for Art's Sake, which seems to have meant something then. It did not please Shaw of course; few things did unless he thought of them first. But art for propaganda's sake is even worse. And a critical magazine whose primary object is not to think intelligently but to think in such a form as to exploit a set of political ideas of whatsoever color always ends up by being critical only in the colloquial sense and intelligent only in the sense of a constant and rather labored effort to find different meanings for things than other people have found. So after a while these magazines always perish; they never achieve life, but only a distaste for other people's views of it. They have the intolerance of the very young and the anaemia of closed rooms and too much midnight smoking. And God help you if you have faith in them and meet them in person. But this last is a rather unfortunate jibe since it could be said of most writers. It is an awful thing to admire a man's book and then meet him, and have your entire pleasure in his work destroyed by a few egotistical attitudes, so that not only do you dislike his personality, but you can never again read anything he writes with an open mind. His nasty little ego is always leering at you from behind the words.

Letter to Charles Morton,
28 October 1947.

I had an idea for some time back that I should like to do an article on The Moral Status of the Writer, or more frivolously, The Hell With Posterity I Want Mine Now. Not a frivolous article really. It seems to me that in all this yapping about writers selling themselves to Hollywood or the slicks or some transient propaganda idea, instead of writing sincerely from the heart about what they see around them, – the people who make this kind of complaint, and that includes practically every critic who takes himself seriously, overlook the point (I don't see how they can, but they do) that no writer ever in any age got a blank check. He always had to accept some conditions imposed from without, respect certain taboos, try to please certain people. It might have been the Church, or a rich patron, or a generally accepted standard of elegance, or the commercial wisdom of a publisher or editor, or perhaps even a set of political theories. If he did accept them, he revolted against them. In either case they conditioned his writing. No writer ever wrote exactly what he wanted to write, because there was never anything inside himself, anything purely individual that he did want to write. It's all reaction of one sort or another.

Oh the hell with it. Ideas are poison. The more you reason, the less you create.

Letter to Charles Morton,
18 December 1947.

I have a great idea for an article which I don't want to write but want to read. Some dispassionate intelligent legally inclined man, not too legal, should write a piece explaining not who is a Commie or a Fellow Traveler, but why reasonably intelligent and well-to-do people like these Hollywood characters are Commies or FT's. Fundamentally they are not out to overthrow the government nor do they think they would be better off under Stalin. Most of them would be shot as right deviationists . . .

Letter to James Sandoe,
21 December 1947. By 'Uncle Dugastiviti' one presumes Chandler is referring to Joseph Stalin (known as Dzhugashvili), the then Communist leader of Russia, who still at this point had many admirers in the West.

You and I perhaps had better leave politics alone, since I am the reactionary type, who thinks the only reason Uncle Dugastiviti has no extermination camps is that he is still trying to find out how to get 50,000 miles out of a truck without greasing it.

Letter to Charles Morton,
1 January 1948.

I am one of those people who have to be known exactly the right amount to be liked. I am standoffish with strangers, a form of shyness which whisky cured when I was still able to take it in the requisite quantities. I am terribly blunt, having been raised in the English tradition which permits a gentleman to be almost infinitely rude if he keeps his voice down. It depends on a complete assurance that a punch on the nose will not be the reply. Americans have no manners as such; they have the manners that arise from their natures, and so when their natures are sweet they have the best manners in the world.

Letter to Dale Warren,
8 January 1948.

All my best friends I have never seen. To know me in the flesh is to pass on to better things.

Letter to James Sandoe,
27 January 1948. The 'Hollywood show in Washington' is in reference to the questioning of what was known as 'The Hollywood Ten' by Senator McCarthy's Committee on Un-American Activities.

Yes, I'd like to read George Orwell's essay 'The British People' very much. Orwell, like other clever people, probably including you and me, can be an ass on occasion. But that doesn't mean he is never interesting, perceptive, and very intelligent.

I've just read *The Iceman Cometh*, and I wish somebody would tell me what is so wonderful about this guy O'Neill. Of course, I haven't seen the play. I've only read it. In fact the only play of his that I ever saw was *Strange Interludes*, and you can not only have that but, if necessary I will pay you to cart it away . . . O'Neill is the sort of man who could spend a year in flophouses, researching flophouses, and write a play about flophouses that would be no more real than a play by a man who had never been in a flophouse, but had only read about them. If I am utterly wrong, please instruct me.

You ask me what I think about the Hollywood show in Washington. Well I think it's pretty awful that an investigation of this sort should be conducted by a man who thinks *Abie's Irish Rose* is a novel. I do not think that the Founding Fathers intended this sort of investigation to be conducted with microphones, flash bulbs, and moving picture cameras. Apart from that, until the Supreme Court defines the powers of Congressional committees and limits them (and our present Supreme Court are no bunch of legal

masters) I cannot see where the committee exceeded its rights . . .
I think the ten men who were cited had very bad legal advice.
They were afraid to say they were Communists or to say that they
were not Communists; therefore they tried to raise a false issue. If
they had told the truth, they would have a far better case before
the courts than they have now, and they would certainly have no
worse a case as regards their bosses in Hollywood. If Jack Warner
fires me because I admit to being a Communist, he's in a far more
shaky legal position than if he does the same thing because, through
refusing to answer the questions of the Congressional Committee,
I have brought the moving picture industry into bad repute . . . I
don't mean that these ten men are all convinced and avowed
Communists. I think about three of them are, that at least two
definitely are not, and that the rest don't know what the hell it's all
about. But I ought to qualify my remarks about the boys by saying
that, although I have no sympathy for them, and don't think
anything very awful will happen to them, except that they will
spend a lot of money on lawyers, and the worst kind of lawyers, I
reserve my real contempt for the industry. A business as big as the
motion picture industry ought to be run by men with a few guts,
men with enough moral and intellectual integrity to say that while
these matters are sub judice and while these men have not been
declared guilty of any crime by the courts, the producers are not
going to treat them as guilty . . . Sometimes I feel kind of sorry for
the poor bastards. They are so damned scared they won't make
their second or third million. In fact, they are just so damned scared,
period. What a wonderful thing it would be if the Motion Pictures
Producers Association had said to Mr Thomas, 'Sure, I guess we
have Communists in Hollywood. We don't know who they are.
How would you expect us to? We're not the F.B.I. But even if we
did know, there's an Attorney General in this country. He hasn't
accused these men of any crime. Congress hasn't legislated anything
that would cause their present or future membership in the Communist party to be a crime, and until it does we propose to treat
them just as exactly as we treat anyone else.' You know what would
happen if the producers had the guts to say anything like that? They

would start making good pictures, because that takes guts too. Very much the same kind of guts.

Letter to Frederick Lewis Allen,
editor of Harper's Magazine, *7 May 1948. Chandler refers to the*
magazine's dramatic critic, Eric Bentley.

Bentley is probably the best dramatic critic in the US and, with the possible exception of Mary McCarthy, the only dramatic critic in the US. The rest of the boys are just think-piece writers whose subject happens to be a play. They are interested in exploiting their own personal brand of verbal glitter. They are witty and readable and sometimes cute, but they tell you next to nothing about the dramatic art and relationship of the play in question to that art.

It is not enough for a critic to be right, since he will occasionally be wrong. It is not enough for him to give colorable reasons. He must create a reasonable world into which his reader may enter blindfold and feel his way to the chair by the fire without barking his shins on the unexpected dust mop. The barbed phrase, the sedulously rare word, the highbrow affectation of style – these are amusing, but useless. They place nothing and reveal not the temper of the times. The great critics, of whom there are piteously few, build a home for truth.

In his review of *The Iceman Cometh* that fading wit and tired needlepoint worker, George Jean Nathan says: 'With the appearance of this long awaited work our theater has become dramatically alive again. It makes most of the plays . . . during the more than twelve-year period of O'Neill's absence look comparatively like so much damp tissue paper.' Cute and quite easy, and with two sentences the spuriousness of an entire career seems to stand revealed. A critic who could write that drivel about O'Neill's drivel is *hors concours*. It would be charitable to say that he has lost contact with his brains; it would be far more accurate to say that he has merely made public a truth which was privately known from the beginning: that George Jean Nathan's critical reputation is not founded on his knowing what he is talking about, since obviously he doesn't now and most probably never did, but on a certain personal dexterity and the choice and order of words.

This play, *The Iceman Cometh*, is a sort of touchstone. If that fools you, you are a knuckle-headed sucker for pretentiousness.

It is wrong to be harsh with the New York critics, unless one admits in the same breath that it is a condition of their existence that they should write entertainingly about something which is rarely worth writing about at all. This leads or forces them to develop a technique of pseudo-subtlety and abstruseness which, when acquired, permits them to deal with trivial things as though they were momentous. This is the basis of all successful advertising copy.

In answer to the question as to whether Chandler's novels offered a serious insight of the criminal milieu.

Are you serious? No. Is this a criminal milieu? No, just average corrupt living with the melodramatic angle over-emphasized, not because I am crazy about melodrama for its own sake, but because I am realistic enough to know the rules of the game.

A long time ago, when I was writing for the pulps I put into a story a line like 'he got out of the car and walked across the sun-drenched sidewalk until the shadow of the awning over the entrance fell across his face like the touch of cool water'. They took it out when they published the story. Their readers didn't appreciate this sort of thing: just held up the action. And I set out to prove them wrong. My theory was that they just thought they cared nothing about anything but the action; that really, although they didn't know it, they cared very little about the action. The things they really cared about, and that I cared about, were the creation of emotion through dialogue and description; the things they remembered, that haunted them, were not for example that a man got killed, but that in the moment of death he was trying to pick a paper clip up off the polished surface of a desk, and it kept slipping away from him, so that there was a look of strain on his face and his mouth was half opened in a kind of tormented grin, and the last thing in the world he thought about was death. He didn't even hear death knock on the door. That damn paper clip kept slipping away from his fingers and he just wouldn't push it to the edge of the desk and catch it as it fell.

Letter to Charles Morton,
  referring to an editorial in the Atlantic Monthly, *7 May 1948.*

Dear Charlie,

Your magnificent piece of prose about wedding presents was read at the last meeting of the La Jolla Hermosa Writers Club. For a moment at the end there was a deadly silence, reminiscent of the silence that so discouraged Lincoln after his Gettysburg address. These hardened veterans of the rejection slip, the La Jolla writers, just sat stunned by your eloquence. Tears streamed down their worn faces and their toil-hardened hands tightened convulsively into knots of bone and sinew. Then, suddenly, with a crash of a giant comber on a reef the applause swelled up to a thunder. They came to their feet as one man, although nine tenths of them were women, and screamed with enthusiasm. There were roars of Author! AUTHOR! A U T H O R! and when the president restored order at last (by waving her hand-knitted bloomers) and it was explained that the Author was on the other side of the continent in a place called Boston (Laughter!) a resolution was passed that he be signed up to give a series of lectures on *The American Home and How To Avoid It.*

Your health was then drunk in elderberry wine and a toast proposed by a recently exhumed member of the British colony, an Old Surbitonite complete with tie. There followed a rendering of several arias from *Madame Butterfly* by the Choir of Kept Women from the La Jolla Beach and Tennis Club . . . I think you would have been very pleased and proud and touched. The affair was quite orderly for La Jolla. Two stick pokings, one assault with pearl hatpin, a couple of fountain pen squirtings, and a few spitballs alone marred the perfect harmony of the occasion. There was a slight tendency to cluster at one end and one old lady was pushed a little by another old lady who told her to stick her ear trumpet in her own ear if she had to use it. For a moment it looked as if this disagreement might end in a spot of hair-pulling, but the president quickly began to read a short story of her own composition and the hall emptied in a flash.

Letter to Jamie Hamilton,
10 August 1948. Chandler was unimpressed by British hardboiled writing.
Nor was he that impressed by Graham Greene.

Just read an English opus called *Blonde Iscariot* by Lustgarten. The year's worst for me. Half-cent pulp writing. What the hell's the matter over there?

I am trying desperately to finish *The Little Sister*, and should have a rough draft done almost any day I can get up enough steam. The fact is, however, that there is nothing in it but style and dialogue and characters. The plot creaks like a broken shutter in an October wind . . . Am reading *The Heart of the Matter*, a chapter at a time. It has everything in it that makes literature except verve, wit, gusto, music and magic; a cool and elegant set-piece, embalmed by Whispering Glades . . . There is more life in the worst chapter Dickens or Thackeray ever wrote, and they wrote some pretty awful chapters.

Letter to Jamie Hamilton,
19 August 1948. Carl Brandt was the head of Chandler's new literary
agency in New York.

The end of Greene's book was great. It atones for a lack I had felt before.

The story has its weaknesses. It is episodic and the emphasis shifts around from character to character and it is, as a mystery, overcomplicated, but as a story of people very simple. It has no violence in it at all; all the violence is off stage. If it has menace and suspense, they are in the writing. I think some of it is beautifully written, and my reactions to it are most unreliable. I write a scene and read it over and think it stinks. Three days later (having done

nothing in between but stew) I reread it and think it is great.
So there you are. You can't bank on me. I may be all washed up.

Lately I have been trying to simplify my life so that I need not
rely on Hollywood. I have no longer a business manager or a
secretary. But I am not happy. I need a rest badly and I cannot rest
until this is done and I sometimes think that when it is done it will
feel as tired as I am and it will show.

Assuming, for the moment, that the thing is any good, I feel that
you may rely on receiving some kind of script in a month. It may
need more work, but it will give you a chance to see whether I am
crazy or not. I guess Carl Brandt would tell you, up to a point.

I hope this is some help.

Ray

P. S. It contains the nicest whore I ever didn't meet

Letter to Cleve Adams,
a detective writer, 4 September 1948. Adams had written to Chandler
warning him about plagiarism of him in a detective book called Double
Take, *written by a Roy Huggins. W. T. Ballard, also referred to in the*
letter, was another old Black Mask *writer.*

It's nice to hear from you even in such queer circumstances . . . I
don't know Roy Huggins and have never laid eyes on him. He
sent me an autographed copy of his book *Double Take* with his
apologies and the dedication he says the publishers would not let
him put in. In writing to thank him I said his apologies were either
unnecessary or inadequate and that I could name three or four writers
who had gone as far as he had, without his frankness about it.

I did not invent the hardboiled murder story and I have never
made any secret of my opinion that Hammett deserves most or all
of the credit. Everybody imitates in the beginning. What Stevenson
called playing the 'sedulous ape'. I personally think that a deliberate
attempt to lift a writer's personal tricks, his stock in trade, his
mannerisms, his approach to his material, can be carried too far –
to the point where it is a kind of plagiarism, and a nasty kind

because the law gives no protection. It is nasty for two main reasons. It makes the writer self-conscious about his own work; an example of this is a radio program which ran the use of extravagant similes (I think I rather invented this trick) into the ground, to the point where I am myself inhibited from writing the way I used to. The second reason is that it floods the market with bad money and that drives out the good. But none of these things can be helped. Even if I were granted the absolute power to stop such practices, I doubt that I would know where to draw the line. For one must bear in mind that they can't steal your style, if you have one. They can only as a rule steal your faults.

Since Hammett has not written for publication since 1932 I have been picked out by some people as a leading representative of the school. This is very likely due to the fact that *The Maltese Falcon* did not start the high budget mystery trend, although it ought to have. *Double Indemnity* and *Murder My Sweet* did, and I was associated with both of them. The result is that everybody who used to be accused of writing like Hammett may now be accused of writing like me . . . More power to Mr Huggins. If he has been traveling on borrowed gas to any extent, the time will come when he will have to spew his guts into his own tank.

The law recognizes no plagiarism except that of basic plots. It is far behind the times in its concepts of these things. My ideas have been plagiarized in Hollywood and I have been accused of plagiarism myself, by a guy who said *The Blue Dahlia* was lifted from an original of his. Luckily Paramount were in a position to show that his story never left the story department. Unconscious plagiarism is widespread and inevitable. Throughout his play *The Iceman Cometh* O'Neill uses the expression 'the big sleep' as a synonym for death. He is apparently under the impression that this is a current underworld or half-world usage, whereas it is a pure invention on my part. If I am remembered long enough, I shall probably be accused of stealing the phrase from O'Neill, since he is a big shot. A fellow over in England, named James Hadley Chase, the distinguished author of *No Orchids For Miss Blandish* (which is half-cent pulp writing at its worst), made a practise in one of his books of lifting verbatim or almost verbatim passages from my books and from those of Jack Latimer and Hammett. He was eventually forced to make a public apology in the English equivalent of *Publisher's Weekly*. And he also had to pay the legal costs of three publishers incurred in forcing him to this apology. My American publisher's attorney would not even risk writing a letter to Chase's American publisher warning him about this. They still have some business honor left in England.

As for you and Ballard, I wouldn't know what the idea was at all. We all grew up together, so to speak, and we all wrote the same idiom, and we have all more or less grown out of it. A lot of *Black Mask* stories sounded alike, just as a lot of Elizabethan plays sound alike. Always when a group exploits a new technique this happens. But even when we all wrote for Joe Shaw, who thought that everyone had to write just like Hammett, there were subtle and obvious differences, apparent to any writer, if not to non-writers.

Letter to James Sandoe,
23 September 1948.

Your family sounds wonderful, including animals. Our cat is growing positively tyrannical. If she finds herself alone anywhere she emits blood curdling yells until someone comes running. She sleeps on a table in the service porch and now demands to be lifted up and down from it. She gets warm milk about eight o'clock at night and starts yelling for it about 7.30. When she gets it she drinks a little, goes off and sits under a chair, and comes and yells all over again for someone to stand beside her while she has another go at the milk. When we have company she looks them over and decides almost instantly if she likes them. If she does she strolls over and plomps down on the floor just far away enough to make it a chore to pet her. If she doesn't like them she sits in the middle of the living room, casts a contemptuous glance around, and proceeds to wash her backside . . . When she was younger she always celebrated the departure of visitors by tearing wildly through the house and ending up with a good claw on the davenport, the one that is covered with brocatelle and makes superb clawing, and it comes off in strips. But she is lazy now. Won't even play with the catnip mouse unless it is dangled in such a position that she can play with it lying down. I believe I told you how she used to catch all sorts of very breakable living things and bring them in the house quite unhurt as a rule. I'm sure she never hurt them intentionally. Cats are very interesting. They have a terrific sense of humor and, unlike dogs, cannot be embarrassed or humiliated by being laughed at. There is nothing worse in nature than seeing a cat trying to provoke a few more hopeless attempts to escape out of a half-dead mouse. My enormous respect for our cat is largely based on a complete lack in her of this diabolical sadism. When she used to catch mice – we haven't had any for years – she brought them alive and undamaged and let me take them out of her mouth. Her attitude seemed to be, 'Well, here's this damn mouse. Had to catch it, but it's really your problem. Remove it at once.' Periodically she goes through all the closets and cupboards on a regular mouse-inspection. Never finds any, but she realizes it's part of her job.

Letter to Charles Morton,
27 September 1948. The book referred to was called The Second World War.

I've been reading a book about the war by an English general named Fuller, who was, I believe, retired from the army while still in his prime, due to an incurable case of intelligence. The book makes more sense of the war than anything I had read so far, and also of the double-cross at Versailles that we let Clemenceau put over the Germans after they had surrendered on terms. Here is a man who has absolutely no prejudice in favour of his own countrymen, who can even give Montgomery his due without gagging, who in a short brilliant chapter makes clear that Mac-Arthur's island-hopping campaign in the South Pacific was as masterly a job of daring, imagination, and guts as the Italian campaign was a senseless and incredibly weak piece of strategic bungling. His disgust, both moral and practical and military, at so-called strategic bombing, is withering and precise. He thinks that in spite of our tactical brilliance we are a nation of military amateurs, and God knows history is proving him right. Even the English, who I am quite sure Fuller thinks incapable of an all-out offensive war because there is always some muttonhead in a high place to kill a good idea or block a daring one, – even the English understood that if we did not end up in Berlin and Vienna, we had fought for nothing. I don't think he quite despises Eisenhower, although his temperament makes him go for men like Bradley and Patton, but it's clear he feels that Eisenhower was not a strong enough man for the job, and that at a crucial moment in September 1944 he threw away a quick victory because he couldn't stand up to either Montgomery or Bradley, but had to compromise with both. It's quite a book. The thing that stands out all through is Fuller's belief that an independent air force is a ghastly mistake, because it will insist on fighting with the most expensive, the least profitable and the most uselessly destructive weapon, the heavy bomber, whereas its true function is ground support, interdiction of traffic and supplies, and logistics. When it was so used, usually unwillingly, the effect was immediate and startling; when it was used for saturation raids on cities like Hamburg, Berlin and Leipsig, it was militarily of small consequence and morally put us right beside the man who ran Belsen and Dachau.

Letter to Ray Stark,
a radio agent, 11 October 1948. Ray Stark later sent the letter to Screen Writer Magazine, *with the following note: 'I thought you might be interested in the following that I received from Raymond Chandler prior to the radio dramatization of Philip Marlowe. All the men connected with the show were tremendously helped by this advice – so I thought you might want to pass it on to other writers doing similar shows.'*

The point about Marlowe is to remember that he is a first person character, whether he shows up that way in a radio script or not. A first person character is under the disadvantage that he must be a better person to the reader than he is to himself. Too many first person characters give an offensively cocky impression. That's bad. To avoid that you must not always give him the punch line or the exit line. Not even often. Let other characters have the toppers. Leave him without a gag, insofar as it is possible. Howard Hawks, a very wise hombre, remarked to me when he was doing *The Big Sleep* that he thought one of Marlowe's most effective tricks was just giving the other man the trick and not saying anything at all. That puts the other man on the spot. A devastating crack loses a lot of its force when it doesn't provoke any answer, when the other man just rides with the punch. Then you either have to top it yourself or give ground.

Don't have Marlowe say things merely to score off the other characters. When he comes out with a smash wisecrack it should be jerked out of him emotionally, so that he is discharging an emotion and not even thinking about laying anyone out with a sharp retort. If you use similes, try and make them both extravagant and original. And there is the question of how the retort discourteous is delivered. The sharper the wisecrack, the less forcible should be the way it is said. There should not be any effect of gloating.

Letter to James Sandoe,
17 October 1948.

The psychological foundation for the immense popularity with all sorts of people of the novel about murder or crime or mystery hasn't been scratched. A few superficial and a few frivolous attempts, but nothing careful and cool and leisurely. There is a lot more to this subject than most people realize, even those who are interested in it. The subject has usually been treated lightly because it seems to have been taken for granted, quite wrongly, that because murder novels are easy reading they are also light reading. They are no easier reading than *Hamlet*, *Lear* or *Macbeth*. They border on tragic and never quite become tragic. Their form imposes a certain clarity of outline which is only found in the most accomplished 'straight' novels. And incidentally – quite incidentally, of course, a very large proportion of the surviving literature of the world has been concerned with violent death in some form. And if you have to have significance (the demand for which is the inevitable mark of a half-baked culture), it is just possible that the tensions in a novel of murder are the simplest and yet most complete pattern of the tensions in which we live in this generation.

Letter to Carl Brandt,
12 November 1948. Chandler had just returned from San Francisco.

The thing I love about S.F. is its go to hell attitude. The narrow streets are lined with NO PARKING AT ANY TIME signs and also lined with parked automobiles which look as if they had been there all day. For the first time in my life I saw a lady traffic cop, a real cop too, complete with nickel star and whistle. I saw one other cop. He was driving around with a piece of chalk on the end of a long stick and about once a block he took a swipe at some rear tyre, just to keep his hand in. The taxi drivers are wonderful too. They obey no laws except those of gravity and we even had one who passes street cars on the left, a offense for which you would probably get ninety days in Los Angeles. In case you think I am too cynical about the police, it just isn't possible to be. A committee of Superior Court judges in L.A. has been going into the *habeas corpus* business which seemed to them to be flourishing too richly and taking up too much court time. The chairman just let loose with a statement in which he announced that he was fed up with the racket of arresting bookies, or supposed bookies, then springing them on *habeas corpus* writs, a cost of $500 in bail and anywhere from $200 to $500 legal fees. He said that the vice squad boys seem to have perfected a system whereby they pull in suspected bookies and the moment the boys are booked along comes a lawyer and a bondsman with a writ; when the case is called the boys have lost all the evidence. Five or six of these operations per night could be quite lucrative over a period of time. The point is, of course, that each of these arrests and releases implies a crooked judge, a crooked lawyer, a crooked bondsman, and some crooked cops. No honest judge would set bail so high that the bond cost $500. Last night a couple of the boys didn't get writs. They had to stay in jail, and boy were they sore! The judge got cold feet. The thing that gets me in this lovely civilization is the complete indifference with which the public greets these disclosures.

Letter to Carl Brandt,
26 November 1948.

I worked at MGM once in that cold storage plant they call the Thalberg Building, fourth floor. Had a nice producer, George Haight, a fine fellow. About that time some potato-brain, probably [Edgar] Mannix, had decided that writers would do more work if they had no couches to lie on. So there was no couch in my office. Never a man to be stopped by trifles, I got a steamer rug out of the car and spread it on the floor and lay down on that. Haight coming in for a courtesy call rushed to the phone and yelled down to the story editor (I forget the name and never even met the man) that I was a horizontal writer and for Chrissake send up a couch. However, the cold storage atmosphere got me too quick, and the coteries at the writers table in the commissary. I said I would work at home. They said that Mannix had issued orders no writers to work at home. I said a man as big as Mannix ought to be allowed the privilege of changing his mind. So I worked at home, and only ever went over there three or four times to talk to Haight. I've only worked at three studios and Paramount was the only one I liked. They do somehow maintain the country club atmosphere there to an extent. At the writers table at Paramount I heard some of the best wit I've ever heard in my life. Some of the boys are at their best when not writing.

Letter to Jamie Hamilton,
29 November 1948.

It's nice of Priestley to want to read my stuff. Bless him! I remember him saying, 'They don't write like this at Dulwich.' That may be, but if I hadn't grown up with Latin and Greek, I doubt if I would know so well where to draw the very subtle line between what I call the vernacular style and what I should call an illiterate or *faux naif* style.

Letter to Lenore Offord,
December 1948. Offord was another established crime writer of the day,
and not one Chandler admired.

Most writers have the egotism of actors with none of the good looks or charm.

Letter to James Sandoe,
6 December 1948.

I knew a banker once from Aberdeen, Washington, who served two or three years in federal prison for making unsecured loans from the bank's funds to the ranchers on whom the bank's business was built. He was a perfectly honest man, he didn't make a cent out of what he did. It was during the depression and the ranchers had to have money or go broke. If they went broke, the bank went broke, because its mortgage loans would become worthless . . . This bank undoubtedly broke the banking laws. He admitted it. But who was he defrauding? The stockholders of the bank? He was one himself and the others were all men of property in the neighborhood. The stock was not traded in. There is something tragically wrong with a system of justice which can and does make criminals of honest men and can only convict gangsters and racketeers when they don't pay their taxes. Of course to be fair I must also admit that there is something wrong with a financial system which ensures that every corporation executive during a time of depression will risk going to jail a dozen times a month in his efforts to save his company. I personally believe, and I am not a socialist or anything of the sort, that there is a basic fallacy about our financial system. It simply implies a fundamental cheat, a dishonest profit, a non-existent value.

Letter to Dale Warren,
19 December 1948

Your caliber is all right so far as I can see. You can kill a man with any size gun, but you are more likely to hit him with a small one, unless of course it's a custom-built job like a Mauser x763 (approx .32 caliber) which has an effective range almost as great as a military rifle and must therefore have a terrific kick. I have a .38 Smith and Wesson Special and even that is pretty damn heavy for accurate shooting (which I'm not capable of anyhow). You use so much muscle holding it straight, that you are apt not to be able to relax enough to hold it steady. The frontier boys who used .44's so well had very strong hands and wrists, which was a natural development of constant riding. A Luger is normally nine mm. and that corresponds to a .38.

Letter to Bernice Baumgarten,
editor at Carl Brandt's agency, 29 December 1948. The Young Lions *was a novel by Irwin Shaw.*

I got *The Young Lions* for Christmas. It looks phony as hell in spots. And how do you do something 'with careful deliberation'? And, 'But the girl's expression hadn't changed. She had broken off a twig from a bush and was absently running it along the stone fence, as though she were pondering what he had just said.' The last clause and the 'absently' throw away the effect. You either describe an action and let the reader make the deduction of the inner reaction it expresses, or else you describe the inner reaction and view what she does from within. You don't do it both ways at the same time. A small thing, but it places the stuff for me. I guess I'm just being a stickler. And enjoying it.

Letter to Paul Brooks,
of Houghton Mifflin, January 1949.

I have often wondered what the hell an editor-in-chief was, but I suppose you know. For purposes of identification it identifies nothing to me. Hell, I corresponded with Dale Warren off and on for many years thinking he was a publicity man, and very much impressed. Isn't that wonderful, I said to myself, in Boston even publicity men can speak English. Then he sent me a couple of anthologies he had edited and I was still more impressed. Hell, the guy is almost educated. Then I learned, or thought I learned, he was one of your editors. And THEN he sent me a blurb he had written, and I don't know whether he is a publicity man or not.

Letter to Carl Brandt,
23 January 1949. Chandler had recently attended meetings in Hollywood
to discuss a plan to write a Marlowe film set in England. The film was
never in the end made.

These Hollywood people are fantastic when you have been away for a while. In their presence any calm sensible remark sounds faked. Their conversation is a mess of shopworn superlatives interrupted by four telephone calls to the sentence. Stark is a nice chap. I like him. Everybody at his bagnio is nice. He has done a fine job with the radio show. It could have been on the air five years already, if I had had him in the first place. It has a better rating they tell me than some quite expensive shows. Just the same I came away depressed. I really don't know why. Perhaps it's just Beverly Hills. It was such a nice place before the Phoenicians took it over. Now it's just a setting for an enormous confidence racket.

Letter to Dale Warren,
23 January 1949.

Other writers do things all the time – talk at book marts, go on autographing tours, give lectures, spread their personalities in silly interviews – which I can't help thinking make them look a bit cheap. To them it's part of the racket. To me it's the thing that makes it a racket.

. . . I hate explanation scenes and I learned in Hollywood that there are two rules about them. 1) You can give only a little at a time, if there is much to give. 2) You can only make an exposition scene when there is some other element, such as danger or love making, or a character reversal suspected. Suspense of some sort, in one word.

Letter to Jamie Hamilton,
24 January 1949. It appearing that Chandler might go to London in order to research the British Marlowe film, Hamilton had assured him a great reception there. Hamilton and his staff had also written to Chandler to thank him for sending them parcels during and in the aftermath of the war.

Your remarks about red carpets, though ever so kindly meant, scare me a little. I'm strictly the background type, and my character is an unbecoming mixture of outer diffidence and inward arrogance. It's so very kind of you to make so much of what to me is so very simple a thing. After all what do I do? And if it were anything at all, which it is not, I have in my mind an unforgettable little story of some friends who visited Luxembourg a couple of years ago. They stayed at a very nice hotel where the food and wine were magnificent. The atmosphere was cheerful, people from all the countries of Europe, almost, were there, having their ease. At two tables were English people, only two. At one sat an elderly couple, formerly well-to-do, now not so well-to-do. At the other a demobbed tank officer with his mother. On all the tables of the hotel dining room but these were bottles of wine. This is a true story. The English could not afford wine. Those who had never surrendered drank water in order that those who had surrendered might drink wine. I think this story is wonderful.

Letter to James Sandoe,
regarding the ongoing Nuremberg Trials, 25 February 1949.

I know from my own knowledge that in the first world war, during the final German retreat from the Hindenburg line the machine gun crews left behind to hold up the advance as long as possible were almost always bayoneted to the last man, even though they rose out of the ground and tried to surrender. There is an element of hypocrisy in these war trials that hurts. Hanging generals and politicians and concentration camp people is fine, but when it comes to junior officers and N.C.O.'s I'm not at all easy about it. Their freedom of choice seems to me little more than freedom to prefer death to dishonor, and that's asking too much of human nature.

Letter to Bernice Baumgarten,
11 March 1949.

Every now and then I get a shock by seeing myself through other eyes. In the current number of *Partisan Review* (which incidentally has several very good things in it) a man writing about *Our Mutual Friend* says: 'It is possible that the question of true-to-life did not arise, and that Dickens' contemporaries accepted his dark vision of England and London . . . as readily as we today accept Raymond Chandler's California with its brutal and neurotic crew of killers and private eyes –' etc. Another writer in an avant garde magazine referred to me as 'a Cato of the Cruelties'. Apart from the obvious compliment of being noticed at all by the rarefied intellectuals who write for these publications – and I should understand them well, because I was one of them for many years – I cannot grasp what they do with their sense of humor. Or let me put it a better way: Why is it that the Americans – of all people the quickest to reverse their moods – do not see the strong element of burlesque in my writing? Or is it only the intellectuals who miss that? And as for true-to-life I don't think these cloud dwellers can have much understanding of the kind of world they live in and the kind of world Dickens lived in. There is a strong element of fantasy in the mystery story; there is in any kind of writing that moves within an accepted formula. The mystery writer's material is melodrama, which is an exaggeration of violence and fear beyond what one normally experiences in life. (I said normally; no writer ever approximated the life of the Nazi concentration camps.) The means he uses are realistic in the sense that such things happen to people like these and in places like these. But this realism is superficial; the potential of emotion is overcharged, the compression of time and event is a violation of probability, and although such things happen, they do not happen so fast and in such a tight frame of logic to so closely knit a group of people.

Letter to Charles Morton,
16 March 1949. Chandler had told Morton in an earlier letter that he was on the lookout for a new car. Morton had suggested to him that he buy the new model Jaguar that had recently been launched.

The Jaguar is a knockout, but it is completely out of my price class. There is a last year's model roadster, or runabout or whatever they call them, here in La Jolla, all black with red leather seats and chromium radiators. But even if I felt justified in spending half the money, I'd just feel Hollywoodish and phony to be riding about in the thing. Also, and this may not be so important back there, my soul cringes at the thought of the average American mechanic laying his incompetent hands on a piece of real machinery.

Letter to Alex Barris,
a Canadian journalist who had sent Chandler a number of interview questions about himself, 18 March 1949.

We live in a rather too large one-story house on a corner across the street from the ocean. La Jolla, as you might not know, is built on a point north of San Diego, and is never either hot or cold. So we get two seasons of tourists, one in winter, one in summer. Two years ago the town was very quiet, exclusive, expensive, and almost as dull as Victoria, B.C. on a wet Sunday afternoon in February. Now it is just expensive. There is a lot of shingle here and lots of low soft sandstone cliff which the ocean has wrought into very strange shapes, but very little beach, except at the north end of town where it is much more exposed than down where we live. Our living room has a picture window which looks south across the bay to Point Loma, the westerly part of San Diego, and at night there is a long lighted coast line almost in our laps. Our radio writer came down here to see me once and he sat down in front of this window and cried because it was so beautiful. But we live here, and the hell with it.

As you may know I am a half-breed. My father was an American of a Pennsylvania Quaker family originally and my mother was Anglo-Irish, also of a Quaker family. She was born in Waterford where there is still, I believe, a famous Quaker school – famous to Quakers anyhow. I grew up in England and I served with the 1st Canadian Division in the first war. As a boy I spent a lot of time in Ireland and I have no romantic ideas about the Irish.

What do I do with myself from day to day? I write when I can and I don't write when I can't; always in the morning or the early part of the day. You get very gaudy ideas at night but they don't stand up. I found this out long ago . . . I'm always seeing little pieces by writers about how they don't ever wait for inspiration; they just sit down at their little desks every morning at eight, rain or shine, hangover and broken arm and all, and bang out their little stint. However blank their minds or dim their wits, no nonsense about inspiration from them. I offer them my admiration and take care to avoid their books. Me, I wait for inspiration, though I don't necessarily call it by that name. I believe that all writing that has any life in it is done with the solar plexus. It is hard work in the sense that it may leave you tired, even exhausted. In the sense of conscious effort it is not work at all. The important thing is that there should be a space of time, say four hours a day at least, when a professional writer doesn't do anything else but write. He doesn't have to write, and if he doesn't feel like it, he shouldn't try. He can look out of the window or stand on his head or writhe on the floor. But he is not to do any other positive thing, not read, write letters, glance at magazines, or write checks. Write or nothing. It's the same principle as keeping order in a school. If you make the pupils behave, they will learn something just to keep from being bored. I find it works. Two very simple rules, a. you don't have to write. b. you can't do anything else. The rest comes of itself.

I hate publicity, quite sincerely. I've been through the interview mill and I regard it as a waste of time. The guy I meet in those interviews masquerading under my name is usually a heel I wouldn't even know. I'm an intellectual snob who happens to have a fondness for the American vernacular, largely because I grew up on Latin and Greek. I had to learn American just like a foreign language . . . The literary use of slang is study in itself. I've found that there are only two kinds that are any good: slang that has established itself in the language and slang that you make up yourself. Everything else is apt to be passé before it gets into print. But I'd better not get off on that subject, or I'll be writing for a week.

Letter to Jamie Hamilton,
21 March 1949.

I remember several years ago when Howard Hawks was making *The Big Sleep*, the movie, he and Bogart got into an argument as to whether one of the characters was murdered or committed suicide. They sent me a wire (there's a joke about this too) asking me, and dammit I didn't know either. Of course I got hooted at. The joke was in connection with Jack Warner, the head of Warner Bros. Believe it or not, he saw the wire, the wire cost the studio 70 cents, and he called Hawks up and asked him whether it was really necessary to send a telegram about a point like that. That's one way to run a business.

. . . I know how careful English proof readers are, but a writer who deals in vernacular and on occasion makes up his own language may find the printer making corrections of things he assumed to be errors, but were in fact meant exactly as written. Knopf's printers once had the greatest of difficulty in reconciling themselves to a sentence which read, 'a guy's there and you see him and then he ain't there and you don't not see him', and which to them was clearly a double negative, but was to me a much more forcible way of saying, 'don't miss him', obvious and conventional, but not alive.

I thought it was damn good . . . I thought Basehart did a grand job and one didn't see enough of him. But to me the really shocking thing about the picture was the assumption that the gestapo methods of the police are natural and proper. By what authority do they mark off an area and bring everyone inside it in for questioning? This is nothing but arrest without warrant and without any reasonable presumption of guilty knowledge. By what authority do they force a man they admit to be innocent to continue in the role of decoy, even beaten up? By none except what they have usurped and been allowed to usurp by the gullible public, most of whom, by this time, had their origins in countries where the police made their own laws just as they do here . . . They make illegal searches, illegal arrests, illegal entrapments, and they get their evidence by illegal means. Because a cop has been killed (and the statistics on cop killing would probably show it to be one of the safest jobs in the world) they declare martial law and do exactly what they please. They commit armed assault with impunity, since the use or threat of force while armed and without warrant or reasonable grounds is armed assault.

Letter to Bernice Baumgarten,
31 March 1949, regarding a New York Times *article about him. Also mentioned later in the letter is that year's Best Picture Oscar, which had gone to the British film* Hamlet, *starring Laurence Olivier.*

Mr Steegmuller is quite a guy. He not only quotes from me in quotes but without quotes. And where did I ever say that only my type of detective story is serious literature? My argument is and always has been merely that there is no such thing as serious literature, that the survivals of Puritanism in the American mind make all but the most literate people incapable of thinking of literature without reference to what they call significance, and that most of this so-called serious literature or fiction is the most transient stuff in the world; the moment its message is dated, damn quick, it is dead stuff.

It is one of the (few) charms of not being as young as you were that you can stick your neck out, because you don't give a damn. If a young writer knocks a reigning favorite, he can be accused of envy and malice, and it hurts him and makes him cautious. I get a lot of fun out of sticking pins in the popular balloons. The most fantastic pratfall of the moment is Elizabeth Bowen's last book, which in spots is a screaming parody of Henry James. Jamie Hamilton wrote me that the English critics are tying themselves in knots trying to be polite to her (because of course they know she is potentially a fine writer), knowing all the time that the poor girl is giving an exhibition of what happens when an over-earnest writer completely loses her sense of humor.

There's a lovely fight going on at the Academy. The boys were finally shamed into giving the award more or less on the basis of merit (except the musical award, which stank) and the five major companies which have been contributing to the cost of the show have withdrawn. 'Look fellows,' they say without saying, 'we want the Oscars to go to the best pictures all right, but we're not in business for our health. The best pictures from Hollywood savvy.' They don't care who is best as long as it's them.

Letter to Carl Brandt,
3 April 1949.

The last actual research I did was in 1945 while writing *The Blue Dahlia*, the first story incidentally which betrayed to the public the fact that the head man of the Homicide Bureau, then a very nice guy called Thad Brown (Captain), did not even have a private office. His desk was sat right next to that of a female secretary and his door was always open. Outside there was a bare largish room in which the dicks lounged about and quite literally did not have enough chairs to sit down in all at once. The entrance to this was a dutch door (which we didn't use in the film) and both of these rooms together would have fitted easily into our living room. This was positively all the boys had to work with and out of . . . A very good cop picture I saw recently called *He Walked by Night* shows some excellent technical stuff, but the shots inside Police Head-quarters are much too spacious. You get the impression of a very complex and highly efficient organization staffed by innumerable men. As a matter of fact they are a pretty dumb bunch who operate about on the mental level of plumbers.

Letter to Jamie Hamilton,
4 April 1949.

Frankly I have no idea why Houghton Mifflin are so slow getting out the proofs of the book. Perhaps they have been entangled in the massive job of publishing Churchill. Knopf used to send proofs rather quickly with an air of being in a furious rush, air mail special delivery and all that sort of thing, and when I rushed through them in a state of urgency and mailed them back absolutely nothing would happen for months and months. I could never discover why they had been in such a hurry nor what happened when they got the proofs back. You run into the same thing in Hollywood: wild rush for conferences over some deal, then an exhausted agreement as to terms, and then a completely leisurely – in fact quite dilatory – writing of the contract. I remember once at Paramount, after a new contract had been negotiated to take the place of one I had grown to dislike, the legal department went for weeks without producing even a draft and during all that time of course I was not paid; they always hold your money up until the contract is signed. I then called the legal department and suggested politely that there was no need to write the new contract at all since they had breached the old one by not paying me any salary and there was now no agreement between us. It was fun while it lasted; their screams were audible for blocks. I always like doing business with Jews. They are so excitable, so superficially sharp and tricky, but basically very reliable. They dramatize every business deal and act very tough and then suddenly give way in the most winning manner.

. . . There always seems to come a point in a story where the impetus of the original situation dies down and you have to turn the corner. It's the hardest thing to do and a lot of people (especially Hungarian playwrights) never do it at all.

Letter to staff at Houghton Mifflin,
11 April 1949, in response to the serialization of The Little Sister *which had appeared in* Cosmopolitan *magazine.*

The bastardized anecdote appearing under my name in the current issue of *Cosmopolitan* (may their returns be the largest in history) contains words and sentences I did not write at all, dialogue I would not spew, and lacunae that are comparable to amnesia on one's honeymoon. This is a cadaver of a book, post-mortemed by a drunken body-snatcher and stitched together by a sailmaker with delirium tremens.

Letter to James Sandoe,
14 April 1949.

Have read *The Moving Target* by John Macdonald and am a good deal impressed by it, in a peculiar way. What you say about pastiche is of course quite true, and the materials of the plot situations are borrowed here and there. E.g. the opening set up is lifted more or less from *The Big Sleep*, mother paralyzed instead of father, money from oil, atmosphere of corrupted wealth, and the lawyer-friend villain is lifted straight out of *The Thin Man*; but I personally am a bit Elizabethan about such things, do not think they greatly matter, since all writers must imitate to begin with, and if you attempt to cast yourself in some accepted mold, it is natural to go to examples that have attained some notice or success.

What strikes me about the book (and I guess I should not be writing about it if I didn't feel that the author had something) is first an effect that is rather repellent. There is nothing to hitch to; here is a man who wants the public for the mystery story in its primitive violence and also wants it to be clear that he, individually, is a highly literate and sophisticated character. A car is 'acned with rust' not spotted. Scribblings on toilet walls are 'graffiti' (we know Italian yet, it says); one refers to 'podec osculation' (medical Latin too, ain't we hell?). 'The seconds piled up like a tower of poker chips', etc. The simile that does not quite come off because it doesn't understand what the purpose of the simile is.

The scenes are well handled, there is a lot of experience of some kind behind this writing, and I should not be surprised to find the name was a pseudonym for a novelist of some performance in another field. The thing that interests me is whether this pretentiousness in the phrasing and choice of words makes for better writing. It does not. You could only justify it if the story itself were devised on the same level of sophistication, and you wouldn't sell a thousand copies, if it was. When you say 'spotted with rust' (or pitted, and I'd almost but not quite go for 'pimpled') you convey at once a single visual image. But when you say, 'acned with rust' the attention of the reader is instantly jerked away from the thing described to the pose of the writer. This is of course a very simple example of the stylistic misuse of language, and I think that certain writers are under compulsion to write in recherché phrases as a compensation for a lack of some kind of natural animal emotion. They feel nothing, they are literary eunuchs, and therefore they fall back on an oblique terminology to prove their distinction. It is the sort of mind that keeps avant garde magazines alive, and it is quite interesting to see an attempt to apply it to the purposes of this kind of story.

Letter to Canadian journalist Alex Barris,
16 April 1949.

Do I think *Hamlet* was the best picture of 1948? Definitely not. Olivier was marvellous. Felix Aylmer was top notch, but the camera work was a pain in the neck and a lot of the acting barely acceptable. But I'm glad Hollywood was shamed into giving it to a foreign picture for all that.

18 April 1949. 'Norbert D.' is Norbert Davis, a former Black Mask
man, now destitute.

It was very kind of you indeed to send me a wire about Norbert
D. However right or wrong, I am sending him a couple of hundred
dollars. Who am I to judge another man's needs or deserts? It's a
pretty miserable thing to live off in the country and watch them all
[stories] come back and be scared. He says he has sold one out of
fifteen this last year. Say it's his fault. Say he got big-headed or
drunk and lazy or what have you – what difference does it make?
You suffer just as much when you're wrong. More. Write it off,
call it a waste, forget it, and hope the guy won't hate you for
helping him, or rather for having to ask you to help him . . . I know
that two hundred bucks will not buy me the key to heaven, but
there have been times when it would have looked like it would,
and I didn't have it, and nobody was around to give it to me. I
never slept in the park but I came damn close to it. I went five days
without anything to eat but soup once, and I had just been sick at
that. It didn't kill me, but neither did it increase my love of
humanity. The best way to find out if you have any friends is to go
broke. The ones that hang on longest are your friends. I don't mean
the ones that hang on forever. There aren't any of those.

*Four months later, on 14 August 1949, Chandler would write again to
Brandt: 'I had a letter from N.D.'s wife. It seems he committed suicide a
couple of weeks ago. I hadn't realized it was that desperate a situation.'*

Letter to Dale Warren,
*20 April 1949. Having finally got his much-interrupted fifth novel out of
the way, Chandler was now ready to embark on a more ambitious
Marlowe book, which he would eventually call* The Long Goodbye.

I can't seem to get started doing anything. Always very tough for
me to get started. Thought I could use Bel Air, but then you drag

in the whole phony Hollywood life, and everything becomes scenery, back projections, matt shots, miniatures, papier mâché rocks, tubbed trees, deluges of tropical rain out of which the characters come in, having walked in it for hours, with one damp lapel and two curls out of place. Three feet of film later the suit's pressed and the guy has a fresh carnation in his buttonhole.

Well, it's not as bad as pinning a posthumous V.C. on the saddle bag of a cavalry horse, which they did in *Lives of a Bengal Lancer*.

I see from *The Sunday Times* that your picture *He Walked By Night* didn't get much from Dilys Powell but a remark about the chase through the Sewers. She's damn good too, and usually very fair about American pictures. What's the matter with the films? I rack my brain for an answer, and I have a queer recurring thought that it isn't anything specific, the films aren't so bad, but they're simply no longer a novelty. The medium, the things it can do, have lost the sting. We're back where silent films were when Warners bought the Vitaphone. Except for forced focus there has hardly been a real technical advance in fifteen years, and you don't realize what forced focus does unless you look at a film made in the middle thirties and note that in a medium close shot everything more than ten feet from the camera is a blur.

Letter to Jamie Hamilton,
22 April 1949. Stephen Spender and W. H. Auden were the pre-eminent British poets of the day, and both reported Chandler fans. Cyril Connolly was an equally pre-eminent literary journalist.

I like this fellow Spender very much. In fact I like him better than Auden, about whom I have always had reservations. (I am also disturbed at your remark that Connolly has no conscience.) His account of the silken barbarity of Eton is wonderful, of course, and the way these fellows thought and wrote and talked, at an age when Americans can hardly spell their names, is also most impressive. Nevertheless, there is something about the literary life that repels me; all this desperate building of castles on cobwebs, the long-drawn acrimonious struggle to make something important which we all know will be gone forever in a few years, the miasma of failure which is to me as offensive as the cheap gaudiness of popular success. I believe the really good people would be reasonably successful in any circumstances; that to be very poor and very beautiful is probably a moral failure much more than an artistic success. Shakespeare would have done well in any generation, because he would have refused to die in a corner; he would have taken the false gods and made them over, he would have taken the current formulae and forced them into something lesser men would have thought them incapable of. Alive today he would undoubtedly have written and directed motion pictures, plays, and God knows what. Instead of saying 'This medium is not good,' he would have used it and made it good. If some people had called some of his work cheap (which some of it is), he wouldn't have cared a rap, because he would know that without some vulgarity there is no complete man. He would have hated refinement, as such, because it is always a withdrawal, a shrinking, and he was much too tough to shrink from anything.

Letter to Charles Morton,
2 May 1949.

The cult of failure is embedded in all highbrow aesthetics, and the current slang for this is probably the 'death-wish' . . . In a way, I am inclined to think that all failure (apart from illness or awful bad luck) is really a kind of moral failure. Half or more of the stuff that has survived time would have been judged pure pot-boiler in its day – or in our day, if done now.

Letter to James Sandoe,
regarding Nathaniel West's novel Miss Lonelyhearts, *3 May 1949.*

A powerful, strange and unusual book – not pretty, but to my mind definitely in the class of real as opposed to merely calculated writing.

Sales of the *Cosmopolitan* in La Jolla are not sensational, which
proves that competition in articles on impotence is not serious, as
the incidence of this malady is probably higher in La Jolla than in
any other locality or organization except the annual get-together
of us Chickamauga veterans.

You mention Joan Fontaine as one of your pals. I met her
once, at a lunch with John Houseman, but I knew her husband,
Bill Dozier, quite well. He hired me at Paramount, and gave my
stoop of an agent a rooking on the salary that was memorable,
and remained an unhealed sore until I took Dozier for a hundred
grand when he was boss at U-I. Paramount made a shocking mistake when they let him resign. At U-I it was understandable,
because he was supposed to handle the contract producers while
Bill Goetz handled the independent production units. These one
by one folded and withdrew, leaving Goetz with nothing to do.
Once looking out of Joe Sistrom's window on the U-I lot I happened to see the big boys strolling back from lunch in the exec
dining room in a loose group. I was transfixed with a sinister
delight. They looked so exactly like a bunch of topflight Chicago
gangsters moving in to read the death sentence on a beaten com-
petitor. It brought home to me in a flash the strange psychological and spiritual kinship between the operations of big money
business and the rackets. Same faces, same expressions, same
manners. Same way of dressing and same exaggerated leisure of
movement.

Letter to James Sandoe,
12 May 1949.

I admit that if you can't create a sufficiently dominating detective,
you might compensate to some extent by involving him in the
dangers and emotions of the story, but that isn't a step forward, it's

a step backward. The whole point is that the detective exists complete and entire and unchanged by anything that happens; he is, as detective, outside the story and above it, and always will be. That is why he never gets the girl, never marries, never really has any private life except insofar as he must eat and sleep and have a place to keep his clothes. His moral and intellectual force is that he gets nothing but his fee, for which he will if he can protect the innocent, guard the helpless, and destroy the wicked, and the fact that he must do this while earning a meager living in a corrupt world is what makes him stand out. A rich idler has nothing to lose but his dignity; the professional is subject to all the pressures of an urban civilization and must rise above them in order to do his job. Because he represents justice and not the law, he will sometimes defy or break the law. Because he is human he can be hurt or beguiled or fooled; in extreme necessity he may even kill. But he does nothing solely for himself. Obviously this kind of detective does not exist in real life. The real life private eye is a sleazy little judge from the Burns Agency, or a strong arm guy with no more personality than a blackjack, or else a shyster and a successful trickster. He has about as much moral stature as a stop-and-go sign.

The detective story is not and never will be a 'novel about a detective'. The detective enters it only as a catalyst. And he leaves it exactly the same as he was before.

Letter to Charles Morton,
13 May 1949.

The big publishers will always carry a few prestige writers as window dressing, the rest will be formula writers, and after a while even the formulas will be restricted . . . The higher the cost of production, the more power flows to the people who put up the money.

Letter to Jamie Hamilton,
13 May 1949.

I don't know what's happening to the writing racket in this country.
I get an offer of $1200 a year for the use of my name on the title of
a new mystery magazine. *Raymond Chandler's Mystery Magazine.* I
have nothing to do with the magazine, no control over the contents
and no contact whatever with the editorial policy. It does seem
to me that a line has to be drawn, and I am even willing to argue
that you can rule out ethics and you would still, if you had any
vision, have to draw that line as a matter of policy. But such is the
brutalization of commercial ethics in this country that no one can
feel anything more delicate than the velvet touch of a soft buck.

Letter to James Sandoe,
14 May 1949.

I HATE PUBLICITY. It is nearly always dishonest and quite
always stupid. I don't think it means anything at all. You don't
get any until you are 'copy' and what you get makes you hate
yourself.

Letter to James Sandoe,
20 May 1949. Daniel Chaucer was a pseudonym used by the novelist
Ford Madox Ford.

I suppose every man has among his memories a few books which
for subtle reasons occupy a more exalted place in his mind than they
really deserve. For example: *The Unbearable Bassington, Lavengro,*
The New Humpty-Dumpty by a man named Chaucer of whom
I never otherwise heard, *The New Arabian Nights* etc. Not all of
these were flops, of course, but those that were were not flops to
me.

Letter to James Sandoe,
2 June 1949. Chandler is initially referring to The Day of the Locust,
the novel by Nathaniel West.

The whole book is a suicide note. It is not tragic, not bitter, not even pessimistic. It simply washes its hands of life . . .

Modern outspokenness has utterly destroyed the romantic dream on which love feeds. The synthetic stallions like James Cain have made a fetish of pure animal lust which honester and better men take in their stride, without literary orgasms, and which the middle classes seem to regard as a semi-respectable adjunct to raising a family. The literary glorification of lust leads to emotional impotence, because the love story proper has little or nothing to do with lust. It cannot exist against a background of cheese cake and multiple marriages. There is nothing left to write about but death and the detective story is a tragedy with a happy ending. The peculiar appropriateness of the detective or mystery story to our time is that it is incapable of love. The love story and the detective story cannot exist, not only in the same book – one might almost say the same culture.

Letter to James Sandoe,
16 June 1949.

The sort of semi-literate educated people one meets nowadays . . . are always saying, more or less, 'You write so well I should think you would do a serious novel.' And then you find out that what they mean by a serious novel is something by Marquand or Betty Smith, and you would probably insult them by remarking that the artistic gap between a really good mystery and the best serious novel of the last ten years is hardly measurable compared with the gap between the serious novel and any representative piece of Attic Literature from the Fourth Century BC.

Letter to Jamie Hamilton,
17 June 1949.

I am very uneasy in mind. I seem to have lost ambition and I have no ideas any more . . . I read these profound discussions, say in the *Partisan Review,* about art, what is it, literature what is it, and the good life and liberalism, and what is the definitive position of Rilke or Kafka, and the scrap about Ezra Pound getting the Bollingen award, and it all seems so meaningless to me. Who cares? Too many good men have been dead too long for it to matter what any of these people do or don't do. What does a man work for? Money? Yes, but in a purely negative way. Without some money, nothing else is possible, but once you have the money (and I don't mean a fortune, just a few thousand quid a year) you don't sit and count it and gloat over it. Everything you attain removed a reason for wanting to attain anything. Do I wish to be a great writer? Do I wish to win the Nobel Prize? Not if it takes much hard work. What the hell, they give the Nobel Prize to too many second-raters for me to get excited about it. Besides, I'd have to go to Sweden and dress up and make a speech. Is the Nobel Prize worth all that? Hell, no.

. . . You cannot have art without a public taste and you cannot have a public taste without a sense of style and quality throughout the social structure. Curiously enough this sense of style seems to have very little to do with refinement or even humanity. It can exist in a savage and dirty age, but it cannot exist in an age of the Book of the Month Club, the Hearst press, and the Coca-Cola machine. You can't produce art by trying, by setting up exacting standards, by talking about critical minutiae, by the Flaubert method. It is produced with great ease, in an almost offhand manner, and without self-consciousness. You can't write just because you have read all the books.

Letter to Jamie Hamilton,
22 June 1949.

I think my favorite Hollywood story is about the Warner brothers, Jack and Harry. The day after Hal Wallis (who had been head of production at the studio) ankled and left them flat, there was deep gloom and a horrid sense of catastrophe at the executive lunch table. All the boys huddle down at the bottom of the table to get far away from Jack Warner when he comes in. All but one, a pushing young producer named Jerry Wald (supposed by some to be the original of Sammy Glick in *What Makes Sammy Run*) who sits down near the head of the table. Jack and Harry Warner come in. Jack sits at the head of the table and Harry just around the corner. Jerry Wald is near and all the others as far away as possible. Jack looks at them with disgust and turns to Harry.

JACK: That sonofabitch, Wallis.

HARRY: Yes, Jack.

JACK: A lousy fifty dollar a week publicity man. We build him up from nothing. We made him one of the biggest men in Hollywood. And what does he do to us? He picks up his hat and walks out and leaves us cold.

HARRY: Yes, Jack.

JACK: That's gratitude for you. And take that sonofabitch Zanuck. A lousy hundred a week writer and we took him in hand and built him up and made him one of the biggest men in Hollywood. And what did he do to us? Picked up his hat and walked out on us cold.

HARRY: Yes, Jack.

JACK: That's gratitude for you. Why we could take any sonofabitch we liked and build him up from nothing and make him one of the biggest men in Hollywood.

HARRY: Yes, Jack.

JACK: Anybody at all. (He turns and looks at Jerry Wald) What's your name?

WALD: Jerry Wald, Mr Warner.

JACK: (to Harry) Jerry Wald. Why, Harry, we could take this fellow here and build him up from nothing to be one of the biggest men in Hollywood, couldn't we, Harry?

HARRY: Yes, Jack, we certainly could.

JACK: And what would it get us? We build him up to be a big

man, give him power and reputation, make him one of the biggest names in Hollywood, and you know what would happen, Harry? The sonofabitch would walk out and leave us flat.

HARRY: Yes, Jack.

JACK: So why wait for that to happen, Harry? Let's fire the sonofabitch right now.

Letter to Dale Warren,
9 July 1949. Laski is the novelist Marghanita Laski; Waugh is Evelyn Waugh; Stranger in the Land was a novel by a writer called Ward Thomas.

I have had a bout with a strep throat which was only fun because it gave me a chance to be shot full of penicillin, a very wonderful thing that makes you almost feel that God is on the side of the right people after all. One had begun to doubt it.

. . . I thought Laski's book had a great idea, but she hasn't either the style or the comic invention to put it over. If Waugh had written it, it would have been really something. As for *Stranger in the Land* I thought it well-written in a negative anonymous sort of way, but the subject repelled me. There ought to be a good novel in homosexualism, but this isn't it . . . What I think would be interesting would be a picture of the peculiar mentality of the homosexualist, his sense of taste, his surface brilliance often, his fundamental inability to finish anything . . . I can't take the homo seriously as a moral outcast. He's no more than the other rebels against a sanctimonious and hypocritical society. There is no more disgusting spectacle on earth than the business man at a stag smoker, and this is just the type of man who would come down hardest on the abnormal. The difficulty of writing about a homo is the utter impossibility of getting inside his head unless you are one yourself, and then you can't get inside the head of a heterosexual man. If you ever read the cross examination of Wilde by Edward Carson in the suit against Queensberry, I think you are bound to admit that here were two people shouting across oceans of misunderstanding. The mob impulse to destroy the homo is like the impulse of a wolf pack to turn on the sick wolf and tear him to pieces, or the human impulse to run away from a hopeless disease. This is probably very old and very cruel, but at the bottom of it is a kind of horror, like a woman frightened by a scorpion. All cruelty is a kind of fear. Deep inside us we must realize what fragile bonds hold us to sanity and these bonds are threatened by repulsive insects and repulsive vices. And the vices are repulsive, not in themselves, but because of their effect on us. They threaten us because our own normal vices fill us at times with the same sort of repulsion.

Letter to Paul Brooks,
who planned to publish a collection of Chandler's old pulp stories, 19 July 1949.

You say some of them I will doubtless want to omit. Or in other words they stink. Which? I doubt if I'm the best judge. Well, let's be bloody frank about this. If something dates, or makes you cringe, out. If it is a small thing that can be fixed, I'll try to fix it. If it is inherent in the plot, I can't. Take the story called 'Blackmailers Don't Shoot', the first I ever wrote. It took me five months to write this thing, it has enough action for five stories and the whole thing is a goddam pose. 'Finger Man' was the first story I felt at home with. 'Smart Aleck Kill' and 'BDS' are pure pastiche. When I started out to write fiction I had the great disadvantage of having absolutely no talent for it. I couldn't get characters in and out of rooms. They lost their hats and so did I. If more than two people were on scene I couldn't keep one of them alive. This failing is still with me, of course, to some extent. Give me two people snotting at each other across a desk and I am happy. A crowded canvas just bewilders me. (I could say the same of some rather distinguished writers, only they don't know it and I do.) I don't know who was the original idiot who advised a writer, 'Don't bother about the public. Just write what you want to write.' No writer ever wants to write anything. He wants to reproduce or render certain effects and in the beginning he hasn't the faintest idea how to do it.

It has seemed to me for a long time now that in straight novels the public is more and more drawn to the theme, the idea, the line of thought, the sociological or political attitude and less and less to the quality of the writing. For instance, if you were to consider Orwell's *1984* purely as a piece of fiction, you could not rate it very high. It has no magic, the scenes have very little personality . . . where he writes as a critic and interpreter of ideas rather than of people or emotions he is wonderful.

I quite agree with you about the *Asphalt Jungle*. I tried to read it and couldn't. This is a sample of what Hollywood does to writers. The stuff is sound and honest and knows what it is doing. But it has no inner urgency, it just doesn't matter. A man may sit down to write a book with no other motive than to meet a deadline or make a few dollars, but if he is a real writer, that is soon forgotten. In Hollywood they destroy the link between a writer and his subconscious. After that what he does is merely a performance.

As to the introduction I suppose an idea of how to go about it. I'm certainly not going to write about these stories as though I were an elderly Henry James or Somerset Maugham tidying up the shelves for posterity. I'm strictly an amateur and an iconoclast in these matters. I think literary history and criticism are as full of bunk and sheer dishonesty as school history generally.

Sometimes I wonder what my politics would be if I lived in England. Can't imagine myself voting now that its nasty bureaucratic soul has been revealed. If you vote Conservative, what do you vote for? You don't, you just vote against. Very much like the last election here. All very well to talk about the patriotic duty of voting and so forth, but why should it be my duty to choose either of two candidates when I don't believe either has any business in the White House? My English friends tell me that the Labor Party will win the next election by a small majority and that by that time the country will be in such a mess that there will be a schism in the Labor Party between the moderates like Crossman and Attlee and the wild men like Nye Bevan. I wouldn't know. Eventually, I am afraid, even in England, the scoundrels will inherit the revolution. They always have where the revolution was real and internal, not a revolt against foreign domination. And that, to dispose of the subject, is where you can't class the Catholic Church with the Communists. The Catholic Church in spite of its sins and its hypocrisy and its politicking and its fascist tendencies and its nasty unprincipled use of the boycott is capable of internal discussion and growth without liquidation of its best elements. It can tolerate heresy and it is not afraid to go abroad among the heathen . . . It proselytizes constantly, but it does not shoot people in the back of the head because they are forty-eight hours behind the party line.

Letter to Dale Warren,
15 September 1949.

The news from here is rotten. Nervous, tired, discouraged, sick of the chauffeur-and-Cadillac atmosphere . . . disgusted at my lack of prescience in not seeing that this kind of life is unsuited to my temperament . . . Writers who get written about become self-conscious. They develop a regrettable habit of looking at themselves through the eyes of other people. They are no longer alone, they have an investment in critical praise, and they think that they must protect it. This leads to a diffusion of effort. The writer watches himself as he works. He grows more subtle and he pays for it by a loss of organic dash. But since he often achieves a real success in the commercial sense just about as he reaches this stage of regrettable sophistication, he fools himself into thinking that his last book is his best. It isn't. Its success is the result of a slow accumulation. The book which is the occasion of success is more often than not by no means the cause of it.

Letter to James Sandoe,
20 September 1949. Chandler was reading a book called American Freedom and Catholic Power, *by Paul Blanshard.*

I'd like to see a reasoned reply, but where would you get it? The Jesuits seem to have a monopoly on this sort of chore and their casuistical double talk would be disgusting if it were not so logically comical. Any time they get on dangerous ground they simply rule that its solidity is a matter of directed faith and not subject to question by the faithful . . . I suppose I only concern myself with this because the closed mind is the worst enemy of freedom. The highbrows, fantastic as they sometimes are, seem to be about the only people we can rely on for a perpetual challenge to what passes for truth. That's why I read the *Partisan Review.* There's a lot of nonsense in it and some of the terminology used by these rare birds like Allen Tate nearly makes me throw my lunch. But at least they don't take things for granted.

How, after the Katyn Forest and Moscow Treason Trials, the Ukraine famine, the Arctic prison camps, the utterly abominable rape of Berlin by the Mongolian divisions, any decent man can become a Communist is almost beyond understanding, unless it is the frame of mind that simply doesn't believe anything it doesn't like. How can the same decent man become a convert to a religious system that played ball with Franco in Spain, and still does, that never in the history of the world has refused to play ball with any scoundrel who was willing to protect and enrich the Church? Well, I guess nobody wants to hear from me about it.

Letter to Marcel Duhanel,
Raymond Chandler's French publisher, 28 September 1949.
Duhanel worked for Gallimard, under whose umbrella he had published a
number of talented hardboiled American writers in a series called 'Série
Noire'. This influential (and successful) series had brought the likes of
Chandler, Hammett and Cain to a generation of French intellectuals.
Albert Camus was famously to claim that the hero of his epochal novel
L'Étranger had been more influenced by Série Noire than by any literary
fiction. It was from the name of this Gallimard series that the popular
expression 'Film Noir' would also arise.

I have always thought it one of the charms of dealing with publishers that if you start talking about money, they retire coldly to their professional eminence, and if you start talking about literature, they immediately yank the dollar sign before your eyes.

Letter to James Sandoe,
14 October 1949.

Am now reading Marquand's *So Little Time*. As I recall or seem to recall it was rather deprecated when it came out, but it seems to me full of good sharp wit and liveliness and altogether much more satisfying than *Point of No Return*, which I found boring in its total impact, although not boring as one read it. Have also started *A Sea Change* by Nigel Dennis which looks good. But I always like the wrong books anyhow. And the wrong pictures. And the wrong people. And I have a bad habit of starting a book and reading just far enough to make sure that I want to read it and look forward to reading it and then putting it to one side while I break the ice on a couple more. In that way, when I feel dull and depressed, which is too often, I know I have something to read late at night when I do most of it and not that horrid blank feeling of not having anybody to talk or listen to.

Why in God's name don't those idiots of publishers stop putting photos of writers on their dust jackets? I bought a perfectly good book . . . was prepared to like it, had read about it, and then I take a fast gander at the guy's picture and he is obviously an absolute jerk, a really appalling creep (photogenically speaking) and I can't read the damn book. The man's probably quite all right, but to me he is that photo, that oh so unposed-posed photo with the gaudy tie pulled askew, the man sitting on the edge of his desk with his feet in his chair (always sits there, thinks better). I've been through this photograph routine, know just what it does to you.

Letter to John Houseman,
a British producer with whom Chandler had been friendly while at
Hollywood, October 1949.

Your article in *Vogue* was much admired here. I think it was beautifully written and had a lot of style. For me personally it had an effect (aftertaste is a better word) of depression and it aroused my antagonism. It is artistically patronizing, intellectually dishonest and logically unsound. It is the last wimper of the Little Theater mind in you. However, I'm all for your demand that pictures, even tough pictures, and especially tough pictures, have a high moral content. *Time* this week calls Philip Marlowe 'amoral'. This is pure nonsense. Assuming that his intelligence is as high as mine (it could hardly be higher), assuming his chances in life to promote his own interest are as numerous as they must be, why does he work for such a pittance? For the answer to that is the whole story, the story that is always being written by indirection and yet never is completely or even clearly. It is the struggle of all fundamentally honest men to make a decent living in a corrupt society. It is an impossible struggle; he can't win. He can be poor and bitter and take it out in wisecracks and casual amours, or he can be corrupt and amiable and rude like a Hollywood producer. Because the bitter fact is that outside of two or three technical professions which require long years of preparation, there is absolutely no way for a man of this age to acquire a decent affluence in life without to some degree corrupting himself, without accepting the cold, clear fact that success is always and everywhere a racket.

The stories I wrote were ostensibly mysteries. I did not write the stories behind those stories, because I was not a good enough writer. That does not alter the basic fact that Marlowe is a more honorable man than you and I. I don't mean Bogart playing Marlowe and I don't mean because I created him. I didn't create him at all; I've seen dozens like him in all essentials except the few colorful qualities he needed to be in a book. (A few even had those.) They were all poor; they will always be poor. How could they be anything else.

Letter to Jamie Hamilton,
11 November 1949.

This is Armistice Day here, a sort of mixed holiday. Banks and post offices closed, and a few stores, but not many. Big parade of troops and marines and sailors, none of them have any idea what the first world war was like. It was a damn sight worse than they think . . .

While reviewing generally is not very reliable anywhere, I really think that English reviewing is getting absurd. There are far, far too many novelists reviewing other novelists. There is far too much consideration for books that are obviously going to get nowhere, and far too little understanding of what it is in books that makes people read them. And there is a tight group of critics or reviewers who are monotonously willing to say something nice about almost any book at all. Your own book ads show it. These names, supposedly of influence, really can't have any because they show no discrimination to speak of . . . And at the other extreme is that ridiculous publication *The Times Literary Supplement*, which is apparently compiled from the blitherings of a group of aged dons, whose standards of comparisons, points of reference or what have you, seem to be stuck in the year when Jowett translated Plato . . .

P.S. I suppose you know this, but I think it wonderful, from *Fontemara*, by Ignazio Silone:

At the head of all is God, lord of heaven.
Then comes Prince Torlonia, lord of earth.
Then comes the armed guard of Prince Torlonia.
Then come the hounds of the armed guard of Prince
    Torlonia.
Then comes nobody else.
And still nobody else.
And still again nobody else.
Then come the farmers.

Letter to James Sandoe,
19 November 1949.

Why do women write such *ordinary* books? Their observation of everyday life is splendid, but they never seem to develop any color . . .

Letter to Dale Warren,
20 November 1949. Chandler is referring to the Philip Marlowe radio show.

The Marlowe show has gone so soft that even old ladies like it now. I should worry. Who said mystery programs were sadistic? This one is about as sadistic as a frosted marshmallow sundae. The boys who wrote it are on their sixteenth script. Pause and let us have two minutes of silence. That is one hell of a way to make a living. Think of the work, the strain, the deadlines, and for what?

Letter to Jamie Hamilton,
4 December 1949.

Your man Hodge is a superb editor, the rarest kind of man. These trained-seal critics, even the best of them, bore me at least two thirds of the time. Give a man a name of prestige and he is already a fair way to being an ass. I do not suggest that Alan Hodge lacks prestige, but he is still in that happy territory where the man's voice is more important than his name. Surely no one could write better introductions. The Betjemans (I may have spelled this wrong), the Quennels, the Mortimers, etc. are always a little intent on making a good appearance before their admiring public. Hodge is concerned with the book and damn all else.

. . . I expressed myself badly about playwriting. Of course Maugham is right, as he always is. It is more difficult to write plays, harder work, I have no doubt, although I have never even tried to write one. It is also very much more difficult to write screenplays than novels. But it does not, in my opinion, take the same quality of talent. It may take a more exacting use of the talent, a more beautiful job of cabinet work, a finer and more apt ear for the current jargon of a certain kind of people, but it is much more superficial all round. Take any good, but not great, play and put it in fiction form and you have a very slight matter . . . Incidentally, if I knew Maugham, which I fear I never shall, I should ask him for an inscribed copy of *Ashenden*. I've never asked a writer for an inscribed copy and as a matter of fact I attach very little value to such things. (I wouldn't mind having a prompt copy of *Hamlet*.) But I'm a bit of a connoisseur of melodramatic effects, and *Ashenden* is so far ahead of any other spy story ever written, while his novels, the best of them, and good as they are, do not outclass the field. A classic in any manner appeals to me more than the large canvas. *Carmen*, as Mérimée wrote it, 'Hérodias', 'Un Cœur Simple', *The Captain's Doll*, *The Spoils of Poynton*, *Madame Bovary*, *The Wings of the Dove*, and so forth and so on (*A Christmas Holiday*, by God too), these are all perfect. Long or short, violent or still, they do something that will never be done as well again. The list, thank God, is long, and in many languages.

Too bad you are such an old, old man of 50, or not quite. (Fiftieth year means 49 over here.) Too bad, I have sympathy with you. It is a bad age. A man of fifty is not young, not old, not even middle-aged. His wind has gone and his dignity has not yet arrived. To the young he is already old and stodgy. To the really old he is fat and pompous and greedy. He is a mere convenience to bankers and tax collectors. Why not shoot yourself and be done with it?

Letter to James Sandoe,
4 December 1949. Theodor Geisel, the La Jolla-based author of the Dr
Seuss children's books, was also involved in the following incident.

Max Miller found a cat the other day with a coyote trap on its foot.
We tunnelled through some Manzanita to get it and the poor damn
cat's foot was all maggots, must have been wearing the trap for days
and days. So gentle and no scratching or yelling when we took the
trap off. I'm haunted by its almost inevitable end because I can't
find the owner. It still has two toes and is doing fine at the vets, but
I can't give it a home and what the hell can I do? A great big
affectionate tom cat all scarred up with many battles, not a whimper
in its character, and no place to go, no one who cares to give it a
home.

Letter to James Sandoe,
28 December 1949.

That feeling you get in English books and so seldom in ours that
the country with all its small details is a part of their lives and that
they love it. We are so rootless here. I've lived half my life in
California and made what use of it I could, but I could leave it
forever without a pang.

Letter to Jamie Hamilton,
who had secured a signed copy of Ashenden, *5 January 1950.*

Of course I'll write to the old boy, trying not to be too deferential
on the one hand and not too clubby on the other. I have a
feeling that fundamentally he is a pretty sad man, pretty lonely. His
description of his seventieth birthday is pretty grim. I should guess
that all in all he has had a lonely life, that his declared attitude of
not caring much emotionally about people is a defense mechanism,
that he lacks the kind of surface warmth that attracts people, and at
the same time is such a wise man that he knows that however
superficial and accidental most friendships are, life is a pretty gloomy

affair without them. I don't mean that he has no friends, of course; I don't know enough about him to say anything like that. I get my feeling from his writing and that is all.

Letter to Jamie Hamilton,
11 January 1950.

I often wonder why so many English intellectuals turn to Catholicism. But I wonder so many things and as I grow older I have less and less respect for the human brain and more and more respect for human courage. Over here the Catholics are numerous, powerful and mostly quite genial, but the hierarchy is overwhelmingly of Irish origin and the Irish Catholics, always excepting the Jesuits of Maynooth, are pretty crude specimens of high Catholic thinking, compared with the French, English, Scottish, and Italian prelates. Of course I also wonder why people turn to religion at all. As a young man I was very high-church and very devout. But I was cursed with an analytical mind. It still worries me.

Letter to Dale Warren,
15 January 1950. Warren had just sent Chandler the proof of a
biographical sketch, written by Warren, which was to appear on the new
Marlowe dust jacket.

This is the sort of document that makes writers dog themselves out in a velveteen smoking jacket, a cap with a tassel, a pipe full of Craven Mixture, and lollygag around admiring themselves instead of putting out a little careful but uneven prose. The piece is a miracle of overstatement. What about my classical profile, my head of wavy brown hair scarcely thinning at the temples, my erect bearing, and smiling Irish eyes and my unfailing courtesy to my social inferiors? What about those early days in the back of a Fifth Street bar, cleaning spittoons with the tail of my shirt, dining off the debris of the free lunch mixed with sawdust. A butt of bullies, a familiar of courtesans, a whipping boy for shamed alcoholics? What about the time I spent under the shadow of the Saint Sulpice in that short but intoxicating affair with a demoiselle from Luxembourg – the one that afterwards became known the world over – but no, that is dangerous ground. Even in Luxembourg they have libel laws – in three languages as a matter of fact. And what about the lost six months I spent in the Hollenthal, trying to persuade a funicular railway to run on the level? You fellows leave out so much that happened, and put so much in that didn't.

Letter to James Sandoe,
25 January 1950.

I am getting sick and tired of all these women writers who are never satisfied to tell you a story; they have to tell you exactly how to think about it every minute, reminding one of John Betjeman's translation of the critical cliché 'thoughtfully written' as 'by a woman and boring'. Between them and the synthetic tough smart alecks there is a wide vacant space into which modestly steals only now and then a decent, honest, controlled and thoroughly likeable job.

Letter to Dale Warren,
7 March 1950.

The contrast between the claims made for books in the ads . . . and the books themselves, when you get them in hand, is so ludicrous that one begins to wonder whether this stuff doesn't overreach itself.

Letter to Leroy Wright,
Chandler's attorney in San Diego, 12 April 1950.

Some time when you are not too busy or when someone in your office is not too busy, would you be good enough to let me know the present status of the licensed private operative. Specifically (but not inclusively):

What authority licenses him? How must he qualify? What are

his rights privileges and duties? What information does he give, and what shows on the license? Must it be in plain view on the wall of his office? How much is his bond? Are his fingerprints on record locally and at the F.B.I. files? Has he automatically a right to carry weapons or must he qualify like anyone else? Is this within the discretion of the Sheriff or whom? Are his weapons registered and testfired? By whom?

How is a complaint made against him? (a) by a private citizen, (b) by a police authority? What is the procedure in hearing such a complaint (assuming the matter to be short of a criminal charge)? On what grounds may his license be canceled? If it is for a specific period (what is the fee?) is it automatically renewed, or must he re-qualify?

To what extent is information given him by a client a privileged communication? (A lot of stories turn on this.) Has he any greater power of arrest than the ordinary citizen? Can he be held without bond as a material witness at the discretion of the D.A.? Has he any kind of badge (not being a uniformed special officer such as the men who patrol baseball parks, movie lots and so on)? What identification, etc. is he required to carry?

Letter to Dale Warren,
16 May 1950.

When I open a book and see writing like 'her appearance was indeed shocking'; 'I felt the first stab of remorse'; 'rich full-bodied beauty' etc. I get the impression that I am reading a dead language, that awful petrified mandarin English which no one can get away with except perhaps Maugham, and not always he.

Letter to Jamie Hamilton,
18 May 1950.

How do you tell a man to go away in hard language? Scram, beat it, take off, take the air, on your way, dangle, hit the road, and so forth. All good enough. But give me the classic expression actually used by Spike O'Donnel (of the O'Donnel brothers of Chicago, the only small outfit to tell the Capone mob to go to hell and live): What he said was: 'Be missing'. The restraint of it is deadly.

Letter to Dale Warren,
14 June 1950.

Strange things the eyes. Consider the question of the cat. The cat has nothing to express emotion with but a pair of eyes and some slight assistance from the ears. Yet consider the wide range of expression a cat is capable of with such small means. And then consider the enormous number of human faces you must have looked at that had no more expression than a peeled potato.

. . . Some invented slang, not all, becomes current among the people it is invented for. If you are sensitive to this sort of thing, I believe you could often, not always, distinguish between the colored up lingo that writers produce and the hard simplicity of the terms that originate in the circle where they are actually made. I don't think any writer could think up an expression like 'mainliner' for a narcotic addict who shoots the stuff into a vein. It's too exact, too pure.

Letter to Jamie Hamilton,
23 June 1950.

Your Paris trip sounds like a typical publisher's jaunt, every meal an interview, and authors crawling in and out of your pockets from morning till night. I don't know how publishers stand these trips. One writer would exhaust me for a week. And you get one with every meal. There are things about the publishing business that I should like, but dealing with writers would not be one of them. Their egos require too much petting. They live over-strained lives in which far too much humanity is sacrificed to far too little art . . . To all these people literature is more or less the central fact of existence. Whereas, to vast numbers of reasonably intelligent people it is an unimportant sideline, a relaxation, an escape, a source of information, and sometimes an inspiration. But they could do without it far more easily than they could do without coffee or whisky.

Letter to Ray Stark,
28 August 1950.

Of course the lawyers always back each other up because they know that if they couldn't hang together they'd hang separately.

Letter to Bernice Baumgarten,
13 September 1950. Chandler had been hired by Warner Brothers to work
on an adaptation of Patricia Highsmith's novel Strangers on a Train, *to*
be directed by Alfred Hitchcock. He would be allowed to work on it from
La Jolla, rather than travel to the studios.

I'm still slaving away for Warner Brothers on this Hitchcock thing, which you may or may not have heard about. Some days I think it is fun and other days I think it is damn foolishness. The money looks good, but as a matter of fact it isn't. I'm too conscientious and, although I do not work nearly as fast as I would have worked twenty years ago, I still work a good deal faster than the job requires or has any reason to expect. For the most part the work is boring, unreal, and I have no feeling that it is the kind of thing I can do better than anybody else. Suspense as an absolute quality has never seemed to me very important. At best it is a secondary growth, and at worst an attempt to make something out of nothing.

Letter to Jamie Hamilton,
28 September 1950. Chandler is initially referring to Jean-Paul Sartre.

God but this fellow could stand a good pruning. He writes superbly at times, but he never knows where to stop. He's just like most of the goddamned Russians.

. . . There seems to be a general feeling about Hitchcock that he has shot his wad, but that is always a dangerous assumption with a man of any talent. He is definitely a man of talent, but he belongs to a type which is rather dull outside its particular skill. Some movie makers, like some writers, seem to do their work without committing more than a small part of their real abilities. They belong to the class I call the amateurs; when they are big enough they are geniuses. Others can do some particular thing extremely well, but you would never think they had it in them merely by meeting them. These are the technicians. I'd say Hitch belongs to this group, but of course I don't really know the man.

> *Letter to James Keddie,*
> *29 September 1950. Keddie had written to Chandler, to ask whether he*
> *would be interested in joining the Baker Street Irregulars, a Sherlock*
> *Holmes fan club. Chandler had turned the offer down ('I do not seem to*
> *find any hollow place in my life which the cult of the master alone could*
> *fill. If I were drawn into any esoteric activity of this sort, I think it would*
> *probably be devoted to the desperate analysis of certain actual crimes which*
> *have never been satisfactorily explained and, of course, never will be.').*
> *Keddie had written again to Chandler, pressing him for his opinion of the*
> *detective stories of Austin Freeman. Chandler replied:*

Where the solution of a mystery turns on the correct analysis of scientific evidence, there arises a question of honesty. I realize that this is a big problem in detective stories – just what honesty is. But if you accept the basic premise, as I do, that in a novel of detection the reader should have been able to solve the problem, if he had paid proper attention to the clues as they were presented and drawn the right deductions from them, then I say that he had no such opportunity if, to evaluate said clues, he is required to have an expert knowledge of archaeology, physics, chemistry, microscopy, pathology, metallurgy, and various other sciences. If, in order to know where a man was drowned, I have to identify the fish scales found in his lungs, then I, as a reader, cannot be expected to tell you where he was drowned . . . In spite of all this, I have a very high regard for Freeman . . . His problems are always interesting in themselves, and the expositions at the end are masterpieces of lucid analysis.

Letter to Charles Morton,
9 October 1950. The Hemingway book referred to was Across the River and into the Trees.

Quite a lapse in our once interesting correspondence, don't you think? Of course it's my fault because the last letter was from you. And you are most correct in saying in it that I owe you a letter . . . Apparently it is what the years do to you. The horse which once had to be driven with a tight rein now has to be flicked with a whip in order to make him do much more than amble . . . Walter Bagehot once wrote (I am quoting from an increasingly unreliable memory) 'In my youth, I hoped to do great things. Now, I shall be satisfied to get through without scandal.' In a sense, I am much better off than he was because I never expected to do great things, and in fact have done much better than I ever hoped to do.

My compliments to Mr Weeks on belonging to that very small minority of critics who did not find it necessary to put Hemingway in his place over his last book. Just what do the boys resent so much? Do they sense that the old wolf has been wounded and that it is a good time to pull him down? I have been reading the book. Candidly, it's not the best thing he's done, but it's still a hell of a sight better than anything his detractors could do. There's not much story in it, not much happens, hardly any scenes. And just for that reason, I suppose, the mannerisms sort of stick out. You can't expect charity from knife throwers obviously; knife throwing is their business. But you would have thought some of them might have asked themselves just what he was trying to do. Obviously he was not trying to write a masterpiece; but in a character not too unlike his own, trying to sum up the attitude of a man who is finished and knows it, and is bitter and angry about it. Apparently Hemingway had been very sick and he was not sure that he was going to get well, and he put down on paper in a rather cursory way how that made him feel to the things he had most valued. I suppose these primping second-guessers who call themselves critics think he shouldn't have written the book at all. Most men wouldn't have. Feeling the way that he felt, they wouldn't have had the guts to write anything. I'm damn sure I wouldn't. That's the difference between a champ and a knife thrower. The champ may have lost his stuff temporarily or permanently, he can't be sure. But when he can no longer throw the high hard one, he throws his heart instead. He throws something. He doesn't just walk off the mound and weep. Mr Cyril Connolly, in a rather smoother piece of knife throwing than most of the second-guessers are capable of, suggests that Mr Hemingway should take six months off and take stock of himself. The implication here apparently is that Hemingway has fully exploited the adolescent attitude which so many people are pleased to attribute him, and should now grow up intellectually and become an adult. But why? In the sense in which Connolly would define the word, Hemingway has never had any desire to be an adult. Some writers, like painters, are born primitives. A nose full of Kafka is not at all their idea of happiness. I suppose the weakness, even the tragedy, of writers like Hemingway is that their sort of stuff demands an immense vitality; and a man outgrows his vitality without unfortunately outgrowing his furious concern with it. The kind of thing Hemingway writes cannot be written by an emotional corpse. The kind of thing Connolly writes can and is. It has its points. Some of it is very good, but you don't have to be alive to write it.

Letter to Jamie Hamilton,
10 November 1950. Hamilton, also keen to update his dust-jacket
biography of Chandler following the latter's adventures in Hollywood, had
asked him for some information about his life.

The wise screen writer is he who wears his second-best suit, artistically speaking, and doesn't take things too much to heart. He should have a touch of cynicism, but only a touch. The complete cynic is as useless to Hollywood as it is to himself.

. . . I have been married since 1924 and have no children. I am supposed to be a hardboiled writer, but that means nothing. It is merely a method of projection. Personally I am sensitive and even diffident. At times I am extremely caustic and pugnacious, at other times very sentimental. I am not a good mixer because I am very easily bored, and to me the average never seems good enough, in people or in anything else. I am a spasmodic worker with no regular hours, which is to say I only write because I feel like it. I am always surprised at how easily it seems at the time, and at how very tired one feels afterwards. As a mystery writer, I think I am a bit of an anomaly, since most mystery writers of the American school are only semi-literate, and I am not only literate but intellectual, much as I dislike the term. It would seem that a classical education might be a rather poor basis for writing novels in a hardboiled vernacular. I happen to think otherwise. A classical education saves you from being fooled by pretentiousness, which is what most current fiction is too full of. In this country the mystery writer is looked down on as sub-literary merely because he is a mystery writer, rather than for instance a writer of social significance twaddle. To a classicist – even a very rusty one – such an attitude is merely a parvenu insecurity. When people ask me, as they occasionally do, why I don't try my hand at a serious novel, I don't argue with them; I don't even ask them what they mean by a serious novel. It would be useless. They wouldn't know. The question is parrot-talk.

Reading over some of the above, I seem to detect a rather supercilious tone here and there. I am afraid this is not altogether admirable, but unfortunately it is true. It belongs. I am, as a matter of fact, rather a supercilious person in many ways.

Letter to Dale Warren,
13 November 1950. 'The Fitzgerald book' refers to a recently published biography of F. Scott Fitzgerald, a writer Chandler had always strongly respected. In fact, it was only an option impasse among the studios that had prevented Chandler, in the 1940s, from working on a movie adaptation of The Great Gatsby.

You don't sound completely satisfied with the Fitzgerald book. I'm sad about that, because Fitzgerald is a subject no one has the right to mess up. Nothing but the best will do for him. I think he just missed being a great writer, and the reason is pretty obvious. If the poor guy was already an alcoholic in his college days, it's a marvel that he did as well as he did. He had one of the rarest qualities in all literature, and it's a great shame that the word for it has been thoroughly debased by the cosmetic racketeers, so that one is almost ashamed to use it to describe a real distinction. Nevertheless, the word is charm — charm as Keats would have used it. Who has it today? It's not a matter of pretty writing or clear style. It's a kind of subdued magic, controlled and exquisite, the sort of thing you get from string quartets.

Letter to Edgar Carter,
15 November 1950.

I am having a feud with Warners. I am having a feud with the gardener. I am having a feud with a man who came to assemble a Garrard changer and ruined two LP records. I had several feuds with the TV people. Let's see who else — oh, skip it. You know Chandler. Always griping about something.

Letter to Charles Morton,
22 November 1950.

Television is really what we've been looking for all our lives. It took a certain amount of effort to go to the movies. Somebody had to stay with the kids. You had to get the car out of the garage. That was hard work. And you had to drive and park. Sometimes you had to walk as far as half a block to the theater. Then people with big fat heads would sit in front of you and make you nervous . . . Radio was a lot better, but there wasn't anything to look at. Your gaze wandered around the room and you might start thinking of other things — things you didn't want to think about. You had to use a little imagination to build yourself a picture of what was going on just by the sound. But television's perfect. You turn a few knobs and lean back and drain your mind of all thought. And there you are watching the bubbles in the primeval ooze. You don't have to concentrate. You don't have to react. You don't have to remember. You don't miss your brain because you don't need it. Your heart and liver and lungs continue to function normally. Apart from that, all is peace and quiet. You are in poor man's nirvana. And if some nasty-minded person comes along and says you look more like a fly on a can of garbage, pay him no mind . . . just who should one be mad at anyway? Did you think the advertising agencies created vulgarity and the moronic mind that accepts it? To me television is just one more facet of that considerable segment of our civilization that never had any standard but the soft buck.

Letter to Gene Levitt,
who had been adapting Marlowe for the radio show, 22 November 1950.

I am only a very recent possessor of a television set. It is a very dangerous medium. And as for the commercials – well, I understand that the concoction of these is a business in itself, a business that makes prostitution or the drug traffic seem quite respectable. It was bad enough to have the sub-human hucksters controlling radio, but television does something to you which radio never did. It prevents you from forming any kind of a mental picture and forces you to look at a caricature instead.

Letter to Alfred Hitchcock,
6 December 1950.

In spite of your wide and generous disregard of my communications on the subject of the script of *Strangers on a Train*, and your failure to make any comment on it, and in spite of not having heard a word from you since I began the writing of the actual screenplay – for all of which I might say I bear no malice, since this sort of procedure seems to be part of the standard Hollywood depravity – in spite of this and in spite of this extremely cumbersome sentence, I feel that I should, just for the record, pass you a few comments on what is termed the final script. I could understand your finding fault with my script in this or that way, thinking that such and such a scene was too long or such and such a mechanism was too awkward. I could understand you changing your mind about things that you specifically wanted, because some of such changes might have been imposed on you from without. What I cannot understand is your permitting a script which after all had some life and vitality to be reduced to such a flabby mess of clichés, a group of faceless characters, and the kind of dialogue every screen writer is taught not to write – the kind that says everything twice and leaves nothing to be implied by the actor or the camera . . .

I think you may be the sort of director who thinks that camera angles, stage business, and interesting bits of byplay will make up for any amount of implausibility in a basic story. And I think you are quite wrong. I also think that the fact that you may get away with it doesn't prove you are right, because there is a feeling about a picture that is solidly based which cannot be produced in any other way than by having it solidly based. A sow's ear will look like a sow's ear even if one hangs it on a wall in a frame and calls it French modern. As a friend and well-wisher, I urge you just once in your long and distinguished career . . . to get a sound and sinewy story into the script and to sacrifice no part of its soundness for an interesting camera shot. Sacrifice a camera shot if necessary. There's always another camera shot just as good. There is never another motivation just as good.

Letter to James Sandoe,
7 December 1950.

You should by all means catch *The Bicycle Thief*, and if possible an English picture called *I Know Where I'm Going*, shot largely on the west coast of Scotland – the coast that faces the Hebrides. I've never seen a picture which smelled of the wind and rain in quite this way, nor one which so beautifully exploited the kind of scenery people actually live with, rather than the kind which is commercialized as a show place. The shots of Corryvreckan alone are enough to make your hair stand on end. (Corryvreckan, in case you didn't know, is a whirlpool which, in certain conditions of the tide, is formed between two of the islands of the Hebrides.)

Letter to Jamie Hamilton,
11 December 1950.

J. A. Spender was editing the *Westminster Gazette* in the days when I worked for it. It seems to me that I have written to you about him before. He was the sort of man who could make a frightened young nobody feel at ease in the company of the cream of patrician society. Spender put me up for the National Library Club in order that I might have the use of its reading room, and I used to browse through the French and German papers looking for odd paragraphs and news items which could be translated and adapted for a column the *Westminster Gazette* ran. Spender thought I could make six guineas a week out of this, but I don't think I ever made more than about three. I wrote quite a lot of verses for him also, most of them now seem to me deplorable, but not all, and a good many sketches, most of a satirical nature – the sort of thing that Saki did so infinitely better. I still have a couple of them somewhere, and they now seem to me very precious in tone. But I suppose they weren't so bad, considering how little valid experience I had to back them up . . . I had only the most limited personal contact with Spender. I would send the stuff in, and they would either send it back or send me the proof. I never collected the proof, didn't even know if I was expected to. I simply took it as a convenient form of acceptance. I never waited for them to send me the money but appeared regularly on a certain day each week at their cashier's office and received payment in gold and silver, being required to affix a penny stamp in a large book and sign my name across it by way of receipt. What a strange world it seems now! I suppose I have told you of the time I wrote to Sir George Newnes and offered to buy a piece of his trashy but successful weekly magazine called *Tit-Bits*. I was received most courteously by a secretary, definitely public school, who regretted the publication was not in need of capital, but said that my approach had at least the merit of originality. By the same devise I did actually make a connection with the *Academy*, then edited and owned by a man named Cowper, who had bought it from Lord Alfred Douglas. He was not disposed to sell an interest in his magazine, but pointed to a large shelf of books in his office and said they were review copies and would I care to take a few home to review . . . I met there also a tall, bearded, and sad-eyed man called Richard Middleton, of whom I think you may have heard. Shortly afterwards he committed suicide in Antwerp, a suicide of despair, I should say. The incident made a great impression on me, because Middleton struck me as having far more talent than I was ever likely to possess; and if he couldn't make a go of it, it wasn't very likely that I could . . . I had no feeling of identity with the United States, and yet I resented the kind of ignorant and snobbish criticism of Americans that was current at that time. During my year in Paris I had run across a good many Americans, and most of them seemed to have a lot of bounce and liveliness and to be thoroughly enjoying themselves in situations where the average Englishman of the same class would be stuffy or completely bored. But I wasn't one of them. I didn't even speak their language . . . All in all, perhaps I ought to have stayed in Paris, although I never really liked the French. But you didn't exactly have to like the French to be at home in Paris. And you could always like some of them. On the other hand, I did like the Germans very much, that is the South Germans. But there wasn't much sense living in Germany, since it was an open secret, openly discussed, that we would be at war with them almost any time now. I suppose it was the most inevitable of all wars. There was never any question about whether it would happen. The only question was when . . . I have just received my copy of the Old Alleynian Yearbook, and although Dulwich is not, I suppose, quite out of the top drawer as public schools go, there is an astonishing number of quite distinguished old boys with enormous strings of letters after their names, titles, peerages, etc. I notice that two of us, though quite undistinguished, have addresses in La Jolla. Apparently there is only one more in all of California, a fellow named Gropius, who seems to have had the same address in San

Francisco for the past thirty years, and probably went to school sometime during the reign of William IV.

Letter to H. N. Swanson and Edgar Carter,
15 December 1950.

Our beautiful black cat had to be put to sleep yesterday morning. We feel pretty broken up about it. She was almost 20 years old. We saw it coming, of course, but we hoped she might pick up strength. But when she got too weak to stand up and practically stopped eating, there was nothing else to do. They have a wonderful way of doing it now. They inject nembutal into a vein of the foreleg and the animal just isn't there any more. She falls asleep in two seconds. Then, after a few minutes, just to make certain, they inject it into the heart directly. Pity they can't do it to people. I watched my mother die under morphine and it took almost ten hours. She was completely unconscious, of course, but how much better if it took two seconds – if it had to be anyhow.

Letter to Dale Warren,
4 January 1951.

I have always been a great admirer of French colloquial slang. I think it's the only body of slang that can compare with ours. German is pretty good too. There is a wonderful precision and daring about French slang. I don't think it has quite the reckless extravagance of ours, but it seems to have more endurance.

Letter to Somerset Maugham,
5 January 1951.

I have seen a number of the television films of your stories and, admirable as the material is, I cannot help feeling a dissatisfaction with the way in which it is presented. There is something wrong with the medium as it is now used. For one thing the acting is not casual enough. The emphasis of stage acting (one might even call it overemphasis) had to be enormously reduced for films, and it seems to me that it must be still further reduced for television. The slightest artifice glares. The feeling of restricted space is so intense that one almost expects the dialogue to be carried on in whispers by a couple of people hiding in the clothes closet. The camera work seems to me to be pretty bad, as bad as the camera work in those English films of the '30s of which we see so many on television now. The settings are so poor that one feels it might be better to do without them altogether and play against a back drop. But the worst thing to me is that the actors, instead of interpreting the story and making it come alive, seem to bulk right between the story and the audience. Their physical presence is overpowering. Their slightest motion distracts the eye. It strikes me that good acting is very much like style in a novel. You should not be too conscious of it. Its effect should be peripheral rather than central. But in television you can hardly be conscious of anything else.

Letter to Jamie Hamilton,
9 January 1951.

All my life I have had cats and I have found that they differ almost as much as people, and that, like children, they are largely the way you treat them except there are a few here and there who cannot be spoiled. But perhaps that is true of children also. Taki had absolute poise, which is a rare quality in animals as well as in human beings. And she had no cruelty, which is still rarer in cats. She caught birds and mice without hurting them, and had no objection whatever to having them taken away from her and released. She even caught a butterfly once . . . I have never liked anyone who disliked cats, because I've always found an element of acute selfishness in their dispositions. Admittedly, a cat doesn't give you the kind of affection a dog gives you. A cat never behaves as if you were the only bright spot in an otherwise clouded existence. But this is only another way of saying that a cat is not a sentimentalist, which does not mean it has no affection.

Letter to James Sandoe,
10 January 1951.

A legal system which can't convict Al Capone of anything but income tax fraud is apt to make the police rather cynical.

Letter to Edgar Carter,
who had been sent a letter by the British magazine Picture Post *with some questions about Chandler, 5 February 1951.*

The *Picture Post* is for people who move their lips when they read. Surely they can get anything they want from my English publisher, Jamie Hamilton, Ltd., 90 Great Russell Street, London, W.C.1. The questions you ask would seem to me to indicate the intellectual level of the editorial department of the *Picture Post*. Yes, I am exactly like the characters in my books. I am very tough and have been known to break a Vienna roll with my bare hands. I am very handsome, have a powerful physique, and change my shirt regularly every Monday morning. When resting between assignments I live in a French Provincial château off Mulholland Drive. It is a fairly small place of forty-eight rooms and fifty-nine baths. I dine off gold plate and prefer to be waited on by naked dancing girls. But of course there are times when I have to grow a beard and hold up in a Main Street flophouse, and there are other times when I am, although not by request, entertained in the drunk tank at the city jail. I have friends from all walks of life. Some are highly educated and some talk like Darryl Zanuck. I have fourteen telephones on my desk, including direct lines to New York, London, Paris, Rome, and Santa Rosa. My filing case opens out into a very convenient portable bar, and the bartender, who lives in the bottom drawer, is a midget named Harry Cohn. I am a heavy smoker and according to my mood I smoke tobacco, marijuana, corn silk, and dried tea leaves. I do a great deal of research, especially in the apartments of tall blondes. In my spare time I collect elephants.

I've known a number of these not-quite writers. No doubt you have also. But in your profession you would get away from them as fast as possible: whereas I've known several of them quite well. I have spent time and money on them and it's always wasted, because even if they make an occasional sale it turns out they have been traveling on someone else's gas. I guess these are the hardest cases, because they want so hard to be professionals that it doesn't take very much encouragement to make them think they are. I knew one who sold a short story (most of which, incidentally, I had written for him) to that semi-slick MacFadden publication that Fulton Oursler used to edit – I forget the name of it. Some cheap outfit bought the picture rights for five hundred bucks and made a very bad B picture with Sally Rand in it. This fellow thereupon got very drunk and went around snooting all his writer friends because they were working for the pulps. A couple of years later he sold a short story to a pulp magazine, and I think that is the total of his contribution to literature in a commercial sense. To hear this fellow and his wife discussing and analyzing stories was a revelation in how much it is possible to know about technique without being able to use any. If you have enough talent, you can get by after a fashion without guts; and if you have enough guts, you can also get by, after a fashion, without talent. But you certainly can't get by with neither. These not-quite writers are very tragic people and the more intelligent they are, the more tragic, because the step they can't take seems to them such a very small step, which in fact it is. And every successful or fairly successful writer knows, or should know, by what a narrow margin he himself was able to take that step. But if you can't take it, you can't. That's all there is to it.

Letter to Jamie Hamilton,
14 February 1951. Jonathan Latimer, mentioned latterly in the letter, was
another of La Jolla's small colony of writers.

Priestley descended on me out of the skies yesterday without
warning, except a telegram from Guadalajara just before he came,
and at a damned inconvenient time, because my wife is not well
and unable to entertain him. However I have done the best I could.
I drove down to Tijuana and picked him up, a damned long
unpleasant drive, if ever there was one, and have installed him in
our best hotel since we have no spare room. He is a likeable, genial
guy; fortunately a great talker, so about all I had to do was click my
tongue against my teeth. He was not entirely satisfied with my
company, for which I do not at all blame him, and suggested gently
as I departed from him late last night at the door of the hotel that
tonight we might possibly meet some of the fellows. So this morning
I burst into tears and threw myself at the feet of Jonathan Latimer,
who knows everybody and likes everybody (whereas I am just the
opposite); so tonight I am going to take him over to Latimer's
house, where will be gathered a reasonable selection of what passes
for intelligent humanity in our city.

Letter to H. F. Hose,
a contemporary of Chandler's at Dulwich, and subsequently a master at
the school, February 1951.

I agree with you that most contemporary writing is rubbish. But
hasn't that always been true? The situation is no different over here,
except that hardly anyone pays much attention to Latin and Greek
any more. I think the English writers generally speaking are apt to
be much more leisurely and urbane than ours, but these qualities
do not seem to carry them very far. I suppose a generation gets the
literature it deserves, just as it is said to get the government it
deserves.

Most of us become impatient with the messiness that is around
us and are inclined to attribute to the past a purity of line which

was not apparent to the contemporaries of that past. The past after all has been sifted and strained. The present has not. The literature of the past has survived and it has prestige on that account, apart from its other prestige. The reasons for its survival are complex. The past is our university; it gives us our tastes and our habits of thought, and we are resentful when we cannot find a basis for them in the present. It is quite possible that they are just the same. You can't build a Gothic cathedral by assembly line methods; you can't get artistic stone masons from the union. For myself, I am convinced that if there is any virtue in our art, and there may be none at all, it does not lie in its resemblance to something that is now traditional, but which was not traditional when it was first produced. If we have stylists, they are not people like Osbert Sitwell – Edwardians who stayed up too late; nor are they pseudo-poet dramatists like T. S. Eliot and Christopher Fry; nor bloodless intellectuals who sit just at the edge of the lamplight and dissect everything to nothing in dry little voices that convey little more than the accents of boredom and extreme disillusion. It seems to me that there have been damn few periods in the history of civilization that a man living in one of them could have realized as definitely great. If you had been a contemporary of Sophocles, I think you might have thought of him almost as highly as you do now. But I think you might have thought Euripides a little vulgar. And if you had been an Elizabethan, I am quite sure you would have thought Shakespeare largely a purveyor of stale plots and over-elaborate rhetoric . . .

Letter to James Sandoe,
20 February 1951.

I have been having another look at the Adelaide Bartlett case, God knows why. I think one of its most confusing elements is that Sir Edward Clarke's defense was so brilliant in contrast to the rather uninspired defense of Maybrick and Wallace that you are almost fooled into ignoring the facts. But the facts, if you look them straight in the eye, are pretty damning. For example:

Edwin Bartlett died of drinking chloroform. Adelaide, his wife, had liquid chloroform procured for her surreptitiously by Dyson, the clergyman, who, if not actually her lover in a technical sense, was certainly doing some very high-powered necking. Her stated reason for wanting the chloroform is nonsense. Edwin was an unattractive and unnecessary husband and a dope as well. If he died she got Dyson and Edwin's money. Edwin's health was excellent in spite of his constant complaining. It was more than usually good the night before he died. His insomnia seems to have been severe, but is not consistent with his hearty appetite. Morphia and chloral hydrate had both been tried on him without effect. He was obviously a hard person to drug. See about the gas at the dentist's. The wine glass which was found smelled of chloroform behind brandy. The chloroform bottle was not found. According to Adelaide it had been on the mantel earlier. The house was not searched, and Adelaide was not searched. Adelaide had opportunity to hide what remained of the chloroform. She admitted to disposing of it later. There are three principal arguments against her guilt: (1) her nursing care seemed genuine and fairly self-sacrificing; (2) she urged a quick post mortem and herself scouted the chance of his having taken the chloroform himself; (3) the difficulty of poisoning Edwin by this method was enormous according to medical testimony, and there was no previous record of murder by this means. But assuming her guilt, the first argument is meaningless. What else would you expect? How else has any poisoner ever acted? As to the second argument, there is no reason to assume, as the judge did, that she knew a delay in the post mortem would be in her favor. How about the theory of 'methinks you protest too much'? He didn't die of jugged hare. There was bound to be an investigation. If you know that, and you have murdered him, how best can you look innocent? The way she did. The judge disposed of the third argument. If she murdered him, it was by a method which had one chance in twenty of succeeding. But she didn't know that. To her it may have looked easy.

The insomnia makes me laugh. I have had insomnia – quite severe insomnia. I did not want a big meal of jugged hare. I did not want a supper of oysters and cake. I did not want a haddock for breakfast – a large haddock – so badly that I would have been willing to get up an hour earlier in order to start eating. I think this guy was a neurotic insomniac. That is to say, if he didn't feel as fresh as a daisy in the morning, he said he hadn't slept more than twenty minutes the night before. But I don't believe his insomnia was severe, I can't believe he would be desperate enough to take the chloroform himself, even though the unpleasantness of it is not a conclusive argument because people used to take castor oil. If you hold your nose, you can swallow almost anything without tasting it. But you do have to believe that this guy was desperate from insomnia and yet had a very fine appetite for his food. It is quite true that the stuff burns. But if you have sniffed enough of it to make you woozy, it might seem that your senses had been blunted. Apart from murder, this seems to be the only possibility. And it is not a very convincing one.

Assuming Adelaide's guilt, her behavior with the bottle must have been entirely to protect Dyson, because if she admits possession of the chloroform, she has to tell how she got it. If she is willing to do that, the best bet is to leave the bottle where it was and stand on the insomnia and Edwin's desperate attempt to overcome it. Dr Leach, the dope, will certainly back her up. Some of the medical history is in favor of it (but not the jugged hare). It makes a neat little problem all right. If she makes him sniff enough chloroform to put him almost under but not quite, and then gives him a nice fat drink of it in circumstances where he doesn't exactly know what he is drinking, just takes things on trust, and he swallows the chloroform and it kills him. The doctors say that if he had been quite unconscious, he wouldn't have swallowed it, and that his swallowing would not be working. But they also seem to think that if he had swallowed it while he were conscious, he would have thrown it up. What they really mean is that they would, or you would, or I would. Edwin is a little bit different from us. You can feed anything to Edwin, and all he wants is to get up an hour early the next morning and start eating more. I think the man had a stomach like a goat. I think he could digest sawdust, old tin cans, iron filings, and shoe leather. I think he could drink chloroform just like you and I could drink orange juice. Anyhow, any argument against his being able to retain it in his stomach is nonsense, because he did retain it in his stomach; so the only real argument is against the difficulty of getting it down his throat. And in Edwin's case that doesn't seem to me a very strong argument. He probably thought he was drinking ginger wine.

Letter to Jamie Hamilton,
27 February 1951.

I wouldn't say that I found Priestley tactless, and I certainly haven't any quarrel with him. He plays the part of the blunt-spoken York-shireman very well. He was very pleasant to me and went out of his way to be complimentary. He is rugged, energetic, versatile, and in a way very professional; this is, everything that comes his way will be material and most of the material will be used rather quickly and superficially. His social philosophy is a little too rigid for my taste and a little too much conditioned by the fact that he finds it impossible to see much good in anyone who has made a lot of money (except by writing of course), anyone who has a public school accent or a military bearing, anyone in short who has a speech or mannerisms above the level of the lower middle class. I think this must be a great handicap to him, because in his world a gentleman of property is automatically a villain. That's a rather limiting viewpoint, and I would say that Priestley is rather a limited man . . . Of course I don't like socialism, although a modified form of it is inevitable everywhere. I think a bunch of bureaucrats can abuse the power of money just as ruthlessly as a bunch of Wall Street bankers, and far less competently. Socialism so far has existed largely on the fat of the class it is trying to impoverish. What happens when all that fat is used up?

Letter to James Sandoe,
6 March 1951. The Kefauver committee had been set up by Washington
to investigate organized crime.

I don't know whether you have a television set, or whether having
one you could have seen films of the Kefauver committee hearings.
I saw part of those held in Los Angeles and found them fascinating.
Obviously nothing that a mystery writer could dream up could be
more fantastic than what actually goes on in the hoodlum empire
which infests this country. Kefauver himself is worth the price of
admission any day — a big powerful guy with absolute poise of
manner and unfailing politeness to the witness, no trace of Southern
accent whatever. He was hardly ever even sarcastic. Nevertheless,
he made these racketeer witnesses very nervous, much more nervous I think than if he had been really tough with them. Even
when he produced a piece of documentary evidence which made
nonsense of what they had been saying, he didn't do it with any air
of pouncing but in an offhand, casual manner as if it didn't really
matter what they said, because it had all been decided somewhere
else what was going to happen to them. I hope it has, although it
is pretty obvious that under our present laws only income tax
evasion could ever really be proved against these fellows. There
was one fascinating little session in which an ex-sheriff of San
Bernardino county described a visit to Big Bear Lake up in the
mountains, where he had heard two women mourning over some
gambling losses their husbands had sustained locally and he found
out where the gambling house was and went there. He said there
were about a hundred and fifty people in the place, two roulette
wheels were operating, at least one crap table, and numerous slot
machines. He circulated around, determined who the managers
and gamblers were, then talked to them and found out that the
house was owned by a man named Gentry, who was the foreman
of the grand jury. He then arrested all the gamblers, confiscated all
the gambling equipment apparently with no opposition at all,
although he was alone and not young, took the gamblers down to
the justices of the peace, where they pleaded guilty and paid fines.

Thereafter he was approached by emissaries of Mr Gentry offering him money to get the gambling equipment back. Kefauver then put Mr Gentry on the stand, the former foreman of the grand jury. Mr Gentry said: (a) that he had never owned any gambling equipment and therefore had never sent anybody to try and buy it back from the sheriff; (b) that he had never owned this house in Big Bear Valley, although he had once had a twenty-six hundred dollar mortgage on it; (c) that he had never lived in it; (d) that the house consisted of a rather small living room, a bedroom, a small kitchen and a bathroom, and that if you could get fifteen people into it, the walls would bulge. Senator Kefauver smiled politely, thanked him, and left it at that.

Letter to Dale Warren,
14 March 1951.

A few years ago a publicity man came to see me, his face shining with triumph and said he had 'set it up' for me to do a guest column for some newspaper lady on vacation. He seemed to think I ought to blush with delight, and he was quite annoyed when I kicked him in the groin and poured a bottle of red ink down his neck.

Letter to Jamie Hamilton,
19 March 1951.

I had a friendly note from Priestley, flawlessly typed on Gracie Fields' stationery. I hear she is giving up California and going to live in Capri. She seems to feel about Los Angeles very much as I do: that it has become a grotesque and impossible place for a human being to live in. Priestley left me with one uncomfortable and probably exaggerated idea, but it is one in which he seems to believe implicitly. He thinks the entertainment world in England and the literary world for that matter, at least from the critical side (stage, films, radio, television, reviewing, etc.) is completely dominated by homosexuals, and that a good fifty per cent of the people active in this area are homosexuals; including, he says, practically all the literary critics … He also mentioned several rather distinguished writers as pansies, whom I had never thought of in that way. And when I said, 'Well, if there are so many of them, why doesn't somebody write a really good novel about it?' He mentioned the name of a *very* distinguished novelist, a notorious case according to him, and said that he had retired from publication for several years and written a long novel about homosexualism from the inside by an expert, but that nobody would publish it. Well, well. These are dangerous thoughts to implant in a young and impressionable mind like mine. Now, every time I read one of these flossy and perceptive book reviewers, I say to myself, 'Well, is he, or isn't he?' And by God, about three quarters of the time I am beginning to think he is. The *Saturday Review of Literature* published an article a couple of weeks ago about twelve new and presumably promising novelists of 1950, together with their photographs. There were only three whom, on their physiognomy, I would definitely pass as male. From now on I'll be looking for them under the bed like an old maid looking for burglars. Maybe I ought to try an article for the *Atlantic* on the subject. I should call it, 'You Too Could Be A Pansy'; or perhaps simply, 'Homo Sapiens'.

Letter to Bernice Baumgarten,
16 April 1951. Ambler is the British thriller writer Eric Ambler, and the
book being referred to is Judgement on Deltchev.

It would seem to me that Ambler has fallen between two stools and that he has succumbed to a danger which afflicts all intellectuals who attempt to deal with thriller material. I know I have to fight it all the time. It is no easy trick to keep your characters and your story operating on a level which is understandable to the semi-literate public and at the same time give them some intellectual and artistic overtones which that public does not seek or demand or in effect recognize, but which somehow subconsciously it accepts and likes. My theory has always been that the public will accept style provided you do not call it style either in words or by, as it were, standing off and admiring it.

There seems to me a vast difference between writing down to the public (something which always flops in the end) and doing what you want to do in a form which the public has learned to accept. It's not so much that Ambler let himself get too intellectual in this story as that he let it become apparent that he was being intellectual. That seems to be the fatal mistake, although I myself liked the book, just as I did not particularly like Helen MacInnes' book *Neither Five Nor Three*. She offends me by dealing with very complicated issues in a sort of half-baked manner like a school girl analyzing Proust. You can't laugh Communism off just as a dirty conspiracy. You have to justify its intellectual appeal to some very brilliant minds and destroy it nevertheless. I guess the lucky writers are those who can outwrite their readers without outthinking them.

Letter to D. J. Ibberson,
an English fan, 19 April 1951.

It is very kind of you to take such an interest in the facts of Philip Marlowe's life. The date of his birth is uncertain. I think he said somewhere that he was thirty-eight years old, but that was quite a while ago and he is no older today. This is just something you will have to face. He was not born in a Midwestern town but in a small California town called Santa Rosa, which your map will show you to be about fifty miles north of San Francisco. Santa Rosa is famous as the home of Luther Burbank, a fruit and vegetable horticulturist, once of considerable renown. It is perhaps less widely known as the background of Hitchcock's picture *Shadow of a Doubt*, most of which was shot right in Santa Rosa. Marlowe has never spoken of his parents, and apparently he has no living relatives. This could be remedied if necessary. He had a couple of years of college, either at the University of Oregon at Eugene, or Oregon State University at Corvallis, Oregon. I don't know why he came to Southern California, except that eventually most people do, although not all of them remain. He seems to have had some experience as an investigator for an insurance company and later as investigator for the district attorney of Los Angeles county. This would not necessarily make him a police officer nor give him the right to make an arrest. The circumstances in which he lost that job are well known to me but I cannot be very specific about them. You'll have to be satisfied with the information that he got a little too efficient at a time and in a place where efficiency was the last thing desired by the persons in charge. He is slightly over six feet tall and weighs about thirteen stone eight. He has dark brown hair, brown eyes, and the expression 'passably good looking' would not satisfy him in the least. I don't think he looks tough. He can be tough. If I had ever had an opportunity of selecting the movie actor who could best represent him to my mind, I think it would have been Cary Grant. I think he dresses as well as can be expected. Obviously he hasn't very much money to spend on clothes, or on anything else for that matter. The horn-rimmed sunglasses do not make him distinctive. Practically everyone in Southern California wears sunglasses at some time or other. When you say he wears 'pyjamas' even in summer, I don't know what you mean. Who doesn't? Were you under the impression that he wore a nightshirt? Or did you mean that he might sleep raw in hot weather? The last is possible, although our weather here is very seldom hot at night. You are quite right about his smoking habits, although I don't think he insists on Camels. Almost any sort of cigarette will satisfy him. The use of cigarette cases is not as common here as in England. He definitely does not use bookmatches which are always safety matches. He uses either large wooden matches, which we call kitchen matches, or a smaller match of the same type which comes in small boxes and can be struck anywhere, including on the thumbnail if the weather is dry enough. In the desert or in the mountains it is quite easy to strike a match on your thumbnail, but the humidity around Los Angeles is pretty high. Marlowe's drinking habits are much as you state. I don't think he prefers rye to bourbon, however. He will drink practically anything that is not sweet. Certain drinks, such as Pink Ladies, Honolulu cocktails and crème de menthe highballs, he would regard as an insult. Yes, he makes good coffee. Anyone can make good coffee in this country, although it seems quite impossible in England. He takes cream, and sugar with his coffee, not milk. He will also drink it black without sugar. He cooks his own breakfast, which is a simple matter, but not any other meal. He is a late riser by inclination, but occasionally an early riser by necessity. Aren't we all? I would not say that his chess comes up to tournament standard. I don't know where he got the little paper-bound book of tournament games published in Leipzig, but he likes it because he prefers the continental method of designating the squares on the chess board. Nor do I know that he is something of a card player. This has slipped my mind. What do you mean he is 'moderately fond of animals'? If you live in an apartment house, moderately is about as fond of them as you can get. It seems to me that you have an inclination to interpret any chance remark as an indication of a fixed taste. As to his interest in women as 'frankly carnal', these are your words, not mine.

Marlowe cannot recognize a Bryn Mawr accent, because there is no such thing. All he implies by that expression is a toplofty way of speaking. I doubt very much that he can tell genuine old furniture from fakes. And I also beg leave to doubt that many experts can do it either, if the fakes are good enough. I pass the Edwardian furniture and pre-Raphaelite art. I just don't recall where you get your facts. I would not say that Marlowe's knowledge of perfume stops at Chanel Number 5. That again is merely a symbol of something that is expensive and at the same time reasonably restrained. He likes all the slightly acrid perfumes, but not the cloying or overspiced type. He is, as you may have noticed, a slightly acrid person. Of course he knows what the Sorbonne is, and he also knows where it is. Of course he knows the difference between a tango and a rumba, and also between a conga and a samba, and he knows the difference between a samba and a mamba, although he does not believe that the mamba can overtake a galloping horse. I doubt if he knows the new dance called a mambo, because it seems to be only recently discovered or developed.

Now let's see, how far does that take us? Fairly regular filmgoer, you say, dislikes musicals. Check. May be an admirer of Orson Welles. Possibly, especially when Orson is directed by someone other than himself. Marlowe's reading habits and musical tastes are just as much a mystery to me as they are to you, and if I tried to improvise, I'm afraid I would get him confused with my own tastes. If you ask me why he is a private detective, I can't answer you. Obviously there are times when he wishes he were not, just as there are times when I would rather be almost anything than a writer. The private detective of fiction is a fantastic creation who acts and speaks like a real man. He can be completely realistic in every sense but one, that one sense being that in life as we know it such a man would not be a private detective. The things which happen to him might still happen to him, but they would happen as a result of a peculiar set of chances. By making him a private detective, you skip the necessity for justifying his adventures.

Where he lives: in *The Big Sleep* and some earlier stories he apparently lived in a single apartment with a pull-down bed, a bed that folds up into the wall and it has a mirror on the under side of it. Then he moved into an apartment similar to that occupied by a character named Joe Brody in *The Big Sleep*. It may have been the same apartment, he may have got it cheap because a murder had taken place in it. I think, but I'm not sure, that this apartment is on the fourth floor. It contains a living room which you enter directly from the hallway, and opposite are French windows opening on an ornamental balcony, which is just something to look at, certainly not anything to sit out on. Against the right-hand wall, nearest to the hallway of the apartment house, there is a door that leads to an interior hall. Beyond that, against the left-hand wall, there is this oak drop leaf desk, an easy chair, etc.; beyond that, an archway entrance to the dinette and kitchen. The dinette, as known in American apartment houses or at any rate in California apartment houses, is simply a space divided off from the kitchen proper by an archway or a built-in china closet. It would be very small, and the kitchen would also be very small. As you enter the hallway from the living room (the interior hallway) you would come on your right to the bathroom door and continuing straight on you would come to the bedroom. The bedroom would contain a walk-in closet. The bathroom in a building of this type would contain a shower in the tub and a shower curtain. None of the rooms is very large. The rent of the apartment, furnished, would have been about sixty dollars a month when Marlowe moved into it. God knows what it would be now. I shudder to think. I should guess not less than ninety dollars a month, probably more.

As to Marlowe's office, I'll have to take another look at it sometime to refresh my memory. It seems to me it's on the sixth floor in a building which faces north, and that his office window faces east. But I'm not certain about this. As you say, there is a reception room which is a half-office, perhaps half the space of a corner office, converted into two reception rooms with separate entrances and communicating doors right and left respectively. Marlowe has a private office which communicates with his reception room, and there is a connection which causes a buzzer to ring in his private office when the door of the reception room is opened. But this buzzer can be switched off by a toggle switch. He has not, and never has had, a secretary. He could very easily subscribe to a telephone answering service, but I don't recall mentioning that anywhere. And I do not recall that his desk has a glass top, but I may have said so. The office bottle is kept in the filing drawer of the desk, – a drawer, standard in American office desks (perhaps also in England) which is the depth of two ordinary drawers, and is intended to contain file folders, but very seldom does, since most people keep their file folders in filing cases. It seems to me that some of these details flit about a good deal. His guns have also been rather various. He started out with a German Luger automatic pistol. He seems to have had Colt automatics of various calibers, but not larger than .38, and when last I heard he has a Smith & Wesson .38 special, probably with a four-inch barrel. This is a very powerful gun, although not the most powerful made, and has the advantage over an automatic of using a lead cartridge. It will not jam or discharge accidentally, even if dropped on a hard surface, and is probably just as effective a weapon at short range as a .45 caliber automatic. It would be better with a six-inch barrel, but that would make it much more awkward to carry. Even a four-inch barrel is not too convenient, and the detective branch of the police usually carries a gun with only a two and a half-inch barrel. This is about all I have for you now, but if there is anything else you want to know, please write to me again. The trouble is, you really seem to know a good deal more about Philip Marlowe than I do, and perhaps I shall have to ask you questions instead of you asking me.

Memo to Juanita Messick,
Chandler's secretary, Easter 1951. Leona was Chandler's maid in La Jolla.

Office will be closed Thursday and Friday. On Friday you should go to church for three hours. On Thursday you will have to be guided by your conscience, if any. Leona won't be here from Wednesday night until the following Monday but she doesn't get paid this time. Some damn nonsense about the child getting married. I suppose the nuns have told her she is to become the bride of Christ. Do Catholics get confirmed at the age of 8? I thought you had to have some idea of what it was all about. I was confirmed by the Bishop of Worcester. He had a beard.

Letter to Sol Siegal,
an executive at Twentieth Century-Fox Studios, 27 April 1951.

There are two kinds of screenwriters. There are the adept technicians, who know how to work with the medium and how to subordinate themselves to the use of the camera and the actors by the director. Their work is polished, effective, and entirely anonymous. Nothing they do bears any stamp of individuality. Then there is the writer whose personal touch must be allowed to come through, because his personal touch is what makes him a writer. Obviously a writer of this kind should never work for a director like Hitchcock, because there must be nothing in a Hitchcock picture which Hitchcock himself might not have written. It is not merely a question of how Hitchcock uses his camera and his actors; the point is that there must be nothing in his pictures which is beyond his range. Eventually there will be a type of director who

162

realizes that what is said and how it is said is more important than shooting it upside down through a glass of champagne.

> Letter to Somerset Maugham,
> 4 May 1951.

Priestley was in La Jolla a couple of months ago, and was kind enough to tell me that I wrote well, and that I should write a straight novel. Of course I have heard this before in other connections. If you write well, you should not be writing a mystery. Mysteries should only be written by people who can't write. I regard this as vicious propaganda from the Edmund Wilson crowd. Obviously you can't expect detective fiction to be anything but sub-literary, to use Edmund Wilson's word, if you insist on weeding out from that field anyone who shows any pretensions to skill or imagination.

Charles Morton, interestingly, had once written to Chandler about an encounter he had had with Edmund Wilson, in a letter dated 24 January 1945: 'We once published a piece by Wilson about a Russian poet – one of the most wonderful poets in the world, he said – but the only hitch was that this poet had never been translated in English. Wilson himself, as he assured us, had been boning up on Russian. As such, Wilson was obviously unique in our circulation, contributors and staff. Being the only guy who had ever heard of this poet, he was naturally the only one who had ever read him, and for some reason or another we chose to let him make free with the matter. As things went along, however, we conceived some curiosity about the poet, and we procured a Russian who translated some of him for us. The poetry, we all agreed, was terrible.'

> Letter to Mr Dana,
> *a publisher at Lippincott, 19 June 1951. The book being referred to was a collection of Charles Morton's journalism.*

You have sent me a massive hunk of galleys of a book allegedly by one Charles W. Morton. You are in a frantic rush. You are holding the presses on the jacket in case I might care to get hysterical and call Mr Morton the greatest American humorist since Hoover. So I am supposed to drop everything, including the week's washing and ironing and such feeble attempts as I may make to earn a living, and dedicate myself to your noble purpose. You have probably been stalling around with this book for six months until someone lit a fire under your chair, and now you are climbing up and down the walls yodeling like a Swiss tenor, because, forsooth, 'the jackets must go press without fail next week, be sure to send them your comment back the fastest way'. I know you publishers. You send the proofs off by air express, and I sit up all night correcting them and send them back to you the same way, and the next thing anybody hears about you, you're sound asleep on somebody's private beach in Bermuda . . . I may read these galleys and I may not. Perhaps I'll go out and cut the back lawn instead.

Letter to Charles Morton,
July 1951.

I wasn't writing to you but to a man named Dana at Lippincott's. Evidently somebody with an important name dropped dead or got jailed for mopery at the last moment, so he had to root around in the weeds for a substitute: so I just had a little fun with him, meaning no harm for anyone. Secretly of course I was delighted that he hit me when I didn't have time to think, because I hate the whole lousy racket. The proper time to praise a writer is after his book has been published, and the proper place to praise him is in something else that is published. You must be well aware that there is practically a stable of puff merchants back in your territory who will go on record over practically anything including the World Almanac, provided they get their names featured. A few names occur with such monotonous regularity that only the fact of their known success as writers keeps one from thinking this is the way they earn their groceries. As a matter of fact I know that payment is sometimes made, because my Hollywood agent once called me up from New York and carefully propositioned me on the subject . . . Over in

England they carry this quote business, though not pre-publication so much, to the point where it is absolutely meaningless. The currency of praise has been so depreciated that there is nothing to say about a really good book. It has all been said already about the second, third, and fourth rate stuff which appears, circulates briefly, and then is forgotten. Anyhow if something comes along that you feel a sort of moral compulsion to praise to all the world if you have the opportunity, are you going to do it through the medium of a promotion department? I should hope to kiss a duck you're not.

Letter to Charles Morton,
5 July 1951.

Many thanks for the signed photograph of yourself in your good suit. That's a nice piece of material kid. You're executive as hell. You look as if you'd just been telling the head of production control that if he couldn't maintain schedule No. BF 7139x21 you'd get someone who could.

Letter to Frederic Dannay,
10 July 1951. Dannay was the co-editor of Ellery Queen crime
magazine, and had written to Chandler asking him to contribute to a
survey in the magazine of the top ten living crime writers.

My list, if I made it, would probably leave out some of those names which will inevitably appear on your list . . . I have liked some very pedestrian stories because they were unpretentious and because their mysteries were rooted in hard facts and not in false motivations cooked up for the purpose of mystifying a reader. I suppose the attraction of the pedestrian book is their documentary quality and this, if it is authentic, is pretty rare, and any attempt to dish it up with chi-chi and glamour turns my stomach completely. I think you are up against a difficult problem, because I think we may take it as granted that a mystery fan would rather read a bad mystery than none at all. You are bound to give some weight to volume of production, and strictly speaking volume of production means absolutely nothing. A writer discloses himself on a single page, sometimes in a single paragraph. An un-writer may fill a whole shelf, he may achieve fame of a sort, he may occasionally concoct a plot which will make him seem to be a little better than he really is, but in the end he fades away and is nothing.

Letter to Jamie Hamilton,
14 July 1951. Chandler is talking about his novel-in-progress, The Long Goodbye.

The trouble with my book is that I wrote about half of it in the third person before I realized that I have absolutely no interest in the leading character. He was merely a name; so I'm afraid I'm going to have to start all over and hand the assignment to Mr Marlowe, as a result of which I'm going to lose a number of good scenes because they took place away from the leading character. It begins to look as though I were tied to this fellow for life. I simply can't function without him.

Letter to Dale Warren,
20 July 1951. Chandler had now seen the released version of Strangers on a Train.

It has no guts, no plausibility, no characters, and no dialogue. But of course it's Hitchcock, and a Hitchcock picture always does have something.

An insurance inventory
filled in by Chandler in August 1951, listing some of his typical office equipment as well as the Chandlers' post-Hollywood furniture.

Equipment

Audiograph
Dictator
Transcriber

Typewriter Control
Hand Microphone
Earphone
Ash Tray Speaker

Remington Typewriter
Underwood Typewriter
Corona Portable

Dumont TV
Zenith Radio

Furniture

1 gold sofa
1 gold and rust sofa
Chrome chairs
Steinway Grand
Boudoir lamps
Chaise Longue

Letter to Dale Warren,
6 August 1951.

I had a couple of very pleasant times with Syd Perelman when he was out here on an assignment, presumably from *Holiday*. There is one hell of a nice guy, easy going, unassuming and without vanity. When Priestley spent about fifty per cent of his time and energy trying to make you realize how good he is, Perelman doesn't give it two minutes. Did I say two minutes? He doesn't give it ten seconds. He acts as though he didn't care, and I don't think it's an act.

Letter to Mr Hines,
the Superintendent of the US Post Office in La Jolla, 13 August 1951.

Dear Mr Hines,

Once in a while I get a special delivery letter. Sometimes they are out in my box, since that is my delivery address, and sometimes they are delivered to the house. Whoever does this lately has developed a habit of arriving at 7:30 in the morning and trying to batter the front door down, thus arousing my wife from sleep which she badly needs. I don't criticize the man at all, since he is probably impelled by a strong sense of duty. But may I, in all courtesy and friendliness, point out: first that a special delivery letter is hardly that urgent, as anything really urgent would come by wire and telephone; and second, that there is a mail slot in the side door of our house at ground level, and that simply dropping the letter in that slot would be my idea of a beautiful job accomplished with tact and consideration. If this should prove impossible to accomplish or should be in violation of some post office rule, then may I request that special delivery be deposited in my box, No 128, just like any other first-class mail. In my case at least it does not really require the red light and siren treatment. When this house was built the mail slot was put in the side door deliberately so that the mail man would not have to climb any steps. Usually, whoever delivers special delivery mail does not know this, so he climbs to the front door, finds no mail slot and is thereby stung to fury.

Yours very sincerely
Raymond Chandler

Letter to S. J. Perelman,
4 September 1951. Perelman was thinking about moving to the West
Coast with his family from Florida.

If you are still interested in Rancho Santa Fe and haven't forgotten all about it by this time, there is no objection there to your keeping tropical birds and a few tropical animals, provided you keep them off the main street and out of the dining room at the Rancho Santa Fe Inn. Rancho Santa Fe is part of the San Dieguito high school district . . . I don't know anything about the scholastic standing of this school, if any. I have heard the California high schools range from putrid to rotten, and I have one relative, fortunately distant, who graduated from the Fairfax high school in Los Angeles while still struggling with the alphabet. As to the La Jolla schools, which might be representative of this part of the state, the only authentic comment I have heard is from a party living across the street from my sister-in-law. This party has four children and is thinking of moving back to Kansas where there is a possibility of them being educated. It seems that they all get 'A's' out here, although they know nothing and do no work. She regards this as very suspicious, inasmuch as before coming to California they did some work and got nowhere near 'A's' at all.

Perelman replied to Chandler a few days later: 'I'm seated in an all-plastic motel overlooking another all-plastic motel which in turn overlooks the Gulf Stream, but there is no man in America but yourself (or for that matter on the earth) who could convey the grisly charm of the establishment. It's roughly three in the afternoon, sun beating down in a fury, and no sound but the occasional flapping of the laundry and the occasional flush of a toilet in the next booth . . . a rush of work has had me on the ropes since just about six weeks ago, and as of day before yesterday I holed up in here to belt out an article. I'd spent the four or five days prior rubbering at Miami beach and points immediately north, and a depressing sight it is, too. I actually had a cocktail (you see what I have to subject myself to for copy) in the Peekaboo Room of the Broadripple Hotel, a conjunction of syllables I wouldn't have believed had I been told about it. I think you will admit that I earn a hard dollar.'

Letter to Jamie Hamilton,
19 September 1951. Chandler had just taken Cissy for a recuperative holiday at a 'dude ranch'.

I don't know if you have ever been to a dude ranch. I had never been to one before. This one is called the Alisal, which in Spanish means a grove of sycamores, according to the publicity. It is a small part of a 10,500 acre cattle ranch, which is one of the few intact Spanish land grants of California and was originally made to the Carrillo family. It has a lovely climate, at least at this time of the year. It is situated in an inland valley, the Santa Ynez valley just north of Santa Barbara, and is almost as dry as a desert, very hot in the daytime, very cool in the mornings, in the evenings and at night. I think it must be pretty awful in the summer. We found the place both very amusing and intensely boring, expensive, badly run but nicely laid out with the usual swimming pool, tennis courts, etc. The kind of place where the people who work in the office wear riding boots, and where the lady guests appear for breakfast in levis riveted with copper, for lunch in jodhpurs with gaudy shirts and scarfs and in the evening either in cocktail gowns or in more jodhpurs and more gaudy shirts and scarfs. The ideal scarf seems to be very narrow, not much wider than a boot lace, and run through a ring in the front and then hangs down one side of the shirt. I didn't ask why; I didn't get to know anybody well enough. The men also wear gaudy shirts, which they change constantly for other patterns, all except the real horsemen, who wear rather heavy wool or nylon and wool shirts with long sleeves, yoked in the back, the kind of thing that can only be bought in a horsy town. I imagine the place is a lot of fun for the right sort of people, the kind who go riding in the morning, swimming or tennising in the afternoon, then have two or three drinks at the bar, and by the time they arrive for dinner are able to be quite enthusiastic over the rather inferior and much too greasy cooking. For us who were rather tired and out of sorts and consequently much too finicky, the place was a trial. But it was fun to see a whole army of quail strolling unconcernedly past the bungalows in the evening and to see birds that looked like jackdaws, which we never see anywhere else, not even in the mountains.

Letter to Jamie Hamilton,
5 October 1951.

I do hope to have a book in 1952, I hope very hard. But dammit I have a great deal of trouble getting on with it. The old zest is not there. I am worn down with worry over my wife. She has lost a lot of ground in the last two years. When I get into work I am already tired and dispirited. I wake in the night with dreadful thoughts.

Cissy has a constant cough which can only be kept down by drugs and the drugs destroy her vitality. It is not TB nor is it anything cancerous, but I am afraid it is chronic and may get worse instead of better. She has no strength and being of buoyant disposition and a hard fighter, she fights herself to the point of exhaustion. I dread, and I am sure she does, although we try not to talk about it, a slow decline into invalidism. And what happens then I frankly do not know.

Letter to Mr Inglis,
a fan, October 1951. Inglis had written to Chandler. At one point in his
letter he speculated that, to a psychologist, Philip Marlowe might appear
emotionally immature.

I'm afraid I can't give you much of an argument about your concept of what you call maturity ... It may be that your 'advanced psychology student' friend was pulling your leg a little, or it may be that the advanced psychology itself has got him into a state of confusion in which he will probably remain for the rest of his life. We seem to be somewhat over supplied with psychologists nowadays, but I suppose that is natural enough, since their jargon, tiresome as it is to me personally, seems to have the same attraction for muddled minds that theological hair-splitting had for people of a former age. If being in revolt against a corrupt society constitutes being immature, then Philip Marlowe is extremely immature. If seeing dirt where there is dirt constitutes an inadequate social adjustment, then Philip Marlowe has an inadequate social adjustment. Of course, Marlowe is a failure and knows it. He is a failure because he hasn't any money. A man who without physical handicaps cannot make a decent living is always a failure and usually a moral failure. But a lot of very good men have been failures because their particular talents did not suit their time and place. In the long run I guess we are all failures or we wouldn't have the kind of world we have. I think I resent your suggestion that Philip Marlowe has contempt for other people's physical weakness. I don't know where you got that idea, and I don't think it's so. I am also a little tired of the numerous suggestions that have been made that he's always full of whisky. The only point I can see in justification of that is that when he wants a drink he takes it openly and doesn't hesitate to remark on it. I don't know how it is in your part of the country, but compared with the country-club set in my part of the country he is as sober as a deacon.

Letter to Carl Brandt,
27 October 1951.

I am having a hard time finishing the book. Have enough paper to make it complete, but must do all over again. I just didn't know where I was going.

Letter to Dale Warren,
7 November 1951.

You ask me how anybody can survive Hollywood? Well, I must say that I personally had a lot of fun there. But how long you can survive depends a great deal on what sort of people you have to work with. You meet a lot of bastards, but they usually have some saving grace. A writer who can get himself teamed up with a director or a producer who will give him a square deal, a really square deal, can get a lot of satisfaction out of his work. Unfortunately that doesn't happen often. If you go to Hollywood just to make money, you have to be pretty cynical about it and not care too much what you do. And if you really believe in the art of the film, it's a long job and you really should forget about any other kind of writing. A preoccupation with words for their own sake is fatal to good film making. It's not what films are for. It's not my cup of tea, but it could have been if I'd started it twenty years earlier. But twenty years earlier of course I could never have got there, and that is true of a great many people. They don't want you until you have made a name, and you have developed some kind of talent which they can't use. The best scenes I ever wrote were practically monosyllabic. And the best short scene I ever wrote, by my own judgement, was one in which a girl said 'uh-huh' three times with three different intonations, and that's all there was to it. The hell of good film writing is that the most important part is what is left out. It's left out because the camera and the actors can do it better and quicker, above all quicker. But it had to be there in the beginning.

Letter to Carl Brandt,
regarding television, 15 November 1951.

However toplofty and idealistic a man may be, he can always rationalize his right to earn money. After all the public is entitled to what it wants. The Romans knew that and even they lasted four hundred years after they started to putrefy.

Letter to Jamie Hamilton,
29 November 1951.

Publishers may apologize to authors and to other publishers and to other writers. But with agents it is enough that you let them live.

Letter to Paul McClung,
11 December 1951. McClung, Chandler's paperback publisher, had
written to Chandler about a line in one of his novels where he implied
having been told, by a doctor, that alcoholism was incurable.

The doctor on whose point of view I founded the opinion you quote has been dead for several years. In any case I doubt very much whether he would have appreciated my revealing his identity to a magazine or a newspaper in connection with an opinion which his profession as a group would consider defeatist and most improper. I remember his saying to me in effect: 'The toughest thing about trying to cure an alcoholic or a user of dope is that you have absolutely nothing to offer him in the long run. He feels awful at the moment no doubt; he feels shamed and humiliated; he would like to be cured of it if it is not too painful, and sometimes even if it is, and it always is. In a purely physical sense you maybe say he is cured when his withdrawal symptoms have passed, and they can be pretty awful. But we forget pain, and to a certain extent we forget humiliation. So your alcoholic cured or your former dope addict looks around him, and what has he achieved? A flat landscape through which there is no road more interesting than another. His reward is negative. He doesn't suffer physically, and he is not humiliated or shamed mentally. He is merely damned dull.' Obviously such a point of view is inconsistent with the Polyanna attitude we impose on the medical profession. They know better, but they have to live too, although there are times when in particular cases one doesn't quite see why.

I put my opinion, which you seem to have taken rather seriously, in the mouth of a crook. In times like these only a crook may safely express opinions of this sort. Any medical man of standing would have to add something like: 'Of course with proper psychiatric treatment, blah, blah, blah –' He would certainly have you on the upbeat. And by mentioning psychiatry he would, for me at least, instantly destroy the entire effect of any frank statement into which he may have ventured, since I regard psychiatry as fifty per cent bunk, thirty per cent fraud, ten per cent parrot talk, and the remaining ten per cent just a fancy lingo for the common sense we have had for hundreds and perhaps thousands of years, if we ever had the guts to read it.

Letter to Dale Warren,
undated. Chandler recalls a conversation with Hitchcock about how far film technique had evolved since its beginning.

To illustrate he said, and of course I'm remembering not quoting: Imagine a man visiting an old flame he hasn't seen in many years. She's married and rich and so on and she has asked him to tea. The audience knows what is to happen. This is how we used to photograph it. Man arrives in taxi, gets out, pays taxi, looks up at house, mounts step, rings, waits, lights cigarette, inside shot of maid approaching door, opens it, man announces self. Yes, sir, will you please come in. Man enters hallway, looks around, is ushered into reception room, looks around, maid leaves, man smiles wistfully, looks at photo on mantel, finally sits down. Maid reaches top of stairs, knocks on door, enters, mistress primping, close shot of her eyes as maid says who has come, cool voice thank you I'll be right down, maid goes, mistress stares at eyes in mirror, little shrug, rises, starts out of room, comes back for a handkerchief, starts out again, camera follows her downstairs, pauses at door, with tender half smile, then with a quick decision opens it, reverse shot man rising as she says come in, they stand staring at each other, close shot of each, and finally 'George! It's been so long!' or some tripe like that, and *then* the scene begins.

They'd sit through all that and like it some, Hitchcock said, because it was motion, the camera was doing and the camera was a wonderful thing. It took moving pictures, it bloody well did. But now?

Taxi arrives, man gets out, pays, starts up steps. Inside house bell ringing maid coming towards door. Quick cut, fainter sound of ringing heard in bedroom upstairs. Mistress at mirror, camera moves in on her face, she knows who it is, the close shot tells you how she feels about it, DISSOLVE the tea wagon is going down the hall. Cut from inside room, man and woman stand close looking at each other. Will he take her in his arms, will the tea wagon get there first? Then the wonderful wonderful dialogue. SHE: Charles – it's been fifteen years. HE: Fifteen years and four days. SHE: I can hardly – (Knock at door) Come in. (Tea wagon comes in) I'm sure you'd like tea. HE: Love it. SHE: It's Oolong. I grow it myself. HE: I always wondered what you did with your spare time. And so on . . .

Letter to Charles Morton,
17 December 1951.

Talking of agents, when I opened the morning paper one morning last week I saw that it had finally happened: somebody shot one. It was probably for the wrong reasons, but at least it was a step in the right direction.

Letter to Jamie Hamilton,
21 December 1951.

Well, Christmas with all its ancient horrors is on us again. The stores are full of fantastic junk and everything you want is out of stock. People with strained, agonized expressions are poring over pieces of distorted glass and pottery, and being waited on, if that is the correct expression, by specially recruited morons on temporary parole from mental institutions, some of whom by determined effort can tell a teapot from a pickaxe.

Letter to James Sandoe,
27 December 1951.

Many thanks for the letter and books. The one on Gertie [Gertrude Stein] seemed to me as subtle as hell, a bit over my head, in fact. Frankly, I don't think the old girl was worth the effort but I can see that an English prof who has to dish out a book now and again is wise to champion a cause that is not too lost and not too won. My own views of Gertie come closer to those of Mrs Porter. She talked a great game, but if she ever cracked ninety, she moved her ball. She had the sort of reputation that depends less on what she did and more on what the intellectuals said about her. When I read Eliot's play *The Cocktail Party* I wondered what all the fuss was about. But of course I knew. There are always enough sterile critics looking around hunting for a piece of stale cake they can wrap up in a distinguished name and sell to the host of snob-fakers that infest all semi-literate societies.

Letter to Carl Brandt,
27 December 1951.

We had a lousy Christmas, thanks. The cook took sick, and the turkey didn't get cooked, and my wife is either in bed or lying down most of the time, trying to slough an obstinate bronchitis. Swanie sent me a tie for Christmas. It is all covered with Sherlock

Holmeses and bloody footprints. I wish Hollywood agents didn't feel they had to give Xmas presents to clients – especially as the presents are a far too accurate a register of a client's standing. A guy who worked his way up to a wrist watch and then slid back to a tie knows exactly what his rating is . . . I wouldn't wear the thing to a post mortem on an Ozark sharecropper.

Letter to William Townend,
Dulwich acquaintance of Chandler's, and part-time writer of adventure
stories, 3 January 1952.

Your publishers are probably quite right to ask you to cut your book. I think we all grow a little more prolix as we grow older. Our memories are so packed with experiences and emotions that all our perceptions are overlaid by a patina of memory. We lose interest in plot which is kindergarten stuff mostly, and we forget that the public has interest in very little else . . . Even a hundred thousand words seems to me too long; eighty thousand ought to be the limit. Only a very rich writer, rich that is in style and illusion, should go beyond eighty thousand words . . . You couldn't cut Proust or Henry James for example, because the things you would be apt to cut would be the very things that make these men worth reading.

Townend had been a friend of P. G. Wodehouse's at Dulwich, and had kept in touch with him since then; Wodehouse had left Dulwich the year before Chandler's arrival. Wodehouse, who now lived most of the year in New York, was in trouble with the British authorities over his wartime activities; while a captive of the Germans, he had made five entertainment radio broadcasts for them.

I agree that it is perfectly absurd that Wodehouse cannot go back to England . . . plenty of people both in England and America are beginning to think that the War Crimes Trials were a bad mistake regardless of whether the people who were tried deserved hanging, which of course most of them did . . . Even if the Hitler government was vicious, it was still a government legally constituted in its own country, and we recognized it as such. Yet in these trials we now say that generals who had sworn an oath of allegiance to their government had no right to be bound by an oath of allegiance. Also, the trials were in effect drumhead court-martials by the victors. An American general writing in the *Saturday Evening Post* about the Battle of the Bulge told how after a bunch of American prisoners had been murdered in cold blood by German tank crews, various American units were taken to see their bodies laid out on the field. He went on to say that thereafter we, that is the Americans, took the two prisoners a day required by Intelligence and no more. That's just another way of saying that we shot every German who tried to surrender . . . Men attacking under fire often shoot prisoners, or rather men who try to make themselves prisoners, for the simple reason that they cannot let the surrendered men get behind them and that they have no way to handle them.

Letter to S. J. Perelman,
9 January 1952.

I guess you've lost interest in Rancho Santa Fe and so have I, but only because in their efforts to keep the place from getting cluttered up with the conveniences of life, the property owners have gone so far in the other direction that there is only one store for food, and that not much of a store, no drugstore, no movie theater . . . and the essential technicians of life, such as plumbers, electricians and carpenters, are probably so scarce that one would find the aristocratic hauteur of their manners even more trying than the union scale . . . I do think Rancho Santa Fe would be a pretty ideal place in which to bring up children, not that I regard that as one of the essential occupations. As for Florida, there must be some attractive spots in it but evidently not those you visited. Why is your wife so mad at Hollywood? After all, there are lots of nice people in Hollywood, far more than there are in La Jolla. The picture business can be a little trying at times, but I don't suppose working for General Motors is all sheer delight.

Letter to Dale Warren,
11 January 1952. A Place in the Sun was a movie adaptation of
Theodore Dreiser's An American Tragedy, *starring Elizabeth Taylor*
and Montgomery Clift.

Last night, inveigled by the critics and the ballyhoo, although I should now know better, we went to see *A Place in the Sun*. This morning, looking through the *Variety* anniversary number, I see it is listed as the number 8 top grosser for 1951, three and a half million dollars domestic gross, which is very high for these times. So for once the New York critics and the public are agreed. My sister-in-law, who likes practically any kind of picture except slapstick, hated it. And I despised it. It's as slick a piece of bogus self-importance as you'll ever see. And to mention it in the same breath as *A Streetcar Named Desire* seems to me an insult. *Streetcar* is by no means a perfect picture, but it does have a lot of drive, a tremendous performance by Marlon Brando, and a skilful if occasionally rather wearisome one by Mrs Vivien Leigh. It does get under your skin, whereas *A Place in the Sun* never touches your emotions once. Everything is held too long; every scene is milked ruthlessly. I got so sick of starry-eyed close-ups of Elizabeth Taylor that I could have gagged. The chi-chi was laid on not with a trowel, not even with a shovel, but with a dragline. And the portrayal of how the lower classes think the upper classes live is about as ridiculous as could be imagined. They ought to have called it 'Speedboats for Breakfast'. And my God, that scene at the end where the girl visits him in the condemned cell a few hours before he gets the hot squat! My God, my God! The whole damn thing is beautifully done technically, and it reeks of calculation and contrivance emotionally. The picture was made by a guy who has seen everything and has never had a creative idea of his own. Not once but twice in the picture he uses the great trick which Chaplin used in *Monsieur Verdoux*, where instead of fadeout to close an act he shoots out a window and watches the darkness turn to daylight. But this slab of unreal hokum makes three and a half million dollars and *Monsieur Verdoux* was a flop. My God, My God! And let me say it just once more. My God!

It's no wonder the people in Hollywood go crazy trying to figure out what the public likes. *Variety* lists 131 pictures which made a million dollars or over, and the list tells a few things, but not very many. A spectacle will bring in the big gross, but it costs so much that it is doubtful whether it really pays off. A big Broadway stage success will pay off much better, because it costs much less. The public will still go to see stars like Spencer Tracy, Humphrey Bogart and James Stewart in pictures which are not up to standard. The public will go to see comics, even if they are not funny. They will go to see war pictures, which is rather unusual. And among the so-called prestige pictures it is obvious that neither the public nor the critics can tell the real thing from the phony. There were only half a dozen melodramas, by which I mean melodrama without a social message, and some very good ones didn't even get back their cost of production.

Letter to the editor of Sequence *magazine,*
undated.

I hate to see the magazine fold. There is so little intelligent writing about films, so little that walks delicately but surely between the avant garde type, which is largely a reflection of neuroticism, and the deadly commercial stuff. I think you have been a little too hard at times on English films, which even when not top notch do give you the feeling of moving around in a civilized world – something which the Hollywood product falls pretty short of as a rule. Even if you had been less intelligent, I should be sorry to see you go. *Sight and Sound* is all very well so far as it goes. I suppose it is subsidized, and everything that is subsidized compromises, and everything that compromises ends up by being negative.

Letter to Bernice Baumgarten,
14 May 1952.

I'm sending you today, probably by air express, a draft of a story which I have called *The Long Goodbye*. It runs 92,000 words. I'd be happy to have your comments and objections and so on. I haven't even read the thing, except to make a few corrections and check a number of details that my secretary queried. So I am not sending you any opinion on the opus. You may find it slow going.

It has been clear to me for some time that what is largely boring about mystery stories, at least on a literate plane, is that the characters get lost about a third of the way through. Often the opening, the mise en scène, the establishment of the background, is very good. Then the plot thickens and the people become mere names. Well, what can you do to avoid this? You can write constant action and that is fine if you really enjoy it. But alas, one grows up, one becomes complicated and unsure, one becomes interested in moral dilemmas, rather than who cracked who on the head. And at that point one should retire and leave the field to younger and more simple men.

Anyhow I wrote this as I wanted to because I can do that now. I didn't care whether the mystery was fairly obvious, but I cared about the people, about this strange corrupt world we live in, and how any man who tries to be honest looks in the end either sentimental or plain foolish. Enough of that. There are more practical reasons. You write in a style that has been imitated, even plagiarized, to the point where you begin to look as if you were imitating your imitators. So you have to go where they can't follow you . . .

Letter to Jamie Hamilton,
21 May 1952. LS is Little Sister.

The book is a bit longer than LS but I think I don't care. I was not writing for speed. I'm bored stiff with the edge of the chair stuff, and much prefer in these times the flat-on-the-back-on-a-comfortable-couch-with-pipe kind of thing. Add a tall cool drink if you can spare it. Anyhow, it's out of my system and the hell with it. What an enormous emptiness there is around the frantic little fire of creation!

Letter to Charles Morton,
29 May 1952.

At its best, and only at its best, the Hollywood product is untouchable; that is it has a pace, a directness, an innate hardness, and a lack of chi-chi camera work and lighting which only a very occasional foreign film, including the British, can match or come anywhere near matching, and usually at the price of a disorganized story, a lot of irrelevant background and too many cute little character touches.

Baumgarten read the manuscript of The Long Goodbye *and wrote to Chandler saying that she was concerned Philip Marlowe had become 'too Christlike and sentimental'. Chandler sacked her by return of post, and never reinstated her.*

Letter to Bernice Baumgarten,
20 July 1952.

Thanks for your note, but I see no reason why you should, even as a matter of form, apologize for speaking what was on your mind. I am not much good at tinkering or revising. I lose interest, lose perspective, and whatever critical sense I have is dissipated in trivialities such as whether it is better to put in 'he said' or let the speech stand alone.

My kind of writing demands a certain amount of dash and high spirits – the word is gusto, a quality lacking in modern writing – and you could not know the bitter struggle I have had in the past year even to achieve enough cheerfulness to live on, much less to put into a book. So let's face it: I didn't get it into the book. I didn't have it to give.

Letter to James Sandoe,
11 August 1952.

I don't know how you feel about it, but I wish to God that Hollywood would stop trying to be significant, because when art is significant, it is always a by-product and more or less unintentional on the part of the writer.

Chandler and Cissy visited England in 1952, sailing via the Panama Canal on account of Cissy's fear of flying.

> *Letter to Paul Brooks,*
> *28 September 1952.*

Today is an English Sunday and by God it's gloomy enough for a crossing of the Styx. I thought England was broke but the whole damn city is crawling with Rolls Royces, Bentleys, Daimlers, and expensive blondes.

Never thought I'd get sick of the sight of a grouse on toast or a partridge, but by God I am.

On my return Oct. 7 via *Mauritania* shall be at the Hampshire House for a few days and will call up to say hello, if you are available. The book (seen from here in perspective) is all right. It had a few changes here though. Bernice is an idiot (I hope).

In England I am an author. In the USA just a mystery writer. Can't tell you why. God knows I don't care one way or the other. I have met:

(1) An Oxford don who writes bad Westerns under a pen name.
(2) A secretary who lunches on bread and butter and straight gin.
(3) A valet who enters without knocking while my wife is having a bath.
(4) A publisher who makes the world's worst martinis.
    And so on.

Back in La Jolla, Chandler changed The Long Goodbye*'s ending, and made some cuts. The pruned material included the following lines:*

I walked away from them and out of the front door and across the lawn to the row of hibiscus bushes inside the fence. I took a few lungfuls of air. It was nice cool stuff, quiet and comforting, and just for a little while I wanted no part of the human race. Just a few lungfuls of clean air that no liar or murderer had breathed. That was all I wanted.

She was dead now and I could take her for what she seemed to be the first time I saw her, and what she did and why she did it could be left to the solemn fools who explain everything and know nothing.

It's the fall guys that make history. History is their requiem.

— I'm a tired and disappointed woman. I'm no bargain for anyone. I need someone to be kind to me.

— You don't need anyone to be kind to you. You've got all the honesty and a large part of the guts in your family. You can tell anybody to go to hell, including me.

— I think you've already been there.

Letter to J. Francis,
a London bookshop-owner Chandler had met, 30 October 1952.

I seem to recall that Edmund Wilson took rather nasty issue with Maugham about Maugham's claim that the writers of straight novels had largely forgotten how to tell a story. I hate to agree with such an ill-natured and bad mannered person as Edmund Wilson, but I think he was right on this point. I don't think the quality in the detective or the mystery story which appeals to people has very much to do with the story a particular book has to tell. I think what draws people is a certain emotional tension which takes you out of yourself without draining you too much. They allow you to live dangerously without any real risk. They are something like those elaborate machines which they used to use and probably still do use to accustom student pilots to the sensation of aerial acrobatics. You can do anything from a wing over to an Immelman in them without any danger.

*5 November 1952. Cissy's 'bad luck' was falling into a taxi while in
London, and damaging her leg.*

Well, Jamie, let's face it. We loved London and we had a lovely
time there. What little inconveniences we happened to have
suffered were all due to our own inexperience and probably would
not have happened and probably would not happen again. All your
people were wonderful to me. It was really extremely touching. I
am just not used to being treated with that much consideration.
There are things I regret, such as losing several days over my
vaccination, such as not going to any of the picture galleries, such
as only seeing one rather poor play, such as not having dinner at
your house. I spent too much time talking about myself, which I
don't enjoy, and too little time listening to other people talking
about themselves, which I do enjoy. I missed seeing something of
the English countryside. But all in all there was a hell of a lot I did
not miss, and all of it good. And for that you above all others are
to be thanked. I'll be writing you again soon. In the meantime my
best love to you and Yvonne, and that goes for Cissy too. I think
the trip did her a lot of good. She had bad luck, but psychologically
she was buoyed up no end . . .

Letter to William Townend,
11 November 1952.

The present generation of English people impressed me very well.
There is a touch of aggressiveness about the working classes and
the non-Public School types which I think is something new and
which I personally do not find at all unpleasant, since it is even
more emphatic in this country. And the real Public School types,
or many of them, with their bird-like chirpings are becoming a
little ridiculous, I thought. I grant you that English food is pretty
dreary. For instance, at the Café Royal we had pork chops, pork
apparently being the only unrationed fresh meat. Now pork chops
are not particularly difficult to cook. I can cook them myself. You

cook them in their own fat, they bring with them everything that is necessary except salt and pepper. Yet these pork chops were badly cooked and were messed up with some kind of sauce, which added nothing to their flavour and probably took away what little they had left. It's this sort of bastard imitation of French cooking, a fussiness without the skill or grace.

Of all the people we met in London, I think we liked best Roger Machell, a director of Jamie Hamilton, a cheerful, rather pudgy, light-hearted character, with a droll sense of humor and the sort of offhand good manners which you rarely find except in a genuine aristocrat. This fellow is an old Etonian, which of course is not conclusive. He is a great grand-nephew of Queen Victoria, he is the grandson of Prince Hohenlohe, and his mother, Lady Something or Other Machell, lives in St James Palace. He was badly wounded in the war and made a joke of it. He seemed to think it was character-istic that he should have been wounded while telephoning London from a French pub. A bomb just dropped on it and blew a piece of a wall through his chest. It just missed killing him, but he seems to show no ill effects now. He said he got a commission as a major in some guards regiment, but he doesn't know how, probably pure luck or someone else made a bad mistake. When he reported one morning to a barracks in London in uniform he found them in the act of the changing of the guard. He said he didn't know whether he was supposed to salute the guard or if the guard was supposed to salute him, so he just sat in his car outside until it was all over. He has the sort of humorous, self-deprecating manner which by sheer magic of personality is never overdone or posey or artificial. He lives handsomely in chambers in the Old Albany, drives a ramshackle old car, mixes perfectly awful martinis in a two-quart water pitcher (two of them would knock you out for a week) and took us on a wonderful tour of London, including the East End bombed-out district, making all the time such comments as, 'Well, let's run down and take a look at the Tower, supposing I can find it,' and 'Over there is St Paul's or something of that sort.' He had us in giggles the whole time, yet he is in no sense of the word an intentional comedian. I claim that a man who can get away with this sort of thing and be perfectly natural about it is a bit of a genius.

Letter to Jamie Hamilton,
7 December 1952.

Just a quick chit to let you know the state of affairs in beautiful La Jolla which has not been beautiful to me lately. Cissy came back from hospital yesterday. She had an intestinal block, probably a long, slow accumulation and a result of the costivating effect (the French word is so much nicer, don't you think) of certain drugs given to her for her cough. It was removed without an operation, but not without pain. Cissy is in bed and we had a nurse last night, but may get by without one tonight.

Anyway, life has been hell and I have done nothing in the way of work at all. In fact, I got so completely exhausted that I had to go in for a check-up myself and was found to be quite anaemic and to be suffering from malnutrition . . . I knew I'd lost my interest in food but I didn't know you could get malnutrition that fast.

Letter to H. F. Hose,
6 January 1953.

Our trip to England was a qualified success. There is a fundamental decency about the English people and a sort of effortless sense of good manners which I find very attractive. English people themselves seem to think that their manners have deteriorated, but they are still far better than anywhere else in the world. Americans can be very polite too, especially when they are trying to sell you something.

Letter to James Sandoe,
4 February 1953.

The only private eye I have met personally was brought to the house one night by a lawyer friend of mine. He did seventeen years as a detective on the San Diego police force. Most of his work consists of digging up info for lawyers, finding witnesses etc. He struck me as a bombastic and not too scrupulous individual. The private eye of fiction is pure fantasy and is meant to be. In California the private eye is licensed to investigate and nothing else. He is licensed by the same authority that licenses beauty parlor operators. His bond, which costs him fifty dollars, is for no other purpose than to protect clients against swindling.

Letter to H. N. Swanson,
14 March 1953.

Did you ever read what they call Science Fiction? It's a scream. It's written like this: 'I checked out with K19 on Adabaran III, and stepped out through the crummaliote hatch on my 22 Model Sirus Hardtop. I cocked the timejector in secondary and waded through the bright blue manda grass. My breath froze into pink pretzels. I flicked on the heat bars and the Bryllis ran swiftly on five legs using their other two to send out crylon vibrations. The pressure was almost unbearable, but I caught the range on my wrist computer through the transparent cysicites. I pressed the trigger. The thin violet glow was icecold against the rust-colored mountains. The Bryllis shrank to half an inch long and I worked fast stepping on them with the poltex. But it wasn't enough. The sudden brightness swung me around and the Fourth Moon had already risen. I had exactly four seconds to hot up the disintegrator and Google had told me it wasn't enough. He was right.'

They pay brisk money for this crap?

Letter to Roger Machell,
15 March 1953. Machell had sent Chandler a copy of an interview with
him, published in John O'London's Weekly.

This is going to be awful, because I'm balling the jack myself and on a Corona yet. On Sunday nobody works but Chandler and he breaks his heart seven days a week and without no music. He calls me small. What is his standard? I have hardly ever weighed less than twelve stone – is that small in England? I have often weighed almost 13 stone. Attired for the street I am an inch short of six feet. My nose is not sharp but blunt, the result of trying to tackle a man as he was kicking a ball. For an English nose it would hardly be called prominent. Wispy hair like steel wool? Nuts. It is limp. Walks with a forward-leaning lope, huh? Chandler cantered gaily into the cocktail lounge, rapidly consumed three double gimlets and fell flat on his kisser, his steel wool hair curling gracefully against the pattern of the carpet. No wonder this man Forster thinks me observant. By his standards anyone who noticed how many walls the room had would be observant.

Memo to Juanita Messick,
1953.

That is a lot of bunk – removing the grid while preheating. Because why? The grid gets hot very quickly during cooking. The meat splatters grease all over it. The meat has to be turned and therefore does not always lie in the same place. What drivel sales people do talk! Take cigarette advertising. Every favorite brand is milder and less irritating than every other. The ideal cigarette has no taste at all. Therefore why smoke? What we need for broiling is a non-spattering steak, a steak containing no grease, fat, or other injurious ingredients, and incidentally, no flavor. What we need is a steakless steak to be broiled on a heatless broiler in a non-existent oven and eaten by a toothless ghost.

Letter to Alan K. Campbell,
the director of the Harvard Summer School, 22 April 1953.

I am replying to your kind letter of April 1st, inviting me to have something to say at a conference of the Harvard Summer School. Naturally, I am grateful and flattered that you should think of me, and I am regretful that largely for personal reasons I cannot be in Boston in August. I say largely for personal reasons, and these reasons are compelling. But I do not say entirely, since it is not within my scheme of living, and I don't see how it could ever be, to get up on a platform and tell anyone about anything. Perhaps I am trying to make a virtue out of diffidence. I hope that is not entirely true, but it may be. I am not a lecturer, nor do I have any qualifications to be one. Too bad. It would be a nice one to drop into the still pool of respectful attention, 'You know I lectured at Harvard last summer. It was rather fun.' Thank you again.

Letter to Jamie Hamilton,
11 May 1953.

I've just read a book you put out by Miriam Bougenicht called *Ring and Come In*. Frankly, I'm getting pretty damn tired of suspense stories by neurotic females and their atmosphere of half-delayed psychiatry. It's one of those books where every line of action, or every line of dialogue immediately has to be followed by a paragraph of analysis, explanation, interior monologue or whatever you call it, so that half way through you start skipping that.

Two things I am annoyed about in *The Journal of Eugène Delacroix*: one is the India Paper, which of course I like very much in some ways but when the tops of the pages are painted they are so hard to turn: the other is reading a book as fine as this in English when I might just as well be reading it in French. I suppose this is an excellent translation, but the style seems to be a bit stuffy compared with the French. Take any sentence at random. Take the second one in the book: 'My keenest wish is to remember that I am writing only for myself.' What a heavy lump of suet that is compared with the lightness and ease of the French, the casual arrangement of the words and so on. Damn translations anyway. We have to have them because there are so many languages we don't know, but they're never the real thing, not even the best of them.

As to my own efforts, I should say I am about four-fifths of the way through. It is almost completely rewritten because of my unfortunate inability to edit anything except changing a word here or there. If it isn't right, I always have to start all over again and rewrite it. It seems easier to me; it isn't easier I know, it just seems easier. Every now and again I get stuck on a chapter, and then wonder why. But there's always a reason, and I have to wait for the reason to come to me.

Letter to Jamie Hamilton,
26 May 1953.

Some titles, not many, have a particular magic which impresses itself on the memory. I guess we would all like to have them, but we can't very often achieve them, and certainly not by trying. Titles like RED SHOES RUN FASTER, DEATH IN THE AFTERNOON, THE BEAUTIFUL AND DAMNED, JOURNEY'S END, LOST HORIZON, POINT OF NO RETURN, etc.

Letter to Alfred Knopf,
16 July 1953.

I am no longer with Brandt & Brandt, and in a way I regret that I was ever persuaded to leave you, although I realize I was no great financial asset to your publishing house. But I did, and a man can't keep jumping about from publisher to publisher . . . I'm a little tired of the kick-'em-in-the-teeth stuff myself. I hope I have developed, but perhaps I have only grown tired and soft, but certainly not mellow. After all, I have fifty per cent Irish blood.

Letter to H. F. Hose,
16 September 1953.

One of the weird problems of our times is the juvenile delinquent. Gangs of young crooks pop up in the most exclusive neighborhoods. Atlanta, Georgia, had a wave of burglaries and vandalism and it was traced to the young of some of the wealthiest families in the city. Our local high school (realschule or grammar school) had a Thieves Club among the children of the best families. The wars have a lot to do with it, no doubt, but much of it would have happened anyway. There is no discipline in the schools because there is no means of enforcing it. And in the homes parents argue with their children, they don't tell them. If I had children, and thank God I never had any, I should send them abroad to school. American schools are rotten, especially in California. If your boy won't behave himself, you can try a military school where he will be taught to behave himself (or expelled), but he won't learn anything else. You can send him to one of the New England snob schools like Groton, if you can afford it but unless you are well off it is not always the kind thing to do. He will meet boys who drive Jaguars and Rileys and have too much spending money and he will feel inferior. Or you can send him to a Jesuit school, regardless of religion. The public schools are trash. About all they learn there is the increasingly simple art of seduction. One of my wife's nephews graduated from high school with the mental equipment of the Lower Fourth, say the middle third of that form. But he has turned out very well. He couldn't have got into a state university, much less a place like Stanford or Pomona, but he faced the problem of earning without any trouble at all. I find that curious, and very American. He did fourteen months in Korea without the trace of old soldier nonsense about him, he is married, and he is very scrupulous about money.

Letter to thriller writer James M. Fox,
January 1954. The 's.o.b.' is J. Edgar Hoover.

All secret police forces come to the same end. I'll bet the s.o.b. has a dossier on everybody who could do him damage. The F.B.I. throws up such a smoke screen that they make the public forget all the tough ones they never broke . . . Practically all secret police forces are fundamentally pretty stupid because it is so damned easy for them to cover up. I don't mean the men in the field, but the desk jockeys.

Letter to Jamie Hamilton,
  16 January 1954.

Los Angeles has nothing for me any more. It's only a question of time until a Gentile has to wear an armband there. The story I am fitfully working on at the moment is laid in La Jolla and will be much shorter and more light-hearted than *The Long Goodbye*. But I'm fed up with the California locale . . . There are things about writing that I love, but it is a lonely and ungrateful profession and personally I'd much rather have been a barrister, or even an actor.

Letter to James M. Fox,
  5 February 1954.

Ninety per cent of mysteries are written by people who can't write.

Letter to James M. Fox,
  16 February 1954. Fox had written to congratulate Chandler on The
  Long Goodbye.

As to the ending or denouement not being a surprise, what ending is to someone in the trade? . . . Very often just for the fun of it I look at the end and then amuse myself with watching the author trying to smudge his fingerprints. And a surprise ending is no good if you don't believe it. If the reader doesn't think he *should* have known, he has been had. The typical mystery is like that thing on *Studio One* last night. An obvious suspect is presented and played up and you immediately eliminate her just because she has been played up. An old man in a wheel chair can get out of it to snitch a drink at the sideboard. Another red herring. The old housekeeper is obviously just what she pretends to be. The youngest sister is in love with the doctor who is going to solve the mystery. So who is left? The sister who got the poison pen letters. So she wrote them to herself. Why? No reason that makes sense. So she did it without knowing what she was doing. At that point I didn't give a damn.

Letter to Paul Brooks,
1 March 1954. Chandler is referring to the US cover of The Long
Goodbye.

Some day, someone ought to explain to me the theory behind dust jacket designs. I assume they are meant to catch the eye without offering any complicated problems to the mind. But they do present problems of symbolism that are too deep for me. Why is there blood on the little idol? What is the significance of the hair? Why is the iris of the eye green? Don't answer. You probably don't know either.

Letter to Hardwick Moseley,
the sales manager at Chandler's publisher, 23 March 1954.

I'm sick as a dog, thank you, with one of those lousy virus infections the doctors have invented to cover up their ignorance . . . For the first time in my life I was reviewed as a Novelist in the London *Sunday Times*. I was discussed on the BBC by as addled a group of so-called intellectuals as ever had soup on their vests. But over here? *The New York Times* which surely should know what it is doing if any newspaper does has twice given books of mine for review to mystery writers who have been waiting for years for the chance to knife me because I have ridiculed the sort of thing they write themselves.

Letter to Roger Machell,
24 March 1954.

There's quite a bit to answer in your good letter but before I get on to it, two or three items I'm afraid of forgetting. 1. For God's sake save your people the anguish and expense of sending me 8 copies of Finnish translations. Four would be more than enough. They do a nice job on them, but Jesus what a language! Everything is backwards. I once hoped to be a comparative philologist (just a boyhood fancy no doubt) and dabbled in such strange lingos as

Modern Greek (there's a debased language – it just looks like Greek, all the richness and variety is gone, all the subtlety, all the charm), Armenian, Hungarian, besides the simpler and more obvious Romance tongues and the Germanic group. I slept with a chart of the 214 key ideographs of the Chinese Mandarin language pinned to the wall at the head of my bed in the Pension Marjollet, 27 Boulevard St Michel, *au cinquième*. But Finnish, hell it's worse than Turkish . . .

Machell and Chandler were discussing the rise of big corporations.

The point is and always from now on will be, that beyond a certain point of size and power it is more tyrannical than the state, more unscrupulous, less subject to any kind of inspection, and that in the end it destroys the very thing it purports to represent – free competition. It can be benign, charming, friendly and full of charity – when it has won the battle. It is not as ruthless as Big Brother because it is too intelligent to think that fear can make men creative; it can't, it can only make them assiduous. It is technically subject to government control but that means nothing, because we live in an economy of overproduction and if you chastise a big corporation like Alcoa or the Du Ponts or Standard Oil of New Jersey, they can create a serious unemployment situation overnight. And, of course, they are the only organizations that can afford large scale research not directly connected with national security.

As for Commercial TV, here is a small true story of the kind of atmosphere the big advertising agencies can create. A few years back the Pepsodent Company took over sponsorship of a radio series on Philip Marlowe as a summer replacement. Their agency was a big firm which also at the time handled Chesterfield cigarettes. The producer told me the story. A company big shot (partner) visited the L.A. office on business, a severe and elegant gentleman immaculate and grey, one of those extraordinary people of our time who seem to be able to reconcile wealth, position, blameless private lives and perfect manners with an idiotic devotion to the latest brand of skin-poisoning detergent or face cream (if the manufacturer is their client, natch). This geek happened to see a junior executive entering the premises that morning smoking a Philip Morris cigarette. He stopped him and said: 'I observe, Mr Jones, that you do not care for the product of our sponsor.' Mr Jones flushed and looked at the cigarette he was holding. 'Oh, I'm extremely sorry Mr Blank. I was rather in a hurry this morning and instead of my own Chesterfields I must have grabbed up one of my wife's cigarettes.' Mr Blank stared at him in silence for a long moment, then, as he turned away, he remarked icily: 'I presume that your wife has an income of her own.'

You know, that sort of thing makes a cold shiver run down my spine.

My alcoholic capacity is down to three doubles and even after that I feel dopy and stupid. I can remember better and brighter days. I can remember being so cockeyed on Scotch that I crawled up to bed on my hands and knees and woke up singing like a lark at seven in the morning. I can remember sitting around with two or three congenial chumps and getting plastered to the hairline in a most agreeable manner. We ended up doing acrobatics on the furniture and driving home in the moonlight filled with music and song, missing pedestrians by a thin millimetre and laughing heartily at the idea of a man trying to walk on two legs.

Letter to the editor of The Third Degree,
a writers' magazine, April 1954.

The idea that writers of fan letters are psychopathic is judging the general by the exceptional. A few of them are of course. If I get a letter (I haven't lately) from a lady in Seattle who says she likes music and sex and practically invites you to move in, it is safe not to answer it. If you get a letter from a schoolboy asking for an autographed photo to hang in his den you ignore that too. But intelligent people write intelligent letters.

Letter to Hardwick Moseley,
6 May 1954.

I am strictly a gin drinker. Irish whisky is tolerable but Scotch and Rye and Bourbon for some reason I could never like. They had a sour mash corn whisky in Oklahoma when it was dry (perhaps it still is, I don't know) which topped them all. It was delivered in flat pints by a greasy but honest character who produced about 14 pints from various pockets. The stuff tasted so awful that it had to be leaded with lemon and ginger ale and sugar and even then you were apt to throw it across the room until your nervous system was paralyzed enough to kill the reflexes.

Letter to James M. Fox,
19 May 1954.

I'm caught talking to myself quite a lot lately. They say that is not too bad unless you answer back. I not only answer back, I argue and get mad.

Letter to James Sandoe,
26 May 1954.

Giving Shakespeare the documentary treatment is really an enormous joke. No writer has ever lived who cared less about that sort of dime-store accuracy.

Letter to Jamie Hamilton,
15 July 1954. Pompadour *was by Nancy Mitford.*

I don't know whether we Americans . . . are more mentally lazy than you English; I rather think we are, but I'm not sure; but I do think we are more resentful of having to do the donkey work of getting interested in something – unless we know in advance that it is worth the effort. For instance *The Go-Between* was a highly praised book, but I started it and dropped it and went back half a dozen times before I got far enough into it to give a damn about anyone. And even then I did a lot of skipping. And I never quite believed the book. I tried to see the world through the eyes of this boy, but I was a twelve year old myself and in much the same period and it just didn't look that way to me. Somehow for me the book lacks dimension. Or I lack it. I've read Maugham's articles in *The Sunday Times* as far as they have come this way. Maugham would have done that story to perfection, but he wouldn't have written it through the eyes of a 12 year old boy. He would have known damn well that it is not possible and he is much too acute to attempt the impossible. Sometimes one thinks that is rather a pity. So long and distinguished a career deserves at least one magnificent failure.

Pompadour is a lot of fun. What a woman, what a world, what a waste! But the world I grew up in is almost as remote. A wonderful world if you were born into exactly the right family, a blasted cold hypocritical cruel world if you were not. Still, at least part of the population had a good time. No one has nowadays except the crooks and the oil millionaires (there may be some distinction here but I was in the oil business for about ten years and the distinction is very fine), and perhaps some of the higher paid civil servants, but they are usually too stupid to know it. What a strange sense of values we had. What godawful snobs! My grandmother referred to one of the nicest families we knew as 'very respectable people' because there were two sons, five golden haired but unmarriagable daughters and no servant. They were driven to the utter humiliation of opening their own front door. The father painted, sang tenor, built beautiful model yachts and sailed a small yawl all over the place. My grandmother was the widow of an Irish solicitor. Her son, very wealthy later on, was also a solicitor and had a housekeeper named Miss Groome who sneered at him behind his back because he wasn't a barrister. The Church, the Navy, the Army, the Bar. There was nothing else. Outside Waterford in a big house with gardens and gardens lived a Miss Paul who occasionally, very occasionally, invited Miss Groome to tea on account of her father had been a canon. Miss Groome regarded this as the supreme accolade because Miss Paul was County. It didn't seem to bother Miss Paul but it sure as hell made a wreck of Miss Groome.

A strange and puzzling thing, the English snobbishness. I was a poor relation and one of my cousins had a short job as some kind of companion to a very well-to-do family living in a suburb not very far away. Later on when I was about seventeen, I think, I was invited over to the house to play tennis. They were rather gaudy people, except the father. A number of the guests were very young girls and young men, all expensively dressed, and several rather drunk. I was in no way expensively dressed, but far from feeling inferior I realized at once that these people were not up to the standard of even Dulwich, and heaven knows what Eton or Rugby would have thought of them. The boys and girls had gone to private schools, but not the right kind. There was a little something about their accents. During the course of an afternoon of rather studied courtesy on my part the family dog chewed up my straw hat with the school ribbon on it. When I left, the head of the family, a very nice man in some kind of 'trade' in the City, insisted on paying for the hat. I coldly refused to accept his money, although in those times it was quite usual for the host to tip a schoolboy at the end of a visit. But this seemed to me different. This was taking money from a social inferior: not to be thought of. Yet they were kind people and full of fun and very tolerant and probably much more worth knowing than my stupid and arrogant grandmother.

Letter to Dale Warren,
10 August 1954.

This country through its enormous capacity for manufacture has worked its way into an economy of overproduction, which needs an enormous artificial wastage of manufactured products. We get that kind of waste in war. In time of peace you have to try to create it artificially by advertising.

Letter to Jamie Hamilton,
27 September 1954.

I have a private hunch that nowadays any government in any so-called democracy, and always excepting the occasional great man, is merely window dressing for obscure and powerful forces which motivate and determine its every action and which it understands no better than the man on the street does.

When I write to Roger I shall have the pleasure of giving him a detailed account of my toe, because he, as a victim of gout, would probably have some small sympathy for me. I've got nowhere over here. Some little time ago I was in the garage where we send our car to be serviced and having about fifteen minutes of time on my hands to converse with the assistant manager, I thought this might be a good opportunity to tell him about my toe. But I didn't even get a complete sentence out. As soon as he realized what I was leading up to he started on a long and detailed account of how he dislocated his thumb. I think the foundations for the accident went back to childhood and to a time when he was about five years old, and from then on the detail was copious. I left him with many expressions of sympathy and by this time I don't think he even knew I had broken my toe. It's been the same everywhere.

If you really want to know what I should really like to write, it would be fantastic stories, and I don't mean science fiction. A dozen or so of them have been rattling around in my head for a great many years, pleading to be put down on paper. But they wouldn't make a thin worn dime. That would just be a wonderful way to become a Neglected Author. God, what a fascinating document could be put together about Neglected Authors . . . there's Aaron Klopstein. Who ever heard of him? I don't suppose you have. He committed suicide at the age of 33 in Greenwich Village by shooting himself with an Amazonian blow gun, having published two novels entitled *Once More the Cicatrice* and *The Sea Gull has no Friends*, two volumes of poetry, *The Hydraulic Face Lift* and *Cat Hairs in the Custard*, one book of short stories called *Twenty Inches of Monkey*, and a book of critical essays entitled *Shakespeare in Baby Talk.*

Well I guess that's enough for now, Jamie. All the best to you.

Act V (1954–1959)

That winter, on 12 December, Cissy died. As well as being his wife, she had been Chandler's only close friend for the last thirty years. The first two months after her death saw Chandler in a mood of stunned acceptance. Thereafter, he was in state of erratic drunkenness and nervous despair which lasted – almost continuously – for the remaining five years of his life. The lonely breakdown would begin in earnest on 22 February 1955, when he tried to shoot himself.

> *Letter to Leonard Russell,*
> *the literary editor of* The Sunday Times *in London, 29 December 1954.*

Your letter of December 15th has just reached me, the mails being what they are around Christmas time. I have received much sympathy and kindness and many letters, but yours is somehow unique in that it speaks of the beauty that is lost rather than consoling with the comparatively useless life that continues on. She was everything you say and more. She was the beat of my heart for thirty years. She was the music heard faintly on the edge of sound. It was my great and now useless regret that I never wrote anything really worth her attention, no book that I could dedicate to her. I planned it. I thought of it, but I never wrote it. Perhaps I couldn't have written it.

She died hard. Her body fought a hundred lost battles, any one of which would have been enough to finish most of us. Twice I brought her home from the hospital because she hated hospitals, and had her in her own bed in her own room with nurses around the clock. But she had to go back. And I suppose she never quite forgave me for that. But when at the end I closed her eyes she looked very young. Perhaps by now she realizes that I tried, and that I regarded the sacrifice of several years of a rather insignificant literary career as a small price to pay, if I could make her smile a few more times.

I had to measure out all her medicines, or else she would have taken them twice or three times over without realizing she had already taken them. The cortisone didn't work, so at the end of the first week in November he took her off that and started her on ACTH, and this, after the first shots, I was able to give her myself hypodermically, as I had been used for several years to give her hypodermic shots of various vitamins. This didn't do much good either. She got lower and lower and more and more depressed, and she was not an easily depressed person. On November 30th she developed pneumonia and had to be taken to the hospital in an ambulance . . . The doctor wanted to try a medicine called ruwaulfia, or African snake root, which apparently has the property of inducing a condition of euphoria without any damage and can be taken indefinitely. He told me at the time that she would have to spend the rest of her life in a sanatorium and that he was hoping the ruwaulfia would put her in such a complaisant mood that she would accept that. The next morning she called up early and demanded to be taken home. By this time she was very ill and very weak, had to be helped to the bathroom, had to have someone stay there with her. She was very miserable, gasped all the time, coughed violently, and said she was in great pain. By December 7th I realized she was dying. In the middle of the night she suddenly appeared in my room in her pyjamas looking like a ghost. We got her back to bed and she tried it once more, but this time the nurse was watching. At three A.M. on the morning of December 8th her temperature was so low that the nurse got frightened and called the doctor, and once more the ambulance came and took her off to hospital. She couldn't sleep and I knew it took a lot of stuff to put her under, so I would take her sleeping pills and she would tie them in the corner of her handkerchief so that she could swallow them surreptitiously when the nurse was out of the room. She was in an oxygen tent all the time, but she kept pulling it away so that she could hold my hand. She was quite vague in her mind about some things, but almost too desperately clear about others. Once she asked me where we lived, what town we lived in, and then asked me to describe the house. She didn't seem to know what it looked like. Then she would turn her head away and when I was no longer in her line of vision, she seemed to forget all about me. Whenever I went to see her she would reach her handkerchief out under the edge of the oxygen tent for me to give her the sleeping pills. I began to be worried about this and confessed to the doctor, and he said she was getting much stronger medicine than any sleeping pills. On the 11th when I went to see her I had none and she reached out under the edge of the oxygen tent with the handkerchief, and when I had nothing to give her she turned her head away and said, 'Is this the way you wanted it?' About noon that day the doctor called me up and said I had better come over and talk to her as it may be the last chance I would have. When I got there he was trying to find veins in her feet to inject demerol. He managed to get her asleep, but she was wide awake again that night. That is she seemed to be wide awake, but I'm not even sure she knew me. She went to sleep again while I was there. A little after noon on December 12th, which was a Sunday, the nurse called up and said she was very low, which is about as drastic a statement as a nurse ever makes. Vinnie's son was here then with Vinnie, and he drove me over to the hospital at fifty miles an hour, breaking all the traffic regulations, which I told him to ignore as the La Jolla cops were friends of mine. When I got there they had taken the oxygen tent away and she was lying with her eyes half open. I think she was already dead. Another doctor had his stethoscope over her heart and was listening. After a while he stepped back and nodded. I closed her eyes and kissed her and went away.

Of course in a sense I had said goodbye to her long ago. In fact, many times during the past two years in the middle of the night I had realized that it was only a question of time before I lost her.

But that is not the same thing as having it happen. Saying goodbye to your loved one in your mind is not the same thing as closing her eyes and knowing they will never open again. But I was glad that she died. To think of this proud, fearless bird caged in a room in some rotten sanatorium for the rest of her days was such an unbearable thought that I could hardly face it at all. I didn't really break until after the funeral, partly because I was in shock and partly because I had to hold her sister together. I am sleeping in her room. I thought I couldn't face that, and then I thought that if the room were empty it would just be haunted, and every time I went past the door I would have the horrors, and the only thing for me was to come in here and fill it up with my junk and make it look the kind of mess I'm used to living in. It was the right decision. Her clothes are all around me, but they are in closets or hidden away in drawers . . . For thirty years, ten months and two days, she was the light of my life, my whole ambition. Anything else I did was just the fire for her to warm her hands at. That is all there is to say.

Letter to Hardwick Moseley,
undated. Leussler was Houghton Mifflin's West Coast rep.

Thank you very much for the two books. I guess it was Leussler's idea because we got talking about Westerns and I said there were only about two people who could or ever could write them – Owen Wister and Eugene Manlove Rhodes – and he brought up Jack Scheefer. I've read *Shane* and it is excellent in its way, but fundamentally rather childish. I guess the trouble with Westerns as a species is a kind of appalling solemnity about such elementary things. This Leussler is a terrible man. He is a kind-hearted guy and would do anything for you, but he will kill you with talk in the process. We had him here to dinner and by 9.30 he had me so exhausted that I went and put my pyjamas on – a hint that would be considered too broad in the best society (if there is any) but it was just right for Leussler. Anything less pointed would have missed him by a yard and I didn't quite feel up to holding up a card with large letters on it saying: FOR CHRIST'S SAKE STOP TALKING AND GO HOME!

Chandler had booked himself a passage to England from New York on the Mauritania. *He had little idea how long he planned to be in England for, or where he would go after that. The house in La Jolla had now been sold.*

> *Letter to Roger Machell,*
> *7 February 1955.*

Perhaps when I get away from this house and all its memories I can settle down to do some writing. And then again I may just be homesick and to be homesick without a home is rather poignant.

Tomorrow it would have been our thirty-first wedding anniversary. I'm going to fill the house with red roses and have a friend in to drink champagne, which we always did. A useless and probably a foolish gesture because my lost love is so utterly lost and I have no belief in any after life. But all the same I shall do it. All us tough guys are hopeless sentimentalists at heart.

Report in the Hollywood Citizen-News, *24 February 1955: 'Raymond Chandler, widely known mystery writer, today was released from the psychopathic ward at San Diego County Hospital where he was taken to hospital following an apparent suicide attempt. Police said Chandler had been drinking heavily since the death of his wife in December.'*

> *Letter to Roger Machell,*
> *5 March 1955.*

Everything is all right with me, or as near as one could hope for. I couldn't for the life of me tell you whether I really intended to go through with it or whether my subconscious was putting on a cheap dramatic performance. The first shot went off without my intending to. I had never fired the gun and the trigger pull was so light that I barely touched it to get my hand in position when off she went and the bullet ricocheted around the tile walls of the shower and went up through the ceiling. It could just have easily have ricocheted into my stomach. The charge seemed to me very weak. This was born out when the second shot (the business) didn't fire at all. The cartridges were about five years old and I guess in this climate the charge had decomposed. At that point I blacked out . . . I don't know whether or not it is an emotional defect that I have absolutely no sense of guilt nor any embarrassment at meeting people in La Jolla who all know what happened. It was on the radio here. I had letters from all over the place, some kind and sympathetic, some scolding, some silly beyond belief. I had letters from police officers, active and retired, from two Intelligence officers, one in Tokyo and one in March Field, Riverside, and a letter from an active professional private eye in San Francisco. These letters all said two things: 1, they should have written to me long before because I hadn't known what my books meant to people, and 2, How in the name of wonder did a writer who had never been a cop come to know them so precisely and portray them so accurately. One man who had served 23 years on the Los Angeles Police said he could put an actual name to practically any cop I put in any of my stories. He seemed to think I must actually have known all these men. This sort of thing staggered me a little because I have always suspected that if a real live police officer or detective read a mystery, it would be just to sneer at it. Who was it – Stevenson possibly – who said, experience is largely a matter of intuition?

In England, I believe, and in some other places, including New York State, attempted suicide, or what looks like it, is a crime. In California it is not, but you do have to go through the observation ward at the County Hospital. With a more than able assist from a friend of mine who does a column in the San Diego paper, I talked myself out of it the next noon but on condition I went to a private sanatorium. This I did. I had more trouble talking myself out of that. I stuck it for six days and then got a feeling I was being strung along with half promises. At that point I announced that I was going to discharge myself. Upheaval. This simply wasn't done. All right, I said, Tell me the law that keeps me here. There wasn't any and he knew it. So finally he conceded that I could leave any time I wished, but would I come to his office and talk to him. I said I would, not because I expected any good from it, but because it would make his case record look better, and in addition, if he was perfectly frank with me, I might be able to help him.

So I came home and since nothing has mattered to me about the whole business except that they shot me so full of dope to keep me tractable that I still have a little hangover from it. Isn't it amazing that people should sit around depressed and bored and miserable in those places, worried about their jobs and their families, longing to go home, subjected every day to Electrical Shock Treatments (they didn't dare try that on me) and in between insulin shock, worrying about the cost of it all and the feeling of being a prisoner, and yet not have the guts to get up and walk out? I suppose it is part of what's the matter with them. If they had more guts they wouldn't be there in the first place. But that's hardly an answer. If I had more guts I shouldn't have let despair and grief get me so far down that I did what I did. But when I found myself dealing with a lot of psychiatric claptrap and with a non-existent authority that tried to make me think it had power, I didn't find that it took any special daring to tell them all what I was going to do and to do it. And in the end strangely enough they almost seemed to like it. The head nurse kissed me and said I was the politest, the most considerate and co-operative and the most resilient patient they have ever had there, and God help any doctor who tried to make me do anything I wasn't convinced I ought to do. And so much for that.

Letter to William Gault,
thriller writer, April 1955. The friend Chandler refers to was 'Red'
Barrow, an old lawyer friend from Chandler's oil days.

I thought I was extremely lucky to get as far as I did in our field, and believe me when I say lucky I am not talking to the birds. Talent is never enough. The history of literature is strewn with the corpses of writers who through no fault of their own missed out on the timing or were just a little too far ahead of their generation. An old and wise friend of mine once said the world never hears of its greatest men; the men it calls great are just ahead enough of the average to stand out, but not far enough ahead to be remote.

Yesterday I finished the rather agonizing business of getting the furniture out of my house and closing it up for the new buyer. When I walked through the empty rooms checking the windows and so on I felt a little like the last man on a dead world. But it will pass. On Wednesday I leave for Old Chatham, New York, to stay with my best friend and on April 12th I sail on the *Mauritania*. I expect to be back about the end of October and to find a house in La Jolla – much smaller of course – because it is an easy place to live in and everybody knows me here.

Thank you for writing and for what you say and I hope you are not exaggerating too much, unconsciously. It would not matter much to me, but it would not be good for you. Because you have it in you to be as good as the best. Don't ever write anything you don't like yourself and if you do like it, don't take anyone else's advice about changing it. They just don't know.

All the best.

Letter to Hardwick Moseley,
24 April 1955. Chandler was now in London, staying at the Connaught Hotel in Mayfair.

I am here at least until May the 8th after which I may have to go and sleep in Green Park. I am not happy and I am terribly hoarse from laryngitis. The racket here is just too intense also; you go to a luncheon with eight people and the next day five of them invite you to a dinner party. So dine, drink and drab is about all you do. I love this hotel, though, but I do not love being stared at and being pointed out to people, and I do not love newspaper interviews.

Letter to Jamie Hamilton,
27 April 1955. Natasha Spender was the wife of poet Stephen Spender;
Sonia was the wife of George Orwell.

Would you please have someone tell the *Daily Sketch* that not only will I not do a piece of writing for them but that I wouldn't use their rotten rag even to stuff up a rat hole. Our press is no bargain, but your gutter press is fantastically bad. You might also call up that nice Mr Harris of the *Standard* and tell him I'm sorry but cannot now put my mind to what he wants, don't feel well enough and simply cannot get my private letters written. I'll write him a note and send him back the tear sheets because I liked him personally.

The whole thing last night was rather weird. Natasha Spender is a charming and devoted hostess and served up a magnificent meal and everybody got tight. They poured it on me a little too thick I imagine. A Sonia somebody said that I was the darling of the British intellectuals and all the poets raved about me and that Edith Sitwell sat up in bed and read my stuff with passion. They said Cyril Connolly had written a piece about me which was considered a classic. The funny part of it was that they seemed quite sincere. Well anyhow it was a lot of fun.

Chandler was drinking morning to night. He was eventually asked to leave the Connaught. He moved into a furnished flat on Eaton Square, one of the smartest Georgian addresses in London.

Letter to Louise Loughner,
a fan who had written to him from San Francisco after his suicide attempt,
21 May 1955.

Please, if you at all care, write to me and tell me about yourself. I may in return send you some ribald nonsense I have been writing over here, mostly in the middle of the night, just to get over the St John's Wood–Chelsea hyperthyroid method of talking. I sleep very little, unfortunately. I am apt to get up around 4 a.m., take a mild drink of Scotch and water and start hammering at this lovely Olivetti 44, which is far superior to anything we turn out in America. It is a heavy portable and put together like an Italian racing car, and you mustn't judge it from my typing.

To get this flat I almost had to be acquainted with royalty and I had to be interviewed and inspected by the manager of the estate. The interview was very formal and by appointment. I was so bloody polite that I began to sicken myself. So I suddenly said to the man: 'I'm naturally a very polite person but I do think that I'm overdoing it a little at the moment.' He laughed and stood up and held out his hand and thanked me for coming in. I said, 'What about the lease?' He said, 'Well, usually we do like some sort of document, but often in practice we tend to rather overlook the necessity.' That's the way they work over here. And that is why for generations they were the bankers of the world.

Letter to Neil Morgan,
friend in La Jolla, 3 June 1955.

I don't think you'd recognize me if you saw me now. I have become so damned refined that at times I loathe myself. I still don't sleep well and often get up at 4 or 5 in the morning, and lately have been indulging in a form of polite pornography, which would probably interest you mildly and I am, therefore, enclosing a couple of samples. You should understand that the basic motif behind this is an attempt to spoof the upper-middle class sort of talk. There can be no greater mistake than to think that we and the English talk the same language.

Mostly I run around with the St John's Wood-Chelsea literary, artistic crowd, and perhaps they are a little special. Of course I know some cockneys too, but the people that I run around with have expressions of their own which need translating. For instance: 'I simply adore her' means 'I'd stick a knife in her back if she had a back.' 'They are absolutely and utterly precious' means 'What rubbish, but that woman never did have any taste.' 'I rather care for that' means 'Give it to me quick.' And 'I'm simply impossibly in love with him' means 'He has enough money to pay for the drinks.'

It has been a wonderful spring, the squares flaming with the most gorgeous tulips three and even four feet high. Kew Gardens is a paradise of green and colour, rhododendrons, azaleas, amaryllis, flowering trees of every kind. It catches you by the throat after the hard dusty green of California. The shops are beautifully dressed and full of all kinds of wonderful things. Harrods is easily the finest department store in the world. Nothing in New York or Los Angeles can equal it. The traffic control system here is superb. The one thing lacking is tender meat. They simply haven't got the storage to age it. You get it at very good hotels like the Connaught, the Savoy or Claridge's, but almost nowhere else.

But the women! If they ever had buck teeth I don't see them now. I've seen glamor girls at parties that would stun Hollywood. And they are so damn honest that they won't even let you pay their taxi fares. Americans are not as a rule successful with the best type of English girls and women. They move too fast and too roughly. There is far too much of this 'Come on, baby, let's hit the hay' motif. They don't like it. They expect to be treated as ladies. They are perfectly willing to sleep with you if they like you and if you treat them with deference, because in a country where women outnumber the men so excessively that is almost inevitable, but they don't want to be treated as easy lays.

Letter to Louise Loughner,
15 June 1955.

At the darkest and most desperate moment of my life, when I had nothing left to fight with and hardly cared to fight, there came to me out of the unknown a spray of flowers and a letter. And suddenly I had all the fight in the world. I beat them at their own game, I out-talked them and out-thought them, so that in the end they sent me home in a limousine, merely because they were dazzled by the display of wit and courage I put up. But why? Solely and entirely because of you. So never, never in the world thank me for anything. The orchids are all yours. And believe me they will be the most beautiful orchids of all time.

. . . I have three eccentricities. No one can buy a drink at my table at any bar; no guest of mine can look at a menu; I will neither pay nor even sign a check in front of a guest nor, except in special cases (I have one friend who is a diabetic) will I even ask them what they want. It will all be arranged in advance, and if the guest is a lady, there will be a special handwritten menu. I suppose this may sound a bit chi-chi, but dammit I'm entitled to a few tricks.

Letter to the Evening Standard,
30 June 1955. Ruth Ellis was a night-club hostess sentenced to be hanged for shooting her racing driver boyfriend.

As a part-time resident and full-time friend and admirer of England, I have always, until now, respected its legal system – as has most of the world. But there is at times a vein of savagery that repels me.

I have been tormented for a week at the idea that a highly civilized people should put a rope around the neck of Ruth Ellis and drop her through a trap and break her neck. I could understand perhaps the hanging of a woman for bestial crime like a multiple poisoning, an axe murder (à la Lizzie Borden) or a baby-farm operator killing her charges, but this was a crime of passion under considerable provocation. No other country in the world would hang this woman.

In France she would get off with a light sentence or none. In America it would be first or second degree manslaughter and she would be out of prison within three to seven years.

This thing haunts me and, so far as I may say, disgusts me as something obscene. I am not referring to the trial, of course, but to the medieval savagery of the law.

Chandler by now had a number of women whom he would take to lunch and dinner and flirt with and confide in. Some were genuinely fond of him and, as he realized, male escorts were something of a rarity in a country whose male population had been decimated by two wars in the space of thirty years. Some were considerately concerned for his mental stability (his suicide attempt was known about) and had formed an unofficial 'Chandler patrol' to keep his diary filled with engagements. One of these minder-companion-fans was an English woman called Jessica Tyndale, who worked for a bank in New York, knew many of the Chelsea set, and whom Chandler had met on the Mauritania.

Letter to Jessica Tyndale,
17 September 1955.

You know, you never really saw me sober and I have been sober now for some weeks – absolutely bone-dry sober. Dull as it may be I intend to remain that way. Something in my chemistry will no longer accept alcohol. There is some sort of chain reaction. I start off with a drink of white wine and end up drinking two bottles of Scotch a day. Then I stop eating. I have to quit and the withdrawal symptoms are simply awful. I shake so that I can't hold a glass of water. One day I vomited eighteen times. My father was an alcoholic and I have lived my whole life in fear of becoming one but until my wife died I always quit drinking on my own power when I felt there was a real need for it. For three years before she died I was dry as a bone.

His six months allowed residence up (after which he would be liable for British taxes), Chandler returned to New York aboard the Queen Elizabeth, *and went to stay with his friend Red Barrow and his family in Old Chatham, upstate New York.*

Letter to Michael Gilbert,
the London solicitor helping Chandler unravel his residency and tax situation, 14 October 1955.

The voyage was hell. Still practicing to be a non-drinker (and it's going to take a damn sight more practice than I have time for). I sat alone in the corner and refused to have anything to do with the other passengers, which did not seem to cause them any grief.

Letter to Jessica Tyndale,
21 October 1955. Chandler, by this point, had begun drinking again.

Any one who can drink a great deal steadily over a long period of time is apt to think of himself as an alcoholic, because liquor is part of his life, and he is terribly let down without it . . . Yet, if we can, we stop altogether for a while (hating every minute of it) until we are completely free of it and then we try to learn to drink. How much can we absorb without either feeling high at the time or let down the next day? This is what we have to find out and we have to be rather cautious about it. If we don't get enough to feel cheered up, it's a waste. It seems to me that there is a certain level to find, and if you find it, you are all right, even if you sometimes slop over a little. If I had found out all about this when I was twenty years old (I did almost no drinking then) I think I should have cut it out absolutely and I should not have felt any worse, because of the resilience one has at that time. But at my age, that no longer makes sense. At my age, there is nothing to replace it. Drinking, after all, except when it is a social ritual, is a rather negative business.

Letter to Helga Greene,
another of the literary Chelsea scene, 13 November 1955. Chandler was
now in La Jolla.

I am sitting on two bed pillows at the writing desk at the Del Charro Hotel. I am smoking a Craven A cigarette which is no match for the Benson and Hedges Superfine but imported cigarettes here are just a little too steep. Am I comfortable? No. Am I happy? No. Am I weak, depressed, no good, and of no social value to the community? Yes. Outside my window is an illuminated swimming pool. Phooey on it! The service here is excellent, the food fair, the price of my room slightly above what I paid at the Connaught, but an infinitely better room. Light wood furniture, two wide couch beds set in a right angle triangle with the heads against a roomy built-in stand with two of those focused reading lights. There is a chest of six drawers (not enough), three closets, a dressing room with side-lights at the table, and a beautiful bathroom, bathtub with sliding glass doors for the shower. There is a built-in electric heater in the bathroom and a built-in electric heater in the bedroom, which is really a bed-sit.

Chandler heard from England that another of his minder-companions, Natasha Spender, had fallen ill. Chandler had developed a special feeling for Natasha, and had believed himself while in London to be looking after her, rather than her looking after him; he felt she was unhappy and vulnerable. He seemed invigorated, with a new sense of purpose, as he repacked his bags in La Jolla.

Letter to Neil Morgan,
18 November 1955.

On the eve of my departure into regions where Eskimos starve and the polar bears wear mittens and galoshes and are still dissatisfied (Anybody ever see a polar bear that liked anybody?), and on the eve of your dive into marriage with a lovely girl – I'm not sure that dive was the word I wanted – may I wish for you the kind of magic that Maeterlinck's donkey could hear: the roses opening, the grass growing and the day after tomorrow coming. May I wish for you the kind of magic vision that birds have, such as on a morning after rain seeing a worm make love to its other end. May I wish for you the knowledge (I'm getting a little heavy-handed here) that Marriages do not Take Place, they are made by hand; that there is always an element of discipline involved; that, however perfect the honeymoon, the time will come, however brief it is, when you will wish she would fall downstairs and break a leg. That goes for her too. But the mood will pass, if you give it time. Here are a few words of sound advice. I know.

1. Ride her on a short rein and never let her think that she is riding you.
2. If the coffee is lousy, don't say so. Just throw it on the floor.
3. Don't let her change the arrangement of the furniture more than once a year.
4. Don't have any joint bank accounts unless she puts in the money.
5. In case of quarrel, remember that it is always your fault.
6. Keep her away from antique shops.
7. Never praise her girlfriends too much.
8. Above all never forget that a marriage is in one way very much like a newspaper. It has to be made fresh every damn day of every damn year.

Letter to Michael Gilbert,
4 January, 1956. Chandler's residency and tax situation was complicated by the fact that — according to British law — a British woman who is divorced from a foreign man (as Chandler's mother had been), and returns to Britain, thereby resumes her British status, as do her children. Chandler was therefore still registered as being British. The complication was adding to Chandler's rootlessness.

I wish you would send me a bill because I read a blood-curdling article about lawyer's fees somewhere lately and it said re. solicitors that every time you called them up (sorry, rang them up) they rushed for their swindle sheets to put down a charge and that if you passed their chambers and they happened to be looking out the window, they entered a modest charge of a guinea. You realize of course that it is only curiosity that makes me want to see the bill. I haven't the remotest intention of paying it.

Letter to Dorothy Gardner,
secretary of the Mystery Writers Association, January 1956.

The trouble with most English mystery writers, however well known in their world, is that they can't turn a corner. About halfway through a book they start fooling about with alibis, analyzing bits and pieces of evidence and so on. The story dies on them. Every book which is any good has to turn the corner. You get to the point where everything implicit in the original situation has been developed or explored, and then a new element has to be introduced which is not implied from the beginning but which is seen to be part of the situation when it shows up. Or I see it that way.

The great fault of American mystery writers, on the other hand, is a lack of texture, a sort of naiveté which probably comes from them not being very well educated or well read. Exceptions here, of course. Always there are exceptions. And the trouble with brutality in writing is that it has to grow out of something. The best hardboiled writers never try to be tough; they allow toughness to happen when it seems inevitable for its time, place and condition.

Chandler rented a flat close to St John's Wood, near Natasha Spender, at 49 Carlton Hill. The drinking continued.

Letter to Neil Morgan in La Jolla,
20 February 1956.

I am having a delightful time here soaking my feet in boiling water to restore the circulation, and lying in bed under four blankets and an eiderdown and an electric pad, and if it ever got out that I used an electric pad I should be spat upon in California. My health has been bad, and every doctor finds something else the matter with me. But what is really the matter with me is that I have no home, and no one to care for in a home, if I had one.

London is wonderful up to a point, but I get very tired of the bitchy women who are all darling, darling, darling when they meet you, but have an assortment of little knives for your back. They don't do it to me as much as your dearest friends . . . It is a technique I have never learned and will never learn. But it is a mistake to think that they are not friends, for in any time of trouble they are. But they live on malicious gossip.

> *Letter to Ian Fleming,*
> *whom Chandler had met — and liked — on his previous trip, 11 April*
> *1956. The review in question was of* Moonraker, *which Chandler had*
> *written for the London* Sunday Times.

I thought my review was no more than you deserved and I tried to write it in such a way that the good part could be quoted and the bad parts left out. After all, old boy, there had to be some bad parts. I think you will have to make up your mind what kind of a writer you are going to be. You could be almost anything except that I think you are a bit of a sadist!

I am not in any Hampstead hospital. I am at home and if they ever put me in a hospital again I shall walk out leaving corpses strewn behind me, except pretty nurses.

As for having lunch with you, with or without a butler, I can't do it yet — because even if I were much better than I am I should be having lunch with ladies.

Chandler would also review Fleming's next Bond novel, Diamonds Are Forever, *for the London* Sunday Times, *writing: 'I don't like James Bond thinking. His thoughts are superfluous. I like him when he is in the dangerous card game: I like him when he is exposing himself unarmed to half a dozen thin-lipped professional killers. I like him when he finally takes the beautiful girl in his arms, and teaches her about one tenth of the facts of life she already knew.'*

> *Letter to Captain Tore Bakke,*
> *4 May 1956.*

Thank you so much for your letter and believe me most of the most intelligent fan mail I have ever received has come from the

Scandinavian countries. You are very kind to have written to me and I thank you sincerely.

Chandler was hospitalized for drink in London and again dried out at his flat. In May, having been in Britain another six months, he realized the seriousness of his position with the tax authorities and returned to New York, where he stayed at the Grosvenor on Fifth Avenue. He was drinking again. Going to visit his friend Red Barrow in the countryside outside New York, he fell down the stairs, and had to spend a few days recuperating in a New York hospital before returning to La Jolla.

Letter to Ian Fleming,
9 June 1956.

I didn't like leaving England without saying good-bye to the few friends I knew well enough to care about, but then I don't like saying good-bye at all, especially when it may be a long time before I come back. As you probably know, I long overstayed the six months allowed, but I had a compelling reason, even if I get hooked for British income tax. I am also likely to lose half my European royalties, which isn't funny. It's all a little obscure to me, but there it is . . .

I am looking forward to your next book. I am also looking forward to my next book.

I rather liked New York this time, having hitherto loathed its harshness and rudeness. For one thing the weather has been wonderful, only one hot day so far and that not unbearable. I have friends here, but not many. Come to think of it, I haven't many anywhere. Monday night I am flying back to California and this time I hope to stick it out and make some kind of modest but convenient home there.

I am wondering what happened to all the chic pretty women who are supposed to be typical of New York. Damned if I've seen any of them. Perhaps I've looked in the wrong places, but I do have a feeling that New York is slowly being downgraded.

I bet you haven't many boy friends who write you two letters in one day. And perhaps it bores you, but since Friday noon I haven't a damn thing to do but write letters, read, take a taxi or bus uptown and potter about a bit, or just go for a walk through the Village, which always fascinated me with its quaint houses, little culs-de-sac, iron railings painted in odd colors, innumerable hidden restaurants, and the people themselves, the way they dress and the look they have of belonging to another world from uptown New York.

Back in La Jolla, Chandler rented a small house at 6925 Neptune Place, and – with the assistance of self-injected vitamin boosters – began work on a seventh Marlowe novel.

Letter to Hardwick Moseley,
20 June 1956.

Anyone as naturally careless as me could fall down those stairs. They are a menace. But I think Barrow might have waited to see whether I had cracked a rib before he began yanking at me. It will be a hell of a long time before I go to Old Chatham again. Also, this couple live such an ingrown, self-sufficient life, in which I think they are perfectly happy, that it's a bit of a bore to be there much, kind as they usually are. You can't go out with Jane Barrow without having every bloody tree pointed out to you and hearing the history of every damned house between Old Chatham and Bennington.

This place really has a climate. You have to go through an English winter to appreciate it. Very seldom hot and very seldom cold, built on a point of land with the Pacific on three sides. I have tried using it as the setting for a story I am trying to write; I have changed the topography a little. I can't make heavies of the cops, because they are nice cops and most of them are friends of mine.

The captain in charge is a grizzled veteran of long service and he told me he had never fired his Smith and Wesson .38 except to qualify on the police target range, as per the standing orders. Sometime last year a man shot his wife in a store here and the cop who came rushing in – too late – was so nervous that he shot a bystander by mistake. (He didn't kill him.)

Letter to Jessica Tyndale,
12 July 1956.

If I sound a little as if I had been smoking reefers, I had a tooth out this afternoon and am still a little on the goof side. No pain at all, but beginning to feel feverish. Wonderful how they do it though. I never knew it was out until he showed me. I supposed they had to strap you down and pull like hell. It was a molar too.

This place is an unfurnished apartment on the ocean front. That is, it was unfurnished. It now has so damn much furniture in it that only a steeple-chaser would feel at home in it. But in spite of having all this lovely (and to me now detestable) furniture, a fine electric stove, a Frigidaire and some cartons which keep me from putting my shirts and underclothes away, in spite of having a small private patio and a large private storeroom, all I have to eat off is one cup, one saucer, one plate, all borrowed. But a full set of sterling silver, oh my yes.

I know now what is the matter with my writing or not writing. I've lost any affinity for my background. Los Angeles is no longer my city, and La Jolla is nothing but a climate and a lot of meaningless chi-chi. I went to a cocktail party a week or so ago and my God there was a man there in a checked dinner jacket and another in a rose moiré dinner jacket. And today in Dutch Smith's shop I saw one in puce. This country is riding the crest of a boom, everybody is making fine wages and everybody is in debt to the ears from instalment buying. God help them if rearmament slows down. There is nothing for me to write about. To write about a place you have to love it or hate it or do both by turns, which is usually the way you love a woman. But a sense of vacuity and boredom – that is fatal. I was the first writer to write about Southern California at all realistically. Now half the writers in the country piddle around in the smog. Los Angeles is just a tired whore to me now.

Letter to Jessica Tyndale,
20 August 1956.

I have just come back from the Las Encinas Sanitarium in Pasadena, a very wonderful place but frightfully expensive. Cost me over $1400. I had to find out if I was off my rocker and didn't know it. And Las Encinas is the place to find out. They have a psychiatrist there that an intelligent man can really respect. They treat all kinds of people, senile old people (with money, natch), incurable alcoholics, guys on benders, a few psychotics who have to be kept in a special locked bungalow, depressed people etc. It's a beautiful place, carefully landscaped, all bungalows, and the atmosphere is absolutely uncritical. The doctors are very attentive, the food magnificent. They kept me in a state of semi-somnolence for several days until I started to eat, and God, how I did eat then. I had some of the best food I've ever had in my life. Then they went through the usual boring program of tests, and after that they went to work on me. I told them the truth very frankly. I said that I had been married so long and so happily that after the slow torture of my wife's death it seemed at first treason to look at another woman, and then suddenly I seemed to be in love with all women.

They gave me tests, apperception tests, Rorschach tests, wood block tests. I haven't had the lowdown on them yet, but I think I was pretty brilliant except on the drawing. I never could draw, couldn't even learn under a drawing teacher at school.

Finally the head guy said: 'You think you are depressed, but you are quite wrong. You are a fully integrated personality and I wouldn't dream of trying to interfere with it by psychoanalysis or anything of that sort. All that's the matter with you is loneliness. You simply cannot and must not live alone. If you do you will inevitably drink, and that will make you sick. I don't care if you live with one woman or twenty, as long as you live with someone. That in my opinion is an absolute.'

I thought he was damned clever to take me to pieces so smoothly. I hadn't expected anything so penetrating.

Letter to Michael Gilbert,
6 September 1956.

La Jolla is no place in which to live . . . There is no one to talk to. All the well-to-do and almost well-to-do crowd accomplish in their lives is an overdecorated home – the house beautiful for gracious living – a wife who, if she was young, plays tennis at the Beach Club, lies on the beach until her visible skin looks like brown sandpaper, shrieking with laughter at some joke which hardly merits more than a mild 'huh'. If she is middle age she is very chic in a tasteless way, talks a great deal about how she is going to have the guest room done over by some jerk with long sideburns, has her husband so tamed that he is afraid to sit down in some of the chairs, and however tired he may be, he must shower and shave and put on his white dinner jacket (in summer) because Mr and Mrs Whoosis are coming over to play bridge, which he hates almost as much as he hates Mr and Mrs Whoosis. Then there are the quite elderly, quite rich retired people. They dress immaculately, are helped into Cadillacs by colored butler-drivers and are driven to the Beach Club, where they sit in perfect silence, or converse in low monosyllabic voices with others of their kind.

Letter to William Gault,
7 September 1956.

If there is anything in life I hate it is going out to dinner alone. I could cook it, but that would be worse. Four days a week I have someone to go with, but the other three are hell. I feel like chucking the whole thing and going back to England to become a resident and pay their bloody taxes.

Hearing that Natasha Spender was on a concert tour of the United States (she was a concert pianist) Chandler arranged to meet her at Phoenix, and take her to Palm Springs for Christmas, after which she was to meet up with friends of hers who lived in Los Angeles, including the English poet Christopher Isherwood.

Letter to Hardwick Moseley,
5 January 1957.

Spent the time since December sixth until last week taking an English friend all over Arizona and part of Nevada, and then Palm Springs. Arizona never had such a going over, perhaps, since this friend is an incorrigible and insatiable sightseer, which I am not. Friend was entranced by the mountain scenery, which is unlike anything in Europe or California. The Dolomites are rugged enough, but the cypresses grow halfway up their sides, whereas everything in Arizona is barren, as though God had quit with the job half done.

Letter to Jessica Tyndale,
18 January 1957.

I met Christopher Isherwood in Santa Monica and liked him. I think he is the only queer I have felt entirely at ease with. I also met Gerard Heard (he wrote a very clever thriller called *A Taste For Honey*) and found him amusing and learned, but much too pontifical. Americans generally seem to be quite content to be lectured at for a whole evening. I resent it, no matter how clever the talk is. Natasha said I was being very hostile to him, but her social standards and mine are quite different. You can't interrupt these people, because they are constantly interrupting one another and someone is always talking. You could interrupt them, but it would take violence. Really one should, because when they realize they are cornering the conversation they become apologetic.

Back in La Jolla alone, Chandler worked on the new Marlowe novel, Playback, based on an unused screenplay he had once written. Though Chandler was now using his telephone more often than ever, he continued his letter-writing. Indeed, at a time when his drinking was taking him to a point of complete disorder, his novel- and letter-writing were generally the only focused parts of his day. His correspondents had now widened to include several new London acquaintances. These included his London secretary Jean de Leon.

Letter to Jean de Leon,
11 *February* 1957. *The Angus Wilson novel referred to is* Anglo–Saxon
Attitudes.

It was very sweet of you to send me some of your poems . . . I am very glad that you can accept your father's death without too much grief. But of course I know from my own experience that it takes time, quite a lot of time, to reconcile oneself, and that so far you are being very brave. I am one of those who do not believe in personal immortality, since I see no reason for it. God probably finds something to preserve, but what, I don't know. He might find even in me, a sensual, sardonic, cynical man, some essence worth preserving, but I don't really think it is anything I could recognize. So much of it is external, environmental, caused by our experiences here on earth, so little of us is pure and undiluted. God knows, but I don't. I share your antipathy to dogmas, but more than that I just will not surrender my right to examine, to dissect, to question. *Credo quia impossibile* seems to me just one of those devices the Catholic Church is too clever at, and yet, taking it broadly and admitting the many corruptions, the Catholic religion is the only one in our world (I'm not considering the religions of the East) which really lives. The Church of England and our Episcopalian church here live in individual priests, but not as a faith. Its services have beautiful words (which it didn't write) and many of its priests are fine people; but the faith itself is barren and tired.

Your theory of poetry may be right; I don't know. I have no theories about writing; I just write. If it doesn't seem to me to be good, I throw it away. There is a certain quality indispensable to writing, from my point of view, which I call magic, but which could be called by other names. It is a sort of vital force. So I hate studied writing, the kind of thing that stands off and admires itself. I suppose I was a born improviser, I calculate nothing in advance, and I believe that whatever one may have done in the past, one always starts from scratch.

I don't deny you your right to be tolerant of homosexuality; one more or less has to in England. But I do think that homosexuals (not bi-sexuals, that is a matter of time and custom), however artistic and full of taste they may seem to be, always lack any deep emotional feeling. They are wonderful with surfaces. I simply could not read Angus Wilson's novel, because it seemed to me he described his characters and did not create them. People of his kind have no real emotional life. They see life through mirrors. As for their having a better understanding of women, be off with you. I know more about women than any of them will ever know, and I don't know very much. They like women who are sympathetic to them, because they are always afraid, even if they act arrogantly. Their physical bravery was proved in the war, but they are still essentially the dilettante type. Some of them, like Isherwood, are very likeable, some of them are repulsive.

But I am not ashamed to be a lover of women. The difficult thing to make another person understand is that I have a code, that I adhere to it, that I have always adhered to it. There was a time in my life as a young man when I could have picked up any pretty woman on the street and slept with her that night. (Bragging again, but it is true.) I didn't do it because there has to be something else and a man like me has to be sure he is not hurting anyone, and he can't know that until he knows more about her. There are lots of cheap women, of course, but they never interested me. There are women who are inaccessible, and I can tell that in five minutes. I always could. There are women who could be had tomorrow but not tonight. That I knew also. There are women who for one reason or another would give themselves wrongly, and who would feel awful about it the next morning. That also I had to know.

Because one doesn't love in order to hurt or destroy. There were girls who could have been scarred for life by giving way to a normal human impulse, but not by me. There were girls who didn't care, but for them I didn't care either. I don't know whether it is a talent or a curse, but I always know. I don't know how I know but I could give you specific instances in which, against all the outward appearances, I knew. Sometimes this haunts me. I feel as though I must be an evil man, that this intuition is given to me only to destroy me. But I guess I don't mind being destroyed very much any more. After all, I was a loving and faithful husband for almost thirty-one years, and I watched my wife die by half-inches and I wrote my best book in the agony of that knowledge, and yet I wrote it. I don't know how. I used to shut myself in my study and think myself into another world. It usually took an hour, at least. And then I went to work. But I always listened. And late at night I would lie on the eight-foot couch reading because I knew that round midnight she would come quietly in and that she would want a cup of tea, but would never ask for it. I always had to talk her into it. But I had to be there, since if I had been asleep, she wouldn't have wakened me, and wouldn't have had her tea.

Do you think I regret any of this? I'm proud of it. It was the supreme time of my life.

Fragment of a carbon
to a letter written in February 1957. The remaining pages, including the details of the addressee, are missing.

A writer has nothing to trade but his life. Most are frustrated bastards with unhappy domestic lives.

Notes from Chandler's notebook,
undated.

Has anyone ever said clearly that what is wrong with the modern family, or modern marriage, is not messy divorce, sexual infidelity or sort like that, but the fact that there is no longer a leisure class, no longer any kind of people who are not in some sense *cornered*. The lawyer may love his wife and children, but his true love is the law. What a man *does* to live is all. Like the house, the mistress, the drunken orgy, the perversion even, marriage is only a convenient arrangement. A man of this age really lives (and dies) for his work.

The more men are ruled by law, the less they are ruled by honor.

The truth of art keeps science from becoming inhuman, and the truth of science keeps art from becoming ridiculous.

A Poem, 'Youth to Age'
undated.

Let him not perish soon,
That scheming greybeard loon.
Let not his eye grow dim,
Fate needs a laugh at him . . .

Young men are vainly warned,
Yet are forever mourned.
Old men remember well,
How sounds the passing bell.
Lie back in lonely chairs
Dreaming of routs and fairs.
Touching with leaden hand
Some still unfaded strand.
Young men may die in May;
Old men must pass away
When winter nights are cold,
Damp, damp the graveyard mold.

Letter to Edward Weeks,
at the Atlantic Monthly, *27 February 1957.*

When I wrote a couple of rather caustic things about Hollywood, writers warned me that I had destroyed myself; but I never had a word of criticism from any important executive. In fact, it was after you published these things that I had the most lucrative assignments. I think Hollywood people are much underrated; they think, many of them, what I think, but they just don't dare say it, and they are really rather grateful to anyone who does. I always knew there was only one way to deal with them. In any negotiation you must be prepared to lay your head on the block. A writer never has anything to fight with but whatever guts the Lord gave him. He is always up against business organizations that have enough power to destroy him in an hour. So all he can do is try to make them understand that destroying him would be a mistake, because he may have something to give them.

I found it quite wonderful to deal with the Moguls. They seemed so ruthless, they conceded nothing, and they knew they could throw me out, that in a sense I was nobody, that I said things to them that a writer in Hollywood simply does not say to the big bosses. But somehow or other they were too clever to resent it. And in the end I almost think they liked me for it. At any rate, they never tried to hurt me. And some of them are very clever people. I wish I could write the Hollywood novel that has never been written, but it takes a more photographic memory than I have. The whole scene is too complex and all of it would have to be in.

Letter to Deirdre Gartrell,
an Australian fan who had written to him, 2 March 1957.

Courage is a strange thing: one can never be sure of it. As a platoon commander very many years ago, I never seemed to be afraid, and yet I have been afraid of the most insignificant risks. If you had to go over the top somehow all you seemed to think of was trying to keep the men spaced, in order to reduce casualties. It was always very difficult, especially if you had replacements or men who had been wounded. It's only human to want to bunch for companion-ship in face of heavy fire. Nowadays war is very different. In some ways it's much worse, but the casualties don't compare with those in trench warfare. My battalion (Canadian) had a normal strength of 1200 men and it had over 14,000 casualties.

Letter to Helga Greene,
18 March 1957.

She was a terrific fighter. If an awkward or unpleasant scene faced her, and at times we all face that, she would march right in, and never hesitate a moment to think it over. And she always won, not because she deliberately put on the charm at the tactical moment, but because she was irresistible without even knowing or caring about it.

Letter to Paul Brooks,
19 March 1957. Chandler had suggested that he might write a book about the modern medical profession.

The book would not be liked by the bigwigs in the medical profession, by the surgeons who perform all sorts of unnecessary operations to get the money, by the hospitals who charge patients for all sorts of unnecessary tests, by the 'operators' who, although often very competent, put every patient they get into a long and expensive routine, no matter how simple his ailment may be to diagnose. Not by the 'come back boys' (I'd like to see you again on Friday) when there is nothing to come back about. Not by the sort of doctor who wants to get you into a hospital so that he can pop in two or three times a day and say a few pleasant words and stick you ten bucks for every time he drops in. Nor by certain types who want to give every medicine by hypodermic and charge you for giving it to you and charge you the material (they say what it costs them) but at four or five times what it costs them. I know them all; I've had dealings with them all. There are many things people don't know about such practices, nor how to beat over-charges. They don't even know the various county medical associations have scales of fees. They don't know that no doctor has a right to make an unrequited call, unless he does not charge for it.

They don't know how to beat an overcharge. Suppose you receive what you think is an exorbitant bill – it happened to me when my wife was ill, and she was ill many times – and I wrote that I considered it exorbitant and explained why. The next thing I knew I was served by a collection agency. Well, it so happened that one of the lawyers we used at that time (I was in the oil business then) volunteered to represent me and my wife, and refused any fee. So we went to court and the doctor sent one of his juniors to testify. On the stand he had to admit he had not himself rendered any of the services involved and did not of his own personal knowledge know anything about them. The attorney immediately moved for a dismissal and got it. He might not have got it from every judge – some of them automatically give judgement for a collection agency – but he got it this time. So I called the doctor and told him what I thought I should pay and he accepted gladly, although he had already lost half of it to the collection agency. I might add that he was personally a very charming man.

Letter to Deirdre Gartrell,
20 March 1957.

I always opened the car door for her and helped her in. I never let her bring things to me. I always brought things to her. I never went out of a door or into a door before her. I never went into her bedroom without knocking. I suppose these are small things – like constantly sending her flowers, and always having seven presents for her birthday, and always having champagne on our anniversaries. They are small in a way, but women have to be treated with great tenderness and consideration – because they are women.

Letter to James Howard,
of the Mystery Writers of America, who had written to Chandler asking
him how he had come to write crime fiction, 26 March 1957.

In 1931, my wife and I used to cruise up and down the Pacific Coast, in a very leisurely way, and at night, just to have something to read, I would pick a pulp magazine off a rack. It suddenly struck me that I might be able to do this stuff and get paid while I was learning. I spent five months on my first novelette, but I did something I have never been able to persuade any other writer to do. I made a detailed synopsis of some story – say by Gardner, he was one of them, and he is a good friend of mine – and then tried to write the story. Then I compared it with professional work and saw where I had failed to make an effect, or had the pace wrong, or some other mistake. Then I did it over and over again. But the boys who want you to show them how to write won't do that. Everything they do has to be, they hope, for publication. They won't sacrifice anything to learn their trade. They never get it into their heads that what a man wants to do and what he can do are entirely separate things, that no writer worth the powder to blow him through a barbed wire fence into hell is ever in his own mind anything but starting from scratch. No matter what he may have done in the past, what he is trying to do now makes him a boy again, that however much skill in routine technical things he may have acquired, nothing will help him now but passion and humility. They read some story in a magazine and get a lift out of it and start banging the typewriter on borrowed energy. They get a certain distance and then they fade.

Letter to William Gault,
31 March 1957.

I've often tried to figure out what makes these teenagers what they often are. Do they think they live in a lost world? Even here in La Jolla, after a very nice party down somewhere at La Jolla Shores, the boys and girls amused themselves by slashing tires on the way home. Why? Why do highschool kids of decent families get fun out of destroying things belonging, for all they know, to people who may have a hard time getting by? Is it a sort of revolt against a world they don't believe in? Is it the result of the war? I don't know, but it is not just us. In London, they have the Teddyboys, so called because they affect clothes of the Edwardian era. They are plenty tough, and their girlfriends too.

Letter to Helga Greene,
16 April 1957.

I remember my first love, but that was a different world. When we met my throat choked up and I could hardly get a word out. To have held her hand would have been ecstasy, to have kissed her would have been unthinkable. But I don't think at that point one is really in love with a particular girl; one is in love with love. Of course one never finds out, because when one meets her later on, if one does, she has long since been married, and usually to some dullard one considers quite unsuitable. Did you ever read a novel by Leonard Merrick, called *Conrad in Quest of His Youth?* Probably not too good by our standards, but I liked it. The moral is, Never Go Back.

Letter to Jean de Leon,
18 April 1957. The Light of Asia *was a nineteenth-century life of* Buddha, *written by Sir Edwin Arnold.*

No, I haven't read *The Light of Asia.* I really feel that formal religions, however liberal in thought, are a little too late for me now. And perhaps – I hope so – I am not the type who runs crying to an Unknown God when he feels alone, desperate, or facing death. I think I shall take it as calmly as I took the dangers in my war so long ago. But one never knows. Anyone can be broken by suffering. Perhaps, in a way, I am lucky to have reached the decision to take my own life and to have failed, since in a sense I have already known what it is to look death in the eye. Neither prayers nor religion could have helped me then. It was between me and myself, so to speak. Of course, torture is something else. I doubt very much that I could have put on as good a show as so many did.

I don't know what I make of Billy Graham. I saw him once on TV and he seemed a well-dressed, pleasant sort of chap, young, good-looking, and so on. But in America we are inclined to regard all such people as 'on the make', I suppose. There have been too many of them over here and they have made too much money.

The flagrant cases seem to me Aimee Semple MacPherson and Father Divine.

Letter to Deirdre Gartrell,
23 April 1957.

Most people make do with what is available and seemingly appropriate to their condition. Ferocious romantics of my sort never make do with anything. They demand the impossible and on very rare occasions they actually achieve it, much to their surprise. I was one of those, one of the perhaps two per cent, who are blessed with a marriage which is forever a courtship. I never proposed marriage formally. My wife and I just seemed to melt into each other's hearts without the need of words.

Letter to Helga Greene,
30 April 1957.

I think today there are much better film writers than I could ever be, because I never quite saw things in the terms of the camera, but always as dramatic scenes between people. I suppose you know the story of the writer who racked his brains how to show, very shortly, that a middle-aged man and his wife were no longer in love with each other. Finally he licked it. The man and his wife got into a lift and he kept his hat on. At the next stop a lady got into the lift and he immediately removed his hat. That is proper film writing. Me, I'd have done a four page scene about it. What this chap did took a few seconds.

A schoolmaster of mine long ago said, 'You can only learn from the second-raters. The first-raters are out of range; you can't see how they get their effects.' There is a lot of truth in this.

The date and addressee of this fragment are unknown.

Gatsby . . . It is not perfect; evasive of the problem often, side-stepping scenes which should have been written, but somehow passing along, crystalized, complete, and, as such things go now-adays, eternal, a little pure art . . . there is such a difference between the real stuff and a whole shelf full of Pulhams and Forsythes and Charlie Grays.

Letter to Helga Greene,
5 May 1957.

I was an executive in the oil business once, a director of eight companies and a president of three, although actually I was simply an over-paid employee. They were small companies, but very rich. I had the best office staff in Los Angeles and I paid them higher salaries than they could have got anywhere else, and they knew it. My office door was never closed, everyone called me by my Christian name, and there was never any dissension, because I made it my business to see there was no cause for it. Once in a while, not often, I had to fire someone – not someone I had picked myself, but someone who had been imposed upon me by the big man – and that I hated terribly, because one never knows what hardship it may mean to the individual. I had a talent for picking out the capabilities of people. There was one man, I remember, who had a genius for filing. Others were good at routine jobs but had no initiative. There were secretaries who would remember everything and secretaries who were wonderful at dictation and typing, but whose minds were really elsewhere. I had to understand them all and use them according to what they were. There was one girl, not pretty and not too bright, who could have been given a million dollars in cash, and a month later, without being asked, she would have known the number of every bill and listed it, and would have, at her own expense, taken a safe deposit box to keep the money in. There was a lawyer on salary in our office (I didn't approve of the idea, but was overruled by the Board) who was very acute but also very unreliable, because he drank too much. I found out just how to use his brain, and he often said and publicly that I was the best office manager in Los Angeles, and probably one of the best in the world. (Eventually, he crashed a police car and I had to get him out of jail.)

Business is very tough and I hate it. But whatever you set out to do, you have to do as well as you know how . . . I remember one time when we had a truck carrying a pipe in Signal Hill (just north of Long Beach) and the pipe stuck out quite a long way, but there was a red lantern on it, according to law. A car with two drunken sailors and two girls crashed into it and filed actions for $1000 apiece. They waited almost a year, which is the deadline here for filing a personal injury action. The insurance company said, 'Oh well, it costs a lot of money to defend these suits, and we'd rather settle.' I said, 'That's all very well. It doesn't cost you anything to settle. You simply put the rates up. If you don't want to fight this case, and fight it competently, my company will fight it.' 'At your own expense?' 'Of course not. We'll sue you for what it costs us, unless you pay without that necessity.' He walked out of the office. We defended the action, with the best lawyer we knew, and he proved that the pipe truck had been properly lighted and then we brought in various barmen from Long Beach (it took money to find them, but it was worth it) and showed that they had been thrown out of three bars. We won hands down, and the insurance company paid up immediately about a third of what they would have settled for, and as soon as they did I canceled the policy, and had it rewritten with another company.

Perhaps all this sounds a little hardboiled. But it wasn't like that really at all. I was just doing what I thought was my job. It's always been a fight, hasn't it? Everywhere you go, everything you do – it all takes it out of you.

Letter to Paul Brooks,
7 May 1957.

I once told a lawyer whom I know very well that it seemed to me that if the American Bar Association got after the hoodlum lawyers without whom highly organized crime could not exist in this country, they might very possibly wrap it up in a matter of months. These boys, and I mean the really big operators, never make a move without legal advice, and these boys are bound to be crooks because they are taking crooked money and assisting crooked operators. Well, this lawyer friend of mine looked at me in a confused manner and changed the conversation. It seems they would rather protect themselves and each other than the public. To a certain extent the same is true about doctors.

> *Letter to Helga Greene,*
> *7 May 1957. Chandler was now considering returning again to London.*

If you go somewhere to study new surroundings, absorb new atmospheres, meet different types of people, you always have at the back of your mind at least a hope of getting some use from it all. I have lost Los Angeles as a locale. It is no longer the part of me it once was, although I was the first to write about it in a realistic way. Now half the writers in America live in or near it, the war has made it an industrial city, and the climate has been ruined partly by this and partly by too much vegetation, too many lawns to be watered, and in a place that nature intended to be a semi-desert. It was hot and dry when I first went there, with tropical rains in winter, and sunshine at least nine-tenths of the year. Now it is humid, hot, sticky, and when the smog comes down into the bowl between mountains which is Los Angeles, it is damn near intolerable.

So naturally I look around for something else to write about. I can't write about England until I feel England in my bones. Love is not enough.

> *Letter to Deirdre Gartrell,*
> *8 May 1957.*

May I comment on the fact that in none of your letters to me have you ever told me about anything external to your own thoughts? You have never described your room, your university, the build-ings, the place, the atmosphere, the climate, what sort of place Armidale is. You may think this unimportant, but to me it indicates a state of mind; a state of mind which must be unhappy. I am interested in Australia, in everything about it, what it looks like,

238

what its houses are like, how many rooms they have and what sort, what flowers grow there, what animals and birds are there, what the seasons are, what the ordinary life of people of your sort consists of. You tell me a great deal about your thoughts, but nothing about the life around you. Do you suppose I became one of the most successful mystery writers of any age by thinking about me – about my personal torments and triumphs, about an unending analysis of my personal emotions? I did not. And you should know that very well. But from you all I hear is about you. This is not said to blame you or accuse you of being egocentric at all.

Letter to Jamie Hamilton,
16 May 1957.

A friend of yours called me a 'flaming egotist'. For a long time I thought myself to be a rather modest man, but I am beginning to believe this friend was right, that all writers are bound to be egotists since they drain their hearts and souls to write at all, and therefore become introspective. I think I have lately become worse, because I have been praised too much, because I live a lonely life and have no hope of anything else from now on.

Letter to the editor of the London Daily Express,
21 May 1957.

I have read in the *Los Angeles Times* Mr Rene MacColl's remarks on certain things which he does not seem to like about my country, and with many of them I am forced to agree. There is another side to America which Mr MacColl seems to have overlooked. We became too rich and too powerful through a sort of genius of production technique, and as a result I think we placed ourselves in a position to dominate the world before we had any real knowledge of how to do it or any real desire to do it. We were just stuck in the Number One spot. For 100 years, as you may remember, England dominated the world and was rather cordially detested by everyone else. That seems to be the price of power. The position we find ourselves in is almost impossible to maintain either gracefully or cleverly.

I admit that most of our values are quite wrong, but they result from something we did not intend to be wrong. I admit that our motor cars tend to be absurd in their design, but we live in an economy of overproduction and fantastic advertising campaigns are waged to make us think that anything six months old belongs with the Pharaohs. I admit that the cost of living here has reached absurd levels, but at least we have clean kitchens and clean bathrooms – and we bathe. Ours is a young, large, and variegated country. We don't know everything. Do you? We try, and have tried very hard, to do what we think we should do in the world, and our workmen occasionally do a day's work, which is more than yours do so far as I have observed. Once on Wimpole Street while waiting for a friend in a doctor's office, I watched two men moving those light-weight fireproof bricks which are extensively used in construction in England. It took two of them to move two of them across the pavement and drop them into a chute – and that seemed to make them very tired. We should have devised a machine to do it in twenty minutes. They were probably at it for two days.

Not everything about us is right, of course; but is everything about England right? It is so easy to write a newspaper article sneering at some other country; but it is not easy to create a civilization in that country, however many men of good will and great ability may try.

Letter to Edgar Carter,

3 June 1957. As Chandler's television agent, Carter was attempting to negotiate a Philip Marlowe television series. There was no lack of interest within the industry, but Chandler was being careful, and had already turned down one set of proposed scripts from NBC, the standard of which he deemed too mediocre. Both NBC and Carter were surprised at the refusal, but Chandler was adamant.

You have to persuade these lunatics that if a show is to last, it must have some sort of special quality, and that quality must be on terms the public can understand and appreciate. I may be wrong, but to me Marlowe is a character of some nobility, of scorching wit, sad but not defeated, lonely but never really sure of himself. Some of this has to go into Philip Marlowe if he is to be any good. Otherwise, he is just another sharp-talking nobody. If it is not possible to achieve this, I think we should forget the whole thing.

Letter to Roger Machell,
3 June 1957.

Of course I wonder about a lot of things, such as whether I should be psychoanalyzed, or hypnotized, or perhaps quietly put to sleep. No doubt you sometimes wonder the same things yourself as what sensitive man does not.

Letter to Roger Machell,
19 June 1957.

It was certainly amusing to read of Montgomery and Eisenhower explaining the errors of both sides, since Montgomery probably never admired anyone but himself and Ike was never a general at all, but rather a bridge player with a talent for making men of different nationalities co-operate, to a certain extent. I imagine that all the really difficult decisions were made by Marshall – and most of them wrong.

Letter to Michael Gilbert,
25 June 1957.

I went to a fancy cocktail party on Saturday night. Ye Gods, almost all the women were overdressed and overjewelled and burnt brown and coarse by the sun (a sign here you don't have to work for a living). I found a rather nice New York girl to talk to. About half the men were going on to a dance at the Beach Club and wore white DJ's, but loud bow ties in all colors. One man wore a violet plaid jacket which should have been burnt on the spot . . . These people are well off and some are rich, but to me they are quite unattractive, their range of conversation limited to Cadillacs, clothes, redecorating or building, personalities, who was drunk enough to paw whose wife last night . . .

Letter to Michael Gilbert,
5 July 1957.

I don't think one can accept or be happy with corrupt people without being a little corrupt oneself. It seems to me a sort of disease which grows almost unnoticed until one doesn't even know what is happening, and when it has happened, one doesn't know that either . . . Perhaps these darling pansies are the symbols of a civilization of the future. If so, let them have it.

Letter to Helga Greene,
11 July 1957. 'Here' is La Jolla.

I think it would be impossible for me to live here. I am not surrounded by old friends, because in order to have friends you have to cultivate them and for years I almost never went out at night and never had anyone to the house. Also the sort of people who one would expect to know are a stupid lot whose lives center around the Beach and Tennis Club. You probably have exactly the same sort of people in England, but in London there are others. Here there are no others.

Letter to Michael Gilbert,
25 July 1957.

It seems that I have had a very severe anaemia – not quite pernicious, but damn close to it. A blood count on the edge of nothing, but that doesn't worry me at all. I have lived my whole life on the edge of nothing.

Letter to Deirdre Gartrell,
25 July 1957.

I don't quite know why you are so close to my heart, but you are. In some mysterious way you have put me inside of you, so that I have to lie awake at night and worry about you – you a girl I have not ever seen. Why? The older you get, the less you know . . .

Letter to Helga Greene,
20 September 1957.

My ideas of what constitutes good writing are increasingly rebellious. I may even end up echoing Henry Ford's verdict on history, and saying to unlistening ears: 'Literature is bunk.' In the meantime, I don't think I should passionately care for either *The Last Angry Man* or the one on the other side of the sheet you so kindly sent me. You are an agent, and have to keep abreast. I may satisfy myself with *Richard II* or a crime novel and tell all the fancy boys to go to hell, all the subtle-subtle ones that they did us a service by exposing the truth that subtlety is only a technique, and a weak technique at that; all the stream-of-consciousness ladies and gents, mostly the former, that you can split a hair fourteen ways from the deuce, but what you've got left isn't even a hair; all the editorial novelists that they should go back to school and stay there until they can make a story come alive with nothing but dialogue and concrete description: oh, we'll allow them one chapter of set-piece writing per book, even two, but no more; and finally all the clever-clever darlings with the fluty voices that cleverness, like perhaps strawberries, is a perishable commodity. The things that last (I admit they sometimes miss) come from deeper levels of a writer's being.

Unknown recipient,
1 October 1957.

I do all my work on yellow paper, sheets cut in half, typed the long way, triple-spaced. The pages must be from 125 to 150 words and they are so short that you don't get prolix. If there isn't a little meat on each, something is wrong.

Letter to Paul Brooks,
proposing he write a cookbook, 28 November 1957.

It will have headlines such as HOW TO BROIL A STEAK — DON'T. HOW TO MAKE A DINNER IN TEN MINUTES. HOW TO MAKE COFFEE THAT DOESN'T TASTE LIKE COLORED WATER OR A STEWED SLIPPER. DISHES THAT TAKE ALL DAY AND THE HELL WITH THEM. REALLY GOOD MASHED POTATOES ARE AS RARE AS VIRGINS, BUT ANY FOOL CAN MAKE THEM IF HE TRIES.

Letter to Wesley Hartley,
a schoolmaster who had written to Chandler with some questions about him from his pupils, 3 December 1957.

I could speak German well enough then to be taken for a German, but now, alas, the language has changed a lot (but I don't think the Germans will ever change). French one never speaks well enough to satisfy a Frenchman. *Il sait se faire comprendre* is about as far as they will go . . . You could tell your lively students . . . that although I did a lot of writing as a young man in London (some publicity or jacket blurb writers have called me English, but I was born in Chicago of a British mother and an American father from a Pennsylvania Quaker family), but I couldn't write fiction to save my life. I couldn't get a character in or out of a room, I couldn't even get his hat off . . . I concentrated on the detective story because it was a popular form and I thought the right and lucky man might finally make it into literature. My books are so considered in England and most of Europe. The Germans and Italians are a little inclined to look down their noses at this sort of fiction. The Germans are a rather stupid type of intellectual snobs, in spite of their language having a magnificent slang. Only the French and ourselves equal or surpass it. The Italians seem to want either tragic stories in which everyone is dirty, never has any decent clothes or money, and everyone is rude to everyone else; or else novels in which the hero spends practically all of his time in bed with some woman. Some years ago some girl wrote for *Esquire* an article called 'Latins Are Lousy Lovers'. It gave great offense and the issue was even banned in Cuba. But I happen to know she was absolutely right. Latins talk a great game and make a rather dignified parade of love-making, but in the actual result the Northern nations and ourselves have them beat to a frazzle.

The great and difficult problem of the writer in our day – if he wants to make a living – is to write something acceptable to the public and yet at the same time write what he thinks is good writing. It is a lonely and uncertain life and however much success you have, you always start from scratch.

Letter to Helga Greene,
4 December 1957. Dwight Macdonald was the senior book critic of the
New Yorker, James Agee *was the author of novel called* A Death in
the Family, *and* The Outsider *was by Colin Wilson.*

I thought Dwight Macdonald's piece on James Agee was piffling, compared with his slow and patient liquidation of *The Outsider*. I could only get half way through it. He says: 'Why are our (American) writers so much more at home with children than with adults?' They're not. Very few writers can write effectively about children. Salinger, for example, can. Irwin Shaw is not bad, but he doesn't quite get it. 'The stained glass of the L. and N. depot smoldered like an exhausted butterfly'. This is Agee. He tried too hard and stuck his foot in his mouth. Anybody seen an exhausted butterfly smoldering lately? The bit about the street car, too long to quote, much admired by Macdonald, was a perfect piece of pretentious and overstrained writing: 'big drops, silent as a held breath, and the only noise the flattering noise on leaves and the slapped grass at the fall of each drop.' More Agee. Macdonald thinks this is magic. Make up your mind Agee; was it silent as a held breath, or wasn't it? 'All right, Mary I hate to go, but it can't be avoided.' Agee. 'The last sentence, in rhythm and word choice, seems to me perfect.' Macdonald. What's the matter with the man? About as perfect as, for example: 'Why isn't dinner ready, Susan? I'm so hungry I could eat the hind leg off a goat.' It says what it says, of course, but why rave about it? Would you rave about a sentence like: 'If we hurry, we may catch the next bus'?

Letter to E. Jack Neuman,
writer and director of the forthcoming Marlowe TV series for NBC,
Chandler having found a writer he liked, 9 December 1957.

. . . To fill up the space a few of what I call my morning limericks, usually indecent.

A charming young lady of France
Had scorned my most careful advance
Till a sunny day
Made her feel very gay,
And I found she was wearing no pance.

A certain young charmer of Ghent
Was rather too clearly enceinte
When her father yelled 'Who??'
She replied with a coo:
'I don't know. He just came – and he went.'

There was a young lady of Spain
Who regarded my love with disdain,
Till one night on champagne
She was feeling no pain,
And we did it again and again.

Letter to Jessica Tyndale,
23 December 1957. Helga Green, a divorcee, had been to stay with
Chandler in California. 'You know who' was Natasha Spender.
Chandler's 'next Marlowe story' was titled Poodle Springs, *but was*
never completed.

Helga and I get along so perfectly that I am amazed. She seemed so aloof when I first met her. We never quarrel, she takes everything in stride, and all is peace and happiness between us, as it never was with you know who. For reasons of her own life and temperament she doesn't want to get married again, and this is all right with me, as long as I can live close to her and go away with her.

I am flying to Palm Springs today to attend a very fancy party at the home of a rich woman to whom my doctor gave me an introduction. She begged me so hard to come that I finally gave in. She is a redhead (with assistance), about fifty, very easy to get along with and a fine dancer. I want to use her home for my next Marlowe story, which I plan to lay in Palm Springs, with Marlowe married to the 8 million dollar girl from *The Long Goodbye*. I think the struggle between them as to whether he is going to live her kind of life or his own might make a good sub-plot. Either she will give in, or the marriage will bust up. I don't know. But I do know that nobody, but nobody, is going to keep Marlowe from his shabby office and his unremunerative practice, his endurance, determination and his sarcastic pity. She'll probably want to redo his office, but she won't get to first base on that either.

Verse from a Christmas poem to Jean Fracasse,
Chandler's new Australian La Jolla secretary.

Is it a dream of poetry and youth
That makes us long too late
Once more to know
The hopes we died for?

Letter to Bernice Evans,
linguist and presenter of a word quiz show on television, 18 January 1958.

There is an old story about us Americans which, to the right mind, tells us a great deal. At a fork in the road there are two signs. One said, TO A CONCERT OF THE MUSIC OF BACH. The

other said, TO A LECTURE ON THE MUSIC OF BACH.
Guess which way the American went.

Letter to Jessica Tyndale,
3 February 1958.

My Sweet and Adorable Jessica:
  Please pardon the effusiveness, but since I finished the goddam
book I have been a little nutty. Tomorrow my copyist will go to
work on the final copy. You know, if it hadn't been for Helga, I'd
never have finished the damn book. She arouses my mind and my
ambition by some strange quality in her own mind. She makes me
want to conquer the earth, which of course I shan't do, but wanting
to is a lot different from my lackadaisical attitude of the past few
years. There are many sweet and adorable women in the world,
and you are one of the sweetest and most adorable, but there is
some sort of chemistry between Helga and me that gives me a
driving impulse. With Helga around I feel as though I could write
anything. What on earth happened between this rather cool, aloof
woman and me? Something very strange . . . somehow, just by the
way she talks and acts, by her simplicity, her lack of pettiness, the
keenness of her mind, she inspires me.

Letter to Robert Campigny,
a French critic, 7 February 1958.

La Pièce que vous avez dernièrement écrite dans *La Revue-Critique*,
sous le titre 'Raymond Chandler et le Roman Policier' m'est
parvenu de la part de mon éditeur à Londres, and mon ami depuis
longtemps, M. Jamie Hamilton, et aussi de la part de Mme Helga
Greene, qui est ce qu'en anglais on appelle 'my literary agent'. Je
ne suis pas trop sûr du mot précis en français.
  Il va sans dire que j'ai eu grand plaisir en lisant ce que vous avez
écrit, et je vous remercie plus que beaucoup pour l'honneur que
vous m'avez fait en écrivant avec tant de soin sur une espèce de
littérature qui est souvent regardé comme peu de chose. Naturelle-

ment, je ne sais pas écrire en français avec la netteté de style que vous possédez. Mais ce que je dis, c'est moi tout seul qui le dit.

. . . l'idée que Madame Christie déjoue ses lecteurs sans farce me paraît presque impossible à croyer. N'est ce pas qu'elle fait ses surprises en détruisant le portrait d'une caractère ou d'un personnage de roman qu'elle a jusqu'à ce moment peintu en couleurs complètement opposées au portrait fini? Tout cela est sans aucune vraie importance, sans doute, et les lecteurs qui ont besoin d'être taquinés par cette espèce de mystère ne se donnent la peine d'être fâchés si le mystère existe seulement parce que ces autres sont trop paresseux de faire l'effort de penser . . .

[*English Translation*: The piece that you wrote recently in the *Revue-Critique* entitled 'Raymond Chandler and the Detective Novel' reached me from the office of my London publisher, my longtime friend, Mr Jamie Hamilton, and also from Mrs Helga Greene, who is what is called in English 'my literary agent'. I am not sure of the correct word in French.

It goes without saying that I took great pleasure in reading what you had written, and I thank you very much indeed for the honor you have given me in writing with such care on a kind of literature which is often considered insignificant. Of course, I cannot write in French with your precision of style, but what I say is said by me alone.

. . . the idea that Mrs Christie baffles her readers without trickery seems almost impossible for me to believe. Isn't it true to say that rather she creates her surprises by destroying the portrait of a character or of a person in a novel whom she has up to this point depicted in colours completely opposed to the finished portrait? All this is doubtlessly without great importance, and readers who need to be teased by this sort of mystery do not take the trouble to become angry if the mystery exists only because others are too lazy to make the effort to think . . .]

I plan my next Marlowe with a background of Palm Springs, Poodle Springs I call it, because every third elegant creature you see has at least one poodle. I have the very house in which Linda Loring might care to live. The house is in La Jolla. It has a sort of offhand elegance and virtuosity which was once fairly usual in England among the upper classes. The people who live in it are clearly rich, but their enormous drawing room, or living room as we call it, escapes that air of having been done by an expensive decorator. It is full of things which I feel sure are priceless, but are treated in the most casual way. It has the largest oriental rug on the floor that I have ever seen. It has space and warmth. You sit in the room and you know that everything in it cost the earth, and you feel perfectly comfortable and at ease. I haven't known many genuine aristocrats in my life, naturally, but the real ones all have a certain way, not only of behaving with perfect ease in any situation, but of being able to impart this ease to others.

You make light of your accident in rock-climbing, but it must have been rather awful just the same. And I do realize how depressing it must be to find oneself on retirement from a position of responsibility, importance, and affection. Retiring is a kind of dying. The best way to revive is certainly what you have in mind. Work like hell at something just a little creative. No man grows old as long as he can create. You may die in the midst of it – so may I, who am older than you are – but you don't die of lethargy.

You can't have everything, even in California.

Letter to 'Lucky' Luciano Lucania,
the Prohibition-era American gangster deported from America after the
Second World War. The London Sunday Times *had commissioned*

Caro Signor Lucania,

I am an American author, not a journalist, not connected with any newspaper. I shall be in Naples shortly and would greatly appreciate the favor of an interview with you and the purpose of this interview would be solely the attempt of one man to understand another and would be in no way or under any circumstances to smear you.

I suppose we are both sinners in the sight of the Lord and it is quite possible that you have not been represented to the public of my country as you really are. I am aware that it is not what a man does, but what it is made to appear in court which decides.

I myself run a certain danger in this because a sympathetic interview with you might possibly make trouble for me, but I am willing to face this danger because the object of my life is to understand people, their motives, their origins, how they became what they are and not ever to judge them.

Some of my questions to you may be rather brutal, but if you decline to answer them, there will be no record that they have been asked. There will be nothing published by me which you do not say, but of course, I cannot be responsible for editorial comment.

I am sincere and I would like you to believe so, but I imagine that it is now very difficult to believe that anyone would approach you sincerely.

If you are receptible to my request, would you kindly reply on this prepaid telegram, to the Ritz Hotel [in London]?

The interview took place later in 1958. The resulting article by Chandler was never published by the newspaper. Helga Greene, who sat in on the Naples interview, had warned the paper that both men had been extremely drunk by the end of it. The article is not really an interview at all, in the purest sense, but it is nonetheless now quite gripping. Chandler had offered the title 'My Friend Luco'.

That is what they call him in Naples where no one I met had an unkind word for him. No doubt the Neapolitan police have, but they haven't been getting very far lately in prosecuting him. Nor has the American Narcotics Bureau, which at present is under the control of the Attorney General Brownell, who, as I understand, was campaign manager for the man who prosecuted Luco.

His real name is Charles Luciano Lucania. He is known to the newspaper public as Lucky Luciano. Lucky in what way? He is supposed to be a very evil man, the multimillionaire head of a world-wide narcotics syndicate. I don't think he is either. He seemed to me about as much like a tough mobster as I am like the late unlamented Mussolini. He has a soft voice, a patient sad face, and is extremely courteous in every way. This might all be a front, but I don't think I am that easily fooled. A man who has been involved in brutal crimes bears a mark. Luciano seemed to be a lonely man who had been endlessly tormented and yet bore little or no malice. I liked him and had no reason not to. He is probably not perfect, but neither am I.

His story goes back a long time, and many people may have forgotten what a monster he was made out to be. He was born in Sicily and taken to America as a child by his parents. He grew up in a tough section of New York. Italian and Sicilian immigrants are usually too poor to live anywhere but in tenement districts. At seventeen he admits to having been involved in some kind of narcotics business. Later on, during the prohibition era, he became a bootlegger or proprietor of gambling houses. So, considering his handicaps, he must have been a very able man.

Of course these were illegal activities under the law, but few Americans except bluenoses and fanatics ever believed in prohibition. Most of us went to speakeasies and bought bootleg liquor quite openly, the 'most of us' including judges, police officers and government officials. I remember that in one night club in Culver City, a town near Los Angeles where the Metro Goldwyn Studios are situated, two policemen were always on duty – not to keep you from getting liquor, but to keep you from bringing your own instead of buying it from the house.

Prohibition was one of our worst mistakes. It enriched the mobs and made them powerful enough to organize on a nation-wide scale, so that today they are almost untouchable. As for gambling, in some form or other it is legal or countenanced almost everywhere in America. Betting on horse races at pari-mutual tracks is more than legal; it is a valuable source of revenue to the various states.

Every so often we try to salve our consciences by selecting a highly publicized scapegoat in order to create the illusion that our laws are being rigidly enforced. In 1936 Luciano had reached a position of sufficient eminence to be selected. Some such scapegoats are guilty, some half or doubtfully guilty, and some – not many, I hope – are framed.

I believe Luciano was deliberately framed by an ambitious prosecutor. He was outside the law, technically speaking, but I don't believe the crime with which he was charged: compulsory prostitution, and for which he was convicted, had anything to do with his real activities. He was first of all tried in the press, which is an unfortunate part of our way of life, since if a man is abused long enough and hard enough, his actual trial in court makes him guilty at the beginning. Judge Jerome Frank in his posthumous book *Not Guilty* says of a certain case: 'The prosecution as one of its principal witnesses used a stool pigeon, a prostitute and drug addict who was getting her drugs from the government as her pay for informing on others.' If a government agency can stoop to this, it is hardly surprising that so many Americans, including myself, regard a man's fate in court as a game of blackjack or vingt-et-un. What happens to you depends on how the cards fall, how good a lawyer you have, if you can afford a good one, how stupid or intelligent the jury is, and most of them are hopelessly stupid, because intelligent men can usually find a way of escaping jury duty.

One of the worst menaces to any real justice is the big-time newspaper columnist. They are out to create sensation at whatever cost; they care nothing about the fate of the people they attack, and still less about truth. In a way they are worse than the crooks they attack. One columnist, whose name I fortunately forget, said that a prominent film star had taken a million dollars in cash to Luciano in Cuba. This film star, whom I happen to know, has never laid eyes on Luciano, and I very much doubt that Luciano ever had a million dollars, or anything like it.

So he came to trial before twelve good men and true, whose minds, if they could read, had already been corrupted by the press, and if they could not read, there was always radio.

Every witness against Luciano was facing prosecution for a crime, and not for the first time. The prosecutor secluded a number of brothel madams in 'protective custody', ostensibly to protect them. During this seclusion they were no doubt thoroughly coached on what evidence to give and how to give it, and promised immunity if they did the job properly. Of course, there is no legal record of this. The principal witness against Luciano was a man held on a burglary charge. If convicted he would have been a fourth time loser, which in New York State would have required an automatic life sentence – a real one, not a nominal one. He would probably have testified that his own mother was a multiple poisoner, if immunity had been promised to him. He said that he had known Luciano for eight or nine years and that Luciano had recently offered him a job at $40 a week as a collector from houses of prostitution. This makes me laugh almost hysterically, but not with pleasure. If he had said $400 a week or $1,000, I might have kept a straight face. But $40 a week for that? Absurd. It gives me some slight pleasure to know that this witness later, after the prosecutor was out of office, recanted his testimony and said that he had only seen Luciano in a bar.

A judge may be the most honorable man in the world, but he can't do more than instruct the jury to the best of his ability. If their minds have already been made up for them, he is helpless. Perhaps it may seem that in Luciano's case the sentence was rather excessive, but I am no judge of that. He got 30 to 50 years – quite a chore.

He served ten years and then, by some rather unusual executive procedure, he was released and sent to Sing Sing to be deported. He was pardoned on the grounds that he had given the armed forces valuable information for the invasion of Sicily. The armed forces must have laughed their heads off. About all Luciano could have told them about Sicily was that it was an island. They probably already knew more about Sicily than the Sicilians. The real reason for his release could surely have been only one thing: that his lawyers has secured evidence that he had been framed and were prepared to use it against the prosecutor, now an important political figure. He had built his career on spectacular convictions. But he never got what he wanted. We Americans are not fools. At times we may look foolish, but in the pinch we can tell a cat from a leopard.

Luciano went to Rome, but the police made his life impossible. He went to Cuba, and the American Narcotics people jumped on his back. He went to Naples. The police there watched him constantly. He changed his residence every few months. No use. America has become an empire. Its money and influence penetrate everywhere outside the Iron Curtain. Nothing can give him back his life or his freedom. The job on him was too thorough.

No one knows all the facts. I can only go by my feeling about a man. If Luciano is an evil man, then I am an idiot. The man who convicted him has had his reward – and also his failure. I'd rather be an idiot than live with his soul, if he has one.

Verse from an untitled poem,
written by Chandler in spring 1958.

But always lay the grave
In waiting, and the silence and the maggot (naught)
This was at last the honor which they bought.
Man is too often nobler than his fate.

Letter to Dale Warren,
17 June 1958. Chandler is referring to his seventh Marlowe book,
Playback.

Please don't praise the book; sell it!

Concerning horror stories about plumbing in British hotels:

If a country has destroyed itself in two wars, it cannot immediately achieve the American kitchen.

Letter to Luther Nichols,
books editor of the San Francisco Examiner, *who had sent Chandler some interview questions, September 1958.*

1. Yes, I think the hardboiled dick is still the reigning hero, but there is getting to be rather too many of him. The principal challenger is, I think, the novel of pure suspense. The best of these seem to be written by women.
2. I wouldn't call any writer psychoneurotic. We're all crazy to some extent. It's a hard lonely life in which you are never sure of anything.
3. [Regarding whether crime fiction might lead to increased crime.] No effect whatsoever except that a man contemplating a murder might pick up an idea of how to do it and escape afterwards. But the crime was already there.
4. [Regarding the future of mystery writing.] A decline of the hardboiled story on the basis of Gresham's law. They are too numerous, too violent, and too sexy in too blatant a way. Not one in fifty is written with any sense of style or economy. They are supposed to be what the reader wants. Good writers write what they want and make the reader like it. The hard-hitting story will not die completely but it will have to become more civilized. The mystery story in some form will never die in the foreseeable future.
5. I don't worry about the reviewers. I've had it both ways, and that is how it should be. Some are stupid, even vicious, but so are some writers.

Letter to Helga Greene,
1 October 1958. Following his meeting with Lucky Luciano, Chandler now had an idea for a new story:

. . . about a man who tried to get out of the Syndicate organization, but he knew too much, and he got a tip that a couple of pros were being sent to wipe him out. He has no one to turn to for help, so he goes to Marlowe. The problem is what can Marlowe do without getting in front of the guns himself. I have some ideas and I think the story would be fun to write. Needless to say, if the killers fail, others will take care of them. You don't fail the syndicate and go on living. The discipline is strict and severe, and mistakes are simply not tolerated. The only syndicate boss who was ever convicted of murder was Lepke Buchhalter, at one time head of Murder Inc. in Brooklyn and head of a 'protection' racket in New York. I don't know how they got him, but he and one of his top men did finally go to the chair. They put Costello in prison for a while and they may still be after him, but they won't get far, I should think. These boys all have good business fronts and very clever, although crooked, lawyers. Stop the lawyers and you stop the Syndicate, but the Bar Associations are simply not interested.

Chandler wrote the story, unpublished on his death. It was the last piece of writing he ever completed, and the first short story he had written since his pulp days. It begins:

He sat down carefully and I sat opposite and we looked at each other. His face had a sort of foxy eagerness. He was sweating a little. The expression on my face was meant to be interested but not clubby. I reached for a pipe and the leather humidor in which I keep my Pearce's tobacco. I pushed cigarettes at him.

'I don't smoke.' He had a rusty voice. I didn't like it any more than I liked his clothes, or his face. While I filled the pipe he reached inside his coat, prowled in a pocket, came out with a bill, glanced at it and dropped it across the desk in front of me. It was a nice bill and clean and new. One thousand dollars.

'Ever save a guy's life?'

'Once in a while, maybe.'

'Save mine.'

The story also contained the line:

the women you get and the women you don't get – they live in different worlds. I don't sneer at either world. I live in both myself.

Letter to Hardwick Moseley,
   5 October 1958.

Hardwick, I need money, cash money, not assets. I need it because for a year and eight months I have been supporting my Australian secretary and her two children. Hell, I even deeded the British and Commonwealth rights in *Playback* to Jean . . .

Letter to Roger Machell,
   14 October 1958. Chandler had become embroiled with his new secretary's ongoing divorce.

Her filthy rotten screwy bastard of a husband (this is one case in which I do not feel it noble to speak well of the dead. I knew him) made a holograph will a few days before he died disinheriting his wife and children and leaving what he had to his brother, who is a screwball, too. Jean has no one to look to but me and it's becoming rather a drain.

   Since I am on an alcohol-free diet, due to hepatitis, my mind seems to lack a little or a lot of its exuberance. Very few writers can write on alcohol but I am one of the exceptions. I don't miss alcohol physically at all, but I do miss it mentally and spiritually.

Letter to Helga Greene,
   22 October 1958.

I've always had a sneaking idea that a professional failure was always a moral failure. There are writers who look the situation squarely in the face and decide that they are willing to be poor if they can write well enough to satisfy their souls. I respect them, but a lack of appreciation is narrowing. Henry James felt it. It tends to make a writer exaggerate the very things that keep the public away from him. I am not a mercenary writer, but I do feel that in this tangled generation a writer who cannot face the rather cynical realities of his trade is lacking in more than popularity.

258

Letter to Catherine Barth,
Executive Secretary of the Mystery Writers of America. The organization
had just asked Chandler to become its President. 7 February 1959.

I spoke to you on the telephone to thank you for the great honor
the Mystery Writers of America have done me; but that does not
seem quite enough – especially as the real work has to be done by
the Executive Vice-President, Herbert Brean, and the Executive
Committee, who seem to do all the work and get none of the
praise.

I am sure you realize that I take this honor as a token of a long
career, and that I do not take it very personally. I have reached a
stage in my career where I have nothing to fear.

Letter to Maurice Guinness,
21 February 1959.

I think I may have misunderstood your desire that Marlowe should
get married. I think I may have picked the wrong girl. But as a
matter of fact, a fellow of Marlowe's type shouldn't get married,
because he is a lonely man, a poor man, a dangerous man, and yet
a sympathetic man, and somehow none of this goes with marriage.
I think he will always have a fairly shabby office, a lonely house, a
number of affairs, but no permanent connection. I think he will
always be awakened at some inconvenient hour by some inconvenient person, to do some inconvenient job. It seems to me that
is his destiny – possibly not the best destiny in the world, but it
belongs to him. No one will ever beat him, because by his nature
he is unbeatable. No one will ever make him rich, because he is
destined to be poor. But somehow, I think he would not have it
otherwise, and therefore I feel that your idea that he should be
married, even to a very nice girl, is quite out of character. I see him
always in a lonely street, in lonely rooms, puzzled but never quite
defeated.

Four weeks after writing that letter, Chandler was taken to hospital by ambulance from his rented home in La Jolla, suffering from pneumonia. He died three days later.

THE END

Chandler had left the following instructions in a letter to his lawyer, written two years before his death. 'Wright' was Leroy Wright, who had helped Chandler draw up his will in La Jolla.

P.S. Wright failed to cover one point and I failed to mention it in the letter attached, but I shall. That is that I want either a Church of England or Episcopalian church service, depending on where I die, I wanted to be cremated, and I want my eyes to go to a cornea bank, if they want them. Since the eyes have to be removed, I am told, within half an hour after death to be of any use, and immediately refrigerated, it would seem that this would require some instrument duly executed between me and some organization, such as an eye hospital. The mutilation of a corpse, except for autopsy or embalmment (the last is compulsory in this country) is illegal, so the right to do this should probably be given to me in a proper document.

As to the funeral service, I will not, if I have anything to say about it, have it anywhere but in a church, and there is to be nothing but the formal service for the dead – no poems read, no speeches, no goddam tame person in a funeral parlor or chapel. I don't know where I was baptized, although I know from my mother that I was baptized, but I was confirmed in the Church of England by the Bishop of Worcester, and as a young man was very devout. My wife had her service in an Episcopal church, although neither of us had ever been inside it. The vicar was a friend of mine, but I don't think that was the reason. I think one is entitled to it.

R.

Index